THE MIRACLE THEATRE

THE MIRACLE THEATRE

The Chichester Festival Theatre's Coming of Age

Leslie Evershed-Martin
O.B.E. SB St.J

Founder of the Chichester Festival Theatre

. . . There is no question at all
but that in getting this theatre
built he performed a miracle . . .

Lord Olivier

DAVID & CHARLES
Newton Abbot London North Pomfret (Vt)

To my wife, Carol, and my sons David and Barry who, whilst being my severest critics, gave me unfailing loyalty and invaluable help in founding the theatre

Quotation on title page taken from
the Prologue in *The Impossible Theatre*,
Published by Phillimore & Co, Chichester

British Library Cataloguing in Publication Data

Evershed-Martin, Leslie
The miracle theatre: the Chichester
Festival Theatre's coming of age.
1. Chichester Festival Theatre—History
I. Title
792'.09422'62 PN2596.C52C5

ISBN 0-7153-9021-X (hardback)
0-7153-9085-6 (paperback)

Typeset by ABM Typographics Limited, Hull
and printed in Great Britain
by Redwood Burn Limited, Trowbridge, Wilts.
for David & Charles Publishers plc
Brunel House Newton Abbot Devon

Published in the United States of America
by David & Charles Inc
North Pomfret Vermont 05053 USA

Contents

Acknowledgements

In the preparation of this book I would like to acknowledge the permission given to me by many newspapers and magazines for extracts to be published. I apologise to anyone I have been unable to trace, either the source or the authorship, but trust they will appreciate the fact that the extracts were too interesting to miss.

I would like to thank the generosity of my many friends who have given assistance. Especially Lord Hugh Cudlipp for his invaluable guidance; Mr Reg Davis-Poynter for his specialised advice; Mr Robert Selbie for his anecdotes; Mr John McKerchar for financial details; Miss Anne Hillier for selection of photographs; Mr Paul Rogerson for list of concerts and Mrs Anne Payne for typing. Also the various photographers for donations of photographs.

Fishbourne,
Chichester
OCTOBER 1986

Foreword by Lord Olivier O.M.

It seems incredible to me that more than twenty-five years have passed since Leslie Evershed-Martin's brainchild gave birth to the Chichester Festival Theatre – and even more incredible that it was that long ago that I was its first theatre director.

From a slow start (panned by the critics) we launched forth into that fortunate production of *Uncle Vanya*, with the late lamented Michael Redgrave heading a wonderful cast and, from that moment, we have not looked back. We have trodden water now and again, but we have not looked back.

The number of 'stars' who have appeared there again and again during this twenty-five year period, and who consider it one of the perks of the job to do so, is most gratifying. To name them all would double the size of this book, but to mention a few would, I think, show the attraction Chichester has, not only for the members of the audience, but for the actors and actresses as well.

John Mills, Alec Guinness, John Gielgud, Omar Sharif, Maggie Smith, Joan Plowright, Googie Withers, Donald Sinden, Derek Jacobi and marvellous people of that ilk, indeed the cream of British theatre, have all drawn in the crowds while enjoying their stints there.

My fellow directors have all, in their ways, added to the ambience of the Chichester Festival Theatre. Sir John Clements was the longest serving member of us all, and produced wonderful things in his reign. Keith Michell, Peter Dews, Patrick Garland and newest incumbent John Gale, have all kept up the high standard and have not been afraid to experiment with new plays – some of which have lived well at Chichester, but died there too, and some of which have transferred to the West End with great results.

Let us celebrate the achievements of this renowned theatre and long may it flourish and prosper.

Olivier
OCTOBER 1986

CHAPTER 1
Onwards from 1962

> . . . and you and I, uncle, dear uncle, shall see a life that is bright, lovely, beautiful. We shall rejoice and look back at these troubles of ours with tenderness, with a smile and we shall rest.
> I have faith, uncle; I have fervent passionate faith. We shall rest . . .
>
> . . . .
>
> 'We did *not* rest . . . but that is another story.'

Those were the closing words of *Uncle Vanya* and the closing words of my first book *The Impossible Theatre* which told the story of how the Chichester Festival Theatre was conceived and born.

So here, now, is the story of the twenty-one years that followed the momentous first season in 1962. That season of never-to-be-forgotten excitement and glamour. It was a season which was also fraught with deep anxieties alongside the almost dreamlike delights and successes.

The fervors of the preparatory years of 1959–61 and the crowning glory of the opening year of 1962 can never be repeated but they can be savoured in retrospect. The following years of consolidation, leading to expansion, also had their interwoven dramas and these I hope to reveal as dispassionately as I can. New anxieties and unexpected difficulties, and some sparkling triumphs, arose and disappeared, so I hope the reader will enjoy some of these experiences as I try to relate them.

After twenty-two seasons, engulfed within twenty-one years, it is a time for stocktaking and, whereas in commerce this could be regarded as a dreary process, stocktaking of an adventure such as ours can be stimulating.

We had been catapulted into the history of world theatre. We had gained international recognition by virtue of the fact that Sir, now Lord, Olivier became our first Artistic Director. His appointment had been reported by the world's press and the significance of this step in his career was acknowledged as being an important one for him as a preliminary to the National Theatre. Incidentally it also established Chichester so that many critics soon readily, and derisively, dubbed us as part of the Establishment. This was hardly correct when we were branching out anew from orthodox theatre buildings and presentations.

Olivier is reported as having said to his wife, Joan, at the end of the first season:

> 'Well we've done it, after all; after all that, after all those terrors it finally seems to turn out that we have done it, that we have launched the theatre, that it can open again next year, and that the season has not been a fiasco, and that the Chichester Festival will not go down in history as the theatre that was once open for ten weeks.'

After the first season the momentum had to be maintained and Olivier sometimes felt that perhaps he had set too high a standard for us to be able to retain. Despite the schoolmaster attitude of the critics, who wanted to instruct him how he would have to behave when he was in charge of the National Theatre, the tremendous success of *Uncle Vanya*, the third play, could not be denied and this, with its galaxy of stars, set the seal on the first season. The second play *The Broken Heart* was agreed to be a failure but *The Chances*, the first play, opened the season in the right festive spirit although Olivier always contends he failed there as well. It is remembered as a delightful production by practically all those who saw it and even now it is quoted in reminiscences of that first year.

Splendid beginnings are not, in themselves, proof that success will continue and we must now be judged by our record in the years that followed. I want to establish the fact that our success has been phenomenal with ever-increasing audiences and subsequent longer seasons.

Started in a district of England which many thought was unsuitable for great theatre and at a time when theatres were being pulled down by the score, we have achieved a reputation unrivalled by many other adventures. We have confounded many of the pessimistic predictions of the 'head waggers', as Tyrone Guthrie described them. This has only been made possible by the combined expertise of famous artistic directors, actors and actresses, the public, the loyal staff and by the clear headed business-like members of the Board of Management. Of course fate, or luck, call it what you like, has also played a part.

I am often asked whether it has fulfilled all my dreams of the early days. Whether or not this is so I hope will be revealed by the story I am about to unfold, of the years up to 1984. The reader can form his, or her, own conclusions.

It is good to feel totally exhausted. It is proof that you have used resources to the full and each one has 'pulled its weight' with the rest.

The first season closed down after ten weeks and everyone in a state of exhaustion disappeared for much needed, and well deserved holidays. This disappearing act has been the pattern ever since, for it must not be forgotten that a theatre such as ours is not like one which takes in touring companies with productions already packaged and set up. It has the task of forming a company each year with all the rehearsing and construction of four completely new productions.

What a forlorn and deserted look the theatre has once the sparkle has died and the tinsel has been stowed away. 'Rehearsal Call' notices left fluttering on notice boards, lipstick messages scrawled across dressing room mirrors, odds and ends of make-up and remnants of wigs strewn on tables together with empty champagne bottles from the 'last night' party.

There stood the building, a solid mass of concrete, the only large building in the park, surrounded by the fourteen seventy-foot elm trees whose doom no one had forecast. If we had known of their fate when disease struck them in 1971, having lived there for approximately 120 years, we might have superstitiously taken fright that the same misfortune might befall the structure of the theatre itself and its promoters. Luckily the theatre building has stood intact and has even bred other buildings attached to it and, touching wood, few of its founder members have departed.

The building, like a hungry monster, a pantomime giant, seemed to be waiting to be fed with the human bodies of the audiences and we, the members of the Board, were committed to see that it was kept alive. A dreadful but exhilarating responsibility which we had accepted when we started the whole affair. No possibility of selling out or handing over to bureaucratic authorities without facing eternal disgrace. I often said that if it had failed in the early days I should have been unable to remain in a close community like Chichester and still hold my head up. I should have had to emigrate to Australia or somewhere.

Fears did beset the Board within the next few months after the season ended, and I will describe these in a later chapter, but just for a short while we did bathe in the euphoria of our present success supported by the world-wide press coverage of our opening months.

Olivier and family went off to Cap Estel in the South of France and the rest scattered. Most of the Board were still around and I resisted the demands for an early meeting. I have never believed in having committee meetings soon after either the theatre season, or after one of my Gala charity days in the city. If they happen too soon after the event they deteriorate into post mortems with all the faults being examined. The troubles are thereby emphasised until members begin to believe it was a failure, instead of a success, which had been achieved.

However, promotion of the theatre went on just the same with talks by some of us to Rotary Clubs, Round Tables, Amateur Drama Clubs, Women's Institutes, school prize givings etc. The emphasis now was on audience development, rather than money, though the need for money was not neglected as there were so many improvements and additions we wanted to make as soon as possible.

We worked on the principle that it was useless to sit back and expect the public to come just because the theatre was there and because the entertainment we offered was of the highest quality. So many theatres, in the past, had taken this attitude and inferred to the public that they almost had a duty to support them and were ever ready to bemoan the fact they found it difficult to survive. Some thought their only effort need be to carry their begging bowls to the Arts Council or their local authority for grants.

As with successful export companies we knew it was necessary to go out and sell our wares and make them attractive. Tyrone Guthrie in a famous and very frank speech on the occasion of a Shakespeare birthday celebration at Stratford-upon-Avon said of the Stratford Memorial Theatre:–

> 'When the time approaches for this theatre to need financial assistance, remember that drama is not a necessity, it is an amenity. It is one of those things which make the difference between civilised and uncivilised people. The minute we go begging on educational grounds we begin to sell the past. Authorities should not be approached cap in hand in cap and gown but in cap and bells, our traditional garb. Not saying Shakespeare is educational but that Shakespeare is fun.'

Which reminds me of the lady who said to Patrick Garland after seeing his production of *As You Like It* in 1983, 'It was so lovely one couldn't believe it was Shakespeare!' This after he had prided himself on keeping to truly Shakespearian traditions.

The theatre, in those early days after the opening season, was under the magnifying glass of the press. There was unending praise, and criticism, but at least we were in the news whatever it was and we were not ignored. To be ignored is the death knell for any entertainment project. We certainly had no need to promote similar publicity and we were grateful for that. Articles in the women's pages of newspapers and magazines discussed the fashions of the audiences seen at Chichester. Many other sources produced articles debating the need of the local restaurants to keep open in the evenings, the future of Sir Laurence, the failure or the success of the auditorium stage, and the waste of keeping the theatre open in the summer and then closing it in the winter.

Unfortunately I am unable to locate the newspaper in which the following article was written in 1967 bit it seems worthy of reproduction here as it was a typical example of praise for our theatre:–

> 'With the announcement of the Chichester Festival Theatre programme for 1967 the seal has been set on its meteoric rise to international fame. It now stands universally acknowledged as one of the world's foremost centres of drama. A success hardly dreamed of in its earliest days. The theatre has provided more desirable publicity for Chichester than any other development in the city for many centuries. It has become its greatest tourist attraction and has carried the name of Chichester to all corners of the world.
>
> Its success is all the more remarkable when one remembers so many other provincial theatres are struggling to keep their heads above water. Many would close their doors tomorrow if they were not subsidised in one way or another. The Chichester theatre is a thriving and bonny infant which promises to grow into a sturdy pillar of dramatic art.
>
> It could serve an even more important role in encouraging other towns and cities to have the foresight and courage to sponsor other projects of their own.'

Not all the articles written about us were as laudatory as this one as will be seen in the chapters about the building and the uses of the theatre and the stage. We have had our share of critics in the city itself, and surrounding district, in the same way as all other towns have had who promote theatres or festivals.

Edinburgh particularly is harassed annually by some of the myopic local inhabitants. Stratford, Ontario, has had bursts of opposition despite the fact that it benefits greatly from the tourists who otherwise would not visit a town so far away from the big cities. It is a peculiar quirk of such communities that some of their citizens resent the success of those who promote events for the good of the public. Luckily in Chichester, from the beginning, we have never had organised opposition but just the same people who turn up now and again to take the opportunity to snipe.

It is difficult to analyse the reasons for these oppositions especially as in our case I have never known any member of the theatre personnel, or supporter, to express criticism of, say, the local football club, the swimming pool or leisure centre projects. In some cases I suppose it is frustration with the fact that the theatre is a success, not a failure, as they had gloomily predicted, and in some cases there is an inference that drama is only for a section of privileged people. This can be seen to be nonsense if anyone glances at the list in the appendix of this book of the varied plays and concerts designed for every taste which we have always provided.

Michael Leach writing in an American newspaper said of Chichester:–

> 'Inevitably the sceptics, the prophets of doom, were present . . . they always are . . . and confounding them is part of the fun.'

During a lifetime of public life I have learnt to take criticism seriously only when it seemed to be unbiased and constructive. It would be foolish not to do so. When it was stupid or malicious I let it be no more than an irritation, then it was easy to throw it off. It has always been amusing to hear those who opposed the theatre at the beginning saying 'Ah, yes, the first year was alright but wait until the second.' Subsequently they would repeat this year after year, adding 'It'll be on the rates in a few years' time, mark my words.'

These began to peter out after about four years but some of them revived hope when the National Theatre departed with Olivier. Luckily we survived this because Olivier persuaded us to have John Clements to succeed him and a solid reputation was built up on Olivier's foundations even if it was of a different nature.

The most pleasing aspect of all this scepticism is when many people have told me 'I had no faith in the project at first and, in fact, thought you were stark staring mad but now I acknowledge I was wrong.' This sort of generous gesture, which takes courage to admit, I appreciated and I found it delightful that there were such people.

Those who did not know of the solid and careful reasoning which I had gone through in the year before we decided to launch the scheme, would honestly have believed it was too risky and that it could fail. If I, myself, had been looking at such a scheme from the outside I might well have been one of the sceptics.

Perhaps I had a theatre for Chichester in my mind for a long time though I was unconscious of the fact until I found a copy of a letter I wrote to the local press in 1952. I was announcing the postponement of a production of *The Vagabond King* in Priory Park in aid of the Eventide Home of which I was founder and chairman. After explaining that it would be wrong to endanger the funds of the charity I said:–

> 'The greatest single factor against making a profit is the cost of building a complete temporary theatre in Priory Park for one week at a cost of £450 [at that time]. If only there was a suitable theatre in Chichester to stage such big shows, that cost could be reduced to something like £50 for hire. The outstanding excellence of the Chichester Amateur Operatic Society certainly deserves such a theatre and we share with them the great disappointment that we shall not be able to sponsor the show for them this time.'

Bank managers and accountants often look at statistics and fail to recognise the determination and devotion of the people behind industrial promotions or those of the entertainment world. Entertainment is probably the most uncertain of adventures and that is why, when we started, the local bank managers discussed our project amongst themselves and agreed to give us only £50 from each of the 'Big Five' banks. I should have acted on Lord Woolton's advice to me that when he was offered a derisory amount for one of his appeals, from someone who could afford a great deal more, he refused the offer saying such a poor example of trust would only lead others to do the same and so he could not afford to accept. (He was then offered ten times as much from the same person.) I did not refuse as I had faith that later, when we succeeded, they would support us in a way worthy of the good it would do for the city from which they made their money. Later on some of them did support concerts and helped in other ways by donations and window displays.

Fifteen years after we started I had a disagreement with a director of one of those banks when he stated at a dinner (I was sitting beside him) that his bank had given a thousand pounds to the theatre when it started, thus contradicting the facts I had just given him. He said he had been briefed before he left for the dinner but my guess was they had muddled it with their support for the Chichester Cathedral Festivities. When I got home and looked up the list of original donors I was able to write to him and prove I was right. By return of post he sent me a cheque for the theatre for £950 which was a splendidly sporting gesture.

Relations with the cathedral have always been extremely amicable.

There was the first service of inauguration on 3 June 1962 when Bishop Wilson preached to a large congregation. He took a benevolent interest in the theatre during the whole of his term of office and with Dean Walter Hussey, who became the theatre's chaplain, they co-operated in every way they could. How excited Bishop Bell would have been to see the creation of a theatre near the cathedral, in his diocese, where he had so enthusiastically promoted religious drama. Unfortunately I had not thought of the idea before he died so he never knew of its possible creation.

It was Bishop George Bell who in 1935 suggested that, following the success of John Masefield's production of *The Coming of Christ* at Canterbury in Whitsun week 1928, T. S. Eliot should be commissioned to write *Murder in the Cathedral* and this was performed at Canterbury in June 1935. Later, in September 1977, Keith Michell produced a splendid performance of it in Chichester Cathedral. It was a personal triumph for him. Those who saw it will never forget the climax where Michell stood precariously on the narrow ledge high up at the foot of the great west window. The cathedral had been cleared of all seats to enable the audience to follow round in a 'walk about' to view the various scenes in all parts of the nave and side chapels. I feel sure Bishop Bell would have approved, and greatly rejoiced, to have seen this presentation in his own cathedral.

The second service took place on 9 June 1963 when Canon Young preached the sermon. He was a wonderful ninety year old character, beloved by many, whose sprightly wit entranced those of the theatre who attended though there were fewer than for the first service. Because of this reduced number we decided it would not be wise to make the service an annual affair lest it should lose its significance in the life of the theatre.

The second Olivier christening at Chichester (the first was in the Bishop's private chapel for Richard on 22 July 1962) took place on 14 July 1963 at St. Mary's Church, Lavant, for their daughter Tamsin. The Olivier family thus forged more permanent links with the history of Chichester and Sussex, in the same way as they had done in East Sussex (Tunbridge Wells) and Brighton.

When Walter Hussey retired, Canon Greenacre became chaplain to the theatre and still remains in that position taking a real interest in the welfare of all theatre personnel and each season's company. Bishop Eric Kemp and Dean Robert Holtby have continued a very happy friendship with everyone and both are constant attenders at the Trust meetings. To show the appreciation of the theatre, in a small way, the costume department, under the direction of Ivan Alderman, designed and made a tunicle (vestment for the crucifer) and this is still used for special occasions in the cathedral.

I always remember Guthrie's vision that when the theatre was opened we would have a grand procession from the cathedral to the theatre consisting of at least five to ten bishops, twenty or thirty deans, canons and other clergy with several choirs from all over Sussex. This was typical of

Guthrie's love of grand and extravagant ceremonial. Instead, for all the special occasions for the first two years, and later for the tenth and twenty-first celebrations, we had either simple evensong or specially designed forms of service which in their simplicity were more moving and impressive.

Our relationships with the Mayor and Corporation of the city have been, on the whole, most friendly despite a small and vociferous minority who sought to damage the theatre by limiting any extensions or by making constant demands for charges to be made for the car park. Special receptions, and in one instance a garden party during the mayoralty of the late Councillor Brookes, have given visible proof of the goodwill of the majority of the councillors.

Since the beginning the Mayor has always entertained all the mayors of Sussex, and nearby Hampshire, to a performance. I wish when I was mayor we had had the opportunity of thus repaying the various mayors for hospitality shown in their cities and towns, but at that time there was no place large enough to entertain them for a ball or a dinner in Chichester.

In 1974 when the reorganisation of the boroughs was carried out the ancient city of Chichester, which had one of the oldest mayoralties in the country with a list of mayors dating back to the year 1231, lost its status and became no more than a parish council, keeping the mayor with a reduced council which had little to do. It was a disastrous change and was as mistaken as the one which altered the National Health Service at the same time. It should never have happened. It transferred power to a District Council of almost fifty members with representatives as far away as Haslemere, on the Surrey border twenty miles, Southbourne on the Hampshire border seven miles and Selsey to the south seven miles.

With the best will in the world how could the majority of members outside the city of Chichester know, or feel, vitally interested in what was right for the citizens of Chichester. Obviously they did their best to put themselves in the picture. Again, how could the members representing the city judge the needs of communities in the surrounding district. Such matters as noise abatement, planning of new buildings, car parking, destruction of trees etc. are matters which can only be judged by those in the immediate vicinity and may seem to be petty, and of no significance, to outsiders who could make up a majority vote. Government by remote control cannot be as sympathetic, and as knowledgeable, as by those who are able to rule their own communities and the results of all this can be seen in my chapter on Controversies.

The privilege of granting the freedom of the city was lost at the time of the reorganisation but after great pressure from the Chichester Member of Parliament, Mr Antony Nelson, and many others, it was restored in 1980 and the Royal Military Police, stationed at the local barracks, were granted the Freedom and I was given the same honour in 1982.

Sybil Thorndike and Laurence Olivier in Uncle Vanya, *1962 (Angus McBean)*

The Military Police have always given good service to the civic life of the city, especially during the term of office in recent years of Lt Col Wood. They have given assistance at all ceremonial parades, including the royal visits to the theatre.

So it is, that whilst I have mentioned a few dissidents, the theatre is surrounded by an extremely happy community and is supported by the huge majority of the citizens.

Claudia Cassidy in the *Chicago Tribune*, 20 August 1963, said:–

> 'Chichester's 16th century coat of arms sheds drops of blood beneath an angry lion crouched with royal blue claws on a field of scarlet. But nothing so fierce seems to have gone into establishing the theatre.'

James Thomas, in the *Daily Express*, 3 July 1976, wrote:–

> 'Now that word Prestige can put a city on the map. The remarkable fact is that Chichester (pop. 21,000) is for ten weeks supporting a theatre which eight times a week seats 1,400, or nearly 6% of the population, at every performance. In a world where provincial theatre is being killed off by the effect of T.V. this theatre is proof that top productions and good actors can give theatre a new lease of life.
>
> In five years the theatre has changed sleepy Chichester into a place where restaurants stay open late, where boutiques window dress the latest goods from America, where top chefs from London send lobster thermidor from kitchens that once had little more than steak and kidney pie. Chichester could set a pattern which will be repeated across the nation and mean that major centres could get live theatre for at least part of the year. Suspicious at first the residents now feel the theatre is an indispensable part of the community.'

Ivan Alderman, speaking on behalf of his colleagues in the costume department in 1963, said of Chichester:–

> 'We welcomed the opportunity of coming to Chichester and are proud to contribute our part towards the success of this new and exciting theatre . . . and do we like the city? Well, of course we do. For in spite of its many supermarkets and numerous inappropriate shop fascias, it still has great beauty, ancient interest and old world charm; qualities we hope and expect to find in our country towns and cities. Yes! We like Chichester and though our manner may not portray our feelings, we really do appreciate, and are more than grateful for, the welcome, the interest, and the kindness shown towards us by the people, especially the Society and the Theatre Board, to whom, may I, on behalf of the whole 'seemingly unruly band' sincerely say 'thank you'.'

On the other hand there are criticisms. On several occasions during the season of 1981 I saw Tom Baker walking the streets of Chichester in the evenings after rehearsals and when I read the article of his interview by the *Chichester Observer*, 3 July 1981, I realised how he felt:–

> 'Where do people go in the evenings? I thought there had been a plague in Chichester the first time I came here, at night. It's spooky like in a film set. It cannot be good to stand at the Chichester Cross and feel spooky. There's no life and that means there is death. There is death in Chichester . . . it is completely dead at night.
>
> Chichester is very beautiful with that wonderful cathedral, but I find it agonisingly boring at night. In the daytime it is fine but it is a shame the precinct cannot stop operating at 6pm at night as I believe they do in other towns. What maddens me is that no one lives in the pretty buildings in your four streets. That is indefensible. All the prettiest buildings are taken up by the trust accountants, the architects, the dentists, TV rental shops, banks and especially the building societies.
>
> They only inhabit them for six hours a day. What use is a bunch of architects in the main streets? The main streets are of use to them but what do they contribute? Nothing. It is disgraceful that flats in the main streets are left empty.
>
> I would have thought buildings and streets were about people . . . you should hear dogs barking and babies crying. Local planners should ensure that business leases have a clause which says flats above premises should be for residential use. I know what they say to that . . . that it is a security risk because there is only one entrance. So what is wrong with building another entrance? They should not get a lease unless the top flat is lived in. I just cannot understand how they can leave all those city centre flats empty.'

The population of Chichester was split fifty-fifty in its opinion on the proposal to have a precinct in the city, but in the end I think more people have come to regard it as a blessing for the city. The pavements were too narrow to contain the large number of pedestrians especially in the summer months. It was necessary to step off the pavement to pass people and this created the constant hazard of being knocked over by the traffic. It always meant looking over one's shoulder. If the traffic was suddenly put back on the streets everyone would see how impossible the situation had become. Now people are able to wander all over the roads in safety and I have found that I have stopped to have conversations with friends and acquaintances which were never possible before the advent of the precinct. The centre of the city in the daytime has become one large social gathering which must be good for the community spirit.

I agree with Tom Baker that there seems to be no good reason why the precinct should not be opened in the evening, to give life by the infusion of traffic, and something should be done to make it easier for the elderly folk to have some sort of small bus service to relieve them of the heavy burdens they now have to trail along in their trolleys and baskets.

In an article in the *The Guardian* by Terrence Rendixon, 6 August 1966 entitled 'A Town like Trollope' he says:–

> 'Chichester is a fat clucking hen of a town . . . So far I have not said a word about cars but they cannot be ignored in a place like Chichester. The town is equipped with several off-street car parks many of them within the Roman walls. These are acting like honey to wasps and the city is accordingly being stung to death.
>
> The council has grandiose and conventional plans for more car parks and a dual ring road but in such a tiny walled town the solution is to go Japanese and leave cars, like shoes, outside. Special electric buses and delivery vans could then ply to and fro between parks beyond the gates . . . Chichester may not quite be a Barchester but Trollope would still feel at home in it.'

As Chichester was midway between the two university cities, namely Southampton with its Gulbenkian Theatre and Brighton's Sussex University with its Gardner Theatre, I had always hoped, and expected, we should have close relationships. In 1965 after studying theatres in Stratford Ontario, New York, Chicago, and Mineapolis I returned home enthusiastically intent on carrying out the scheme I had seen at the Guthrie Theatre in Mineapolis where they had arrangements for students from their university.

The scheme involved integration of drama students in the theatre for six months of their course so that they obtained practical experience with the theatre professionals. I thought this could work to the mutual benefit of our theatre and the Sussex University.

I therefore arranged a lunch in a Brighton restaurant for Lord Fulton, the Vice Chancellor, and Clements to discuss such possibilities with me. Unfortunately both of them seemed to take up guarded positions as though they were defending their own territories and nothing came of the idea.

Whilst I had a friendly association with the next Vice Chancellor, Lord Asa Briggs, from then onwards relationships with the university have dwindled and this is a pity as we could possibly have helped when the Gardner theatre went through a difficult phase.

I have sketched out the atmosphere surrounding our theatre and now comes my view of what happened in the theatre during the years following the opening in 1962. It is not an official history, it is just a personal valuation and I hope the reader will accept it as such.

CHAPTER 2

Board-room Manoeuvres

The last night of the first season on 8 September was, of course, a gala celebration. We all looked at one another and sighed with relief, it had been a success. Amidst the fond farewells and assurances of lasting friendships, sincerely meant at the time but soon forgotten, members of the cast hurried about collecting their possessions from the dressing rooms and loading up cars to hurry back to their more permanent homes. The stars went off to future engagements but many of the supporting players returned home to sit hopefully by telephones awaiting that call which would summon them to the hoped-for fame and prosperity.

Members of the management staff began to feel there was a good possibility of a permanent career at the theatre knowing with genuine pride that they had been, each in his own way, responsible for the success.

But the members of the Board suddenly realised, some with empty hearts, that they had taken on a huge responsibility for the future. There was pressure from some of them, who were not going on holiday, to have an early meeting but, for reasons I have already explained, I was able to defer this for a few weeks.

Whilst recounting the happenings at this stage it may be as well to describe the structure of the management that we had set up. The constitution had been devised in the early days after studying, in detail, the constitutions of other theatres, especially Glyndebourne which was the nearest to our independent state, and by consultation with the Charity Commissioners since we necessarily became a charity registered by them.

The theatre TRUST is a body of appointed people of repute who could be trusted to look after the interests of those of the public who had donated money towards the building of the theatre. The main body consists of people such as the Mayor, the Bishop, the County Director of Education and the Member of Parliament who are elected as being representative of all walks of life, but who are not representatives, or delegates, of any groups or organisations.

The TRUST holds the lease and is responsible for seeing that its terms are carried out. This lease was granted by what was then the Corporation of the City of Chichester but which later became the Chichester District Council.

The Trust is responsible for all the buildings and grounds included in the lease. It meets approximately twice a year to approve the work of its Executive

Council and to formulate policy regarding improvements and extensions.

The PRODUCTIONS COMPANY, also registered as a charity, rents the buildings from the Trust and is responsible for everything that takes place in the buildings and the grounds. It has always been a convenient arrangement that the members of the Trust Executive Council are the same as the Board of the Productions Company. Meetings can then be divided between the business of both and save a duplication of interest.

This system has worked exceedingly well and it always seems a pity to me that when the National Theatre was formed they did not have a similar arrangement. If the Government and the G.L.C. had formed a trust to hold and maintain the buildings it would have taken the impossible burden of these matters away from Peter Hall and the administration. They could then spend all their creative talents on the productions. As it was, in the end, huge debts had to be wiped off. The money allocated to the Arts Council could have been distributed to all other organisations in a fairer way whilst still supporting the National Theatre.

Those who manage theatres in a similar way to ours will readily appreciate the interminable discussions that have to take place, on so many occasions, as to the 'grey' areas of indeterminate responsibilities. This surely must be different for theatres as compared with industries.

There have been those who advocated that the terms of landlord and tenant should apply to a theatre such as ours as they do in the commercial theatre where an impressario rents a theatre with all its lighting, seating and furnishings etc. But when a company, such as our Productions Company, is there for a great many years instead of months or weeks, seats need upholstering and carpets renewing and whole lighting and sound equipments need updating and completely replacing. It then becomes a matter of compromise and negotiation, according to the prosperity of each company at the time, and since the personnel of the various committees is the same it all works out in the end for the good of the theatre as a whole.

The Trust, as landlord, is only really entitled to discuss its own responsibilities of the lease, maintenance of buildings and proposals and sanctioning of new buildings. But it is naturally interested in the fortunes of its tenant so the Productions Company's chairman's report is eagerly listened to at the Trust meetings but the Trust has no power to direct policy of the artistic or administrative aspects of the productions. That does not prevent trustees expressing opinions as anyone may well guess.

At the first Productions Board meeting after the first season, it soon became apparent that because all the members were people of strong personality, they were going to be a very 'awkward squad' for any chairman to handle. The reason why I had hand-picked them in the first instance was because all of them had made successes in their own sphere of work.

The crusade to get the theatre established, the great hunt for money, the tussle with the magistrates, the anxiety of the first season, keeping the theatrical professionals happy and the daily scrutiny of box office receipts to determine whether we should meet our running expenses; all these were over for the moment.

As with the long distance runner there was exhaustion at the winning post and then elation at the success. Very soon there came the realisation that it was not just a 'once-for-all' but the prestige, once won, had to meet the continual challenge of the future. Of course it had been in the back of our minds all along but there had been no time to worry about it when so many other anxieties were pressing on us.

The Board members showed signs of nerves. They realised there was no chance of being released from the responsibilities they had assumed by creating a large building, presenting it to the public as an attraction, and offering it as a source of livelihood for many people.

Whilst I, personally, was somewhat overawed by the prospect of the future I was, at the same time, exhilarated by the knowledge that during the nine weeks of the first season the numbers of people coming to the theatre had increased each week.

Nobody needed to have come if they had preferred not to do so. The critics of the first two plays had not stopped the audiences for *The Chances* though they had reduced the numbers for *The Broken Heart. Uncle Vanya* was acclaimed by the critics, and by the public, so I was assured that we could succeed if we concentrated on the right plays with star performers. It was the first of my 'trinity of principles' and now it was proved, at least, for the time being. Success at the top is always fragile and, like freedom, needs constant vigilance.

Disagreements within the Board, and it was inevitable there would be many such differences of opinion, have, during the twenty-two years, by the good sense of everyone concerned, been kept within the confines of the Minutes. Possibly we had learnt the lesson from the newspaper accounts of disagreements between the boards of management and the profession in some places such as Nottingham, Leeds and the National Theatre. Such publicity only does harm to a theatre at the time and does no good for the participants.

In our case we had all joined in the effort because we believed in the benefit it would give to so many people and we all worked voluntarily. We were not appointed to serve as representatives of any civic authority or organisation. Our sole duty was to see that the money which the public had donated was correctly used in the most economical manner.

Over the twenty-four years of the Board's existence only one or two members have ever drawn travelling expenses to Board meetings in London or Chichester and all the others have themselves paid for all travelling, telephones and postages and all have contributed, according to their means, to the funds. I, and the majority, have never yet had a free seat in the theatre apart from one or two occasions when sponsors have included us in invitations to their parties. I only state these facts as there are always some cynics who like to think no one does these things for the public good without lucratively gaining from them. Britain can be proud of the fact that there is a whole community in its midst that does much needed voluntary work for other people because its members love to do it, for a multitude of charities, to help their fellow beings.

However this story would not be a true and honest account of all that happened in the theatre if I did not relate some of the difficulties that had to be resolved from time to time, particularly those within the Board. Since they are now all in the past they cannot harm the theatre but they will show how the Board as a whole was able to resolve them with good humour and understanding. It is worthy of note that we hardly ever had to resort to actual voting but as soon as a large majority of opinion was established, agreement was made. That is not to say discussions were not, at times, long, arduous and heated.

The first major disagreement that arose was due to the various misgivings, by some, of the way in which the theatre should be managed in the future. One or two of the members had organised factories and businesses. They sincerely believed there was no difference between running a theatre and a factory. Even though I had never had any experience of the theatre world I was certain in my mind that theatre life was very different to that experienced by us lay people. Traditions had grown up through a long history of experience and there were fundamental differences in the artistic outlook on life compared with that of commerce.

At this stage it is quite likely that someone will wonder why we did not include an expert from the theatre on the Board to help in such discussions. I have always resisted this because I was aware of the many varied opinions in the profession. If we had one representative amongst us the Board might get into the habit of believing that person's pronouncements were always correct and would follow that advice implicitly. Luckily our constitution has been proved right and the Board has always consisted of lay people.

Expert advice is called for in all debates affecting the professional side, listened to, and the advice accepted after it has been weighed against all other considerations. In practice the artistic director has nearly always attended our meetings, together with heads of departments whenever their particular sphere of work was debated.

The problem of the management structure has not really ever been completely solved over the years. So much depends on the varied personalities of directors and administrators. There were members who were wholly convinced, and were vociferous in their demands, that an administrator, probably brought in from the world of commerce, should be appointed to be over the whole of the theatre, even over the artistic and general management. I was dead against this as I was certain, especially in the case of Olivier, that it would not be tolerated.

At the meeting when this resolution was finally put I found myself in the position of being the only one against it. The eloquence of the proposers

Royal Hunt of the Sun *(Angus McBean)*

overcame the doubts of the others by the use of the usual 'fear' prophesies. There was nothing I could do but let the idea be presented to Olivier. From my dealings with him I knew exactly what his response would be.

In a letter to me saying he was deeply disturbed by the news and that he would in no way accept such a person he continued:–

> 'I do wish, dear Leslie, in the most human possible of all manners you could put it to my friends on the Board that they would relax, having built the theatre and attained almost all their ambitions in this regard that they could have achieved, and let the 'horrible pros' get on with the job.'

I replied:–

> 'I heartily agree with all you say about last season and the attitude that should be adopted by members of the Board. I must say on their behalf that all members of the theatrical profession do rather veer away from financial control, if they can, and this makes outside business people worry about

> financial results. The great joy of our project is that you and Pieter Rogers have so wonderfully kept things within bounds and we have all taken pride in having made the balance come out on the right side. I feel sure you will be quite happy about the way matters are trending and I am certain we shall always be able to find methods which satisfy both the artistic requirements of the professionals and the natural anxiety of the Board.'

The issue quietened down after I had sent round a discussion paper about management. I was, probably rightly, accused by some of being a dictator and having such determined ideals that I wouldn't listen to other people. I did listen carefully to other ideas. I could hardly do otherwise when they were so forcefully advanced. But when I felt certain in my mind that the ideas were wrong I did dig my heels in and very often would emphasise my point of view too vehemently to win the discussion. If I get extremely earnest about something I tend to overdo the points I am trying to make and so ruin my case. It is something I always try to control but with the theatre, which was so vulnerable in those days, it brought problems which none of us in business, or in our professions, had faced before, except indirectly.

Many said I cared too much for the theatre and I know this was true. Nicholas de Jongh writing in *The Guardian* so many years later (in fact on 10 May 1983) said of me 'the theatre's powerful founder who has had his way with every Festival Board and artistic director since Laurence Olivier departed.' I wish I had; what fun it would have been. The truth was that I accepted the democratic judgements of those who had helped, so wonderfully, to make the theatre possible even if some of the disadvantages of democracy irked a great deal.

One of the oft recurring criticisms levelled at me is that as I am in a profession, which is based on high ideals, I do not have a financial mind. This again is true when it comes to analysing balance sheets and manipulating money. However it is sometimes forgotten that I have had considerable experience in dealing with officials and people doing voluntary work.

I had been chairman of our national professional associations and chairman of the Chichester Group of Hospitals (comprising seven large and small hospitals) after eighteen years of hospital committees. Under my chairmanship we kept to our budgets when many other districts were overspent. This besides my eighteen years on the City Council chairing several committees where financial matters were paramount.

But to return to the problem of management; there is an interesting and provocative article written by Clifford Hanley entitled 'Civil War in the Civic Theatres' (*Illustrated London News*, 20 January 1968) in which he says:–

> 'The curse of Society has always been that the artist, the highest form of evolution, is employed by inferior creatures, Art is at the mercy of the drapers.'

He goes on to ask who is good enough to employ the artists. The conceit of this is only too apparent and is typical of those who overprice their talents. On the other hand it is true that many of the governing bodies of civic theatres have few people on their Boards of Management with real appreciation, or knowledge, of theatre but may be city councillors (often up to 50% of the committee) who are rather flattered to be appointed and who feel that there is a certain prestige in being in charge of the arts. As with most committees and organisations the real work is done by a few people, and their work can be ruined by the bad decisions of a majority who do not have the requisite knowledge.

It cannot be denied that many Boards of Management would not be necessary if only the artistic side could be relied upon to agree a budget at the beginning of a financial year and keep to it.

Mr Hanley also states that theatres (and he is particularly dealing with repertory theatres) not only fail to make profits, they do not even exist to make profits. This is a statement I will deal with in the chapter on Finances.

He further quoted John Neville as saying that 'committee people are tradespeople who think like tradespeople. The draper–butcher–grocer committee men want to have their cake and eat it too, matching prestige with profits.'

This is a typical generalisation which is totally incorrect in its assumption that all committees are of the same composition. He was probably knocking some particular people he knew. Our Board now consists of Lord Bessborough, a renowned scholar and spokesman for the Arts and Electronics in the House of Lords; Lord Cudlipp a former, famous, newspaper chairman and editor; Mrs Henny Gestetner of the world-wide firm of that name; Dr Cyril Read, a former County Director of Education; Mr Victor Behrens, a surveyor and estate agent in Harley Street; Mr Geoffrey Marwood, a former deputy headmaster; Mr Antony Nelson MP for Chichester; Mr John McKerchar, a former managing director of an important factory; Mr Kenneth Fleet, executive editor of finance and industry at *The Times*; with my son David and myself in a profession.

Why do people who write in this fashion wish to widen the gap between the artistic side and those who build, and administer, theatres in order that there should be sufficient places in which the professionals can display their talents? As in industrial concerns there is no reason why the workers and management should not work in happy accord as one team without there being a gap which some people seem to promote for political or mischievous reasons, though Mr Hanley sincerely believes his statements. What a needless waste of time and emotion when all of us have so little time on this earth.

I heartily agree with Mr Hanley when he states that Boards should not try to interfere with, or control, the artistic director and I have always advocated this policy. I deal with how the various directors of our theatre have co-operated with the Board in another chapter.

The Board must swim, or sink, with the artistic director's policy and if there is a consistent run of failures, then it is only right the director should resign. Not even the greatest of impressarios can make sure of every play being a success, many of them would be millionaires if that were possible. I remember Lord Bernard Delfont telling me once that, even with his great experience of a long and successful career, he could never be sure of the success of a play until the first night was half way through. Every director must be allowed his proportion of successes and failures.

The problem of management will, I fear, always be with us. Even after twenty-one years having tried various formulae we are not yet convinced we have discovered the correct system though I have every confidence in the present arrangement with John Gale having been appointed as our director.*

Another difficulty which arose after our first season was the question of leadership. I have never been interested, in the slightest, in the sort of power struggles which take place in the Board-rooms of commercial enterprises. They are completely foreign to my nature. To my mind it is even worse when they take place where everyone is working for a common cause in a voluntary effort. I particularly regret any rivalry between charitable organisations. It destroys the real reason for being together if people cannot work amicably. There can only be frustration and lack of achievement.

Unfortunately one or two members, who are no longer on the Board, could not see this point of view and a sort of 'take over' was contemplated. It almost became an attempt to create 'character assassination' and a whispering suggestion that I wanted the job of being the administrator of the theatre. Nothing could have been more absurd or untrue. I was in the midst of a very successful practice that kept me fully occupied all my days and I thoroughly enjoyed my work. My public life, and the work for the theatre, took up most of my spare time.

Eventually I found myself manoeuvred into a minority of one and I felt I had lost the confidence of the Board with the ideals I was pursuing for the theatre. Therefore on 5 December 1964 (two years after we had opened the theatre) I resigned from the chairmanship of the Productions Company, whilst remaining a member of the Board and chairman of the Trust, a position I have held ever since.

On 10 December the Board passed, in my absence, a unanimous vote of confidence requesting me to remain as chairman. I decided to keep to my decision and I have remained an ordinary member of the Board until this day except for being temporary chairman in 1984. I never regretted my decision as it made it more possible for me to fight for my ideals without the handicap of trying to be neutral as a chairman.

*This book only relates events up to the end of the year 1984. John Gale has been appointed to succeed Patrick Garland, and will be the theatre director at the end of the 1984 season.

I may be wrong but I think in this sort of enterprise the chairman needs to be a leader rather than a neutral referee.

Readers of *The Impossible Theatre* will know the full extent of my founding of the theatre, and all that it entailed, so I will not repeat it here. Suffice to say that it was only natural that I should be called upon, together with Lord Bessborough, for all the radio and television interviews. There were a great number of these as interest in the theatre was intense for at least two years.

This prominence created some feeling that I was getting all the honour and publicity, whilst the many who had given money and worked hard were possibly being left in the background. I never failed to keep on acknowledging the fact that, first of all, I had copied the wonderful example of the people of Stratford, Ontario, and secondly I always paid tribute to those who had so selflessly helped during the critical stages. In fact I still do this to the best of my ability every time an occasion arises and I get great pleasure from doing so.

Nevertheless human nature being as it is, there was still some resentment from a few that tributes were paid to me and finally two members of the Board resigned. Whilst I must say I was relieved at the change in atmosphere I deeply regretted their departure as they had worked tremendously hard and, at times, given excellent advice. I am glad to say both have remained members of the Trust and their friendship remains with us.

David Biart, a local solicitor, and until then secretary to the Board, was elected as chairman for the time being after my resignation but he declined to accept the chairmanship for any length of time owing to the pressure of his own practice. After a few months Mr A. T. Smith became chairman of the Productions Board. A resolution at the time stipulated that it should be for three year terms in the future but in the passage of time this was forgotten and he remained for fifteen years. No one could have been keener or more absorbed in the affairs of the theatre and the arrangement suited me very well as he worked very closely with me, never making a decision without talking it over even when we quite often disagreed. In this way affairs were settled on behalf of, and with, the Board.

Mr Smith resigned as chairman in 1980. As proof of the friendships made throughout our history no one has ever resigned from the Trust in an unfriendly way no matter what position they have held. This is an indication of the amazing loyalty which this theatre seems to engender.

Mrs Henny Gestetner, who had been a member from the beginning and an extremely generous donor in many ways, was elected chairman in 1980 for three years. This policy of changing both artistic directors and chairmen at regular intervals brings in new leaderships with fresh bright ideas.

Although the theatre is run by professionals it will always be different from others, except perhaps Pitlochry, in that all the members of the Board, together with the Theatre Society, were personally involved in the creation and the building of the theatre. Therefore they will always have an intense personal interest in all that goes on. Most of our artistic directors have come to realise this and duly decide to accept the Board meetings where details are examined in more minuteness than would be the case with civic or commercial theatres. How each director has coped with this situation will be shown in another chapter.

Times are changing and it is now necessary to alter the composition of the Board to include some who have not been with us at the beginning. Financial considerations will force themselves on the theatre and the need for influential financial connections will be absolutely necessary in order to keep the theatre stable and prosperous.

CHAPTER 3
The Building

I find it astounding that I have never heard a valid or informed adverse criticism of the appearance of the original building. It may be said that perhaps people were too kind, or good-mannered, to tell me of their objections but I do not think this is true. Everyone seems to enjoy giving an opinion on architecture and I doubt whether they would have been reluctant in this case. I have purposely sought opinions from architects, and other specialists, and they have always praised the conception of such a building placed in a park near a Georgian city with its beautiful cathedral. There could hardly be a more sensitive architectural issue than that of a modern edifice superimposed on such a locality. During the construction period, and after, groups from architects' conferences came to examine its revolutionary construction.

Experts from all over the world came to see the first suspended roof, a system which is now commonly seen in new buildings everywhere. In February 1963 a group of leading French architects visited the theatre to help them in their consideration of plans to build a 'Maison de la Culture' in Lyons.

How thankful I have always been that I happened to know of Philip Powell through his father being a canon of Chichester Cathedral and because I had seen, and admired, his symbolic emblem, the Skylon, at the 1951 Festival of Britain. The scrapbook of memory so often provides the key that unlocks the doors to future endeavours.

As a result of his inspiration the main building has never needed alteration since it was first built, and there are only one or two aspects of it that I would have had different.

One was the vomitories (hateful word) which would have been better as slopes rather than steps so that retreating armies etc could rush off rather than be seen descending step by step however cleverly they camouflage their exits by lowering their heads. It would be impossible to correct this now as the gradient, to be safe, would mean that the slope would extend out into the foyer, almost out to the park! I found at the Sheffield Crucible that they do have slopes but they are of a very steep gradient, which appeared hazardously slippery for some actors to negotiate, and which were not used by the audience as in our case.

The second improvement that could have been made was to provide an orchestra pit. We had left two rows of seats on the same level as the gangway around the stage so that they could be removed for an orchestra. We soon found the fire authorities, quite rightly, could not agree to this arrangement as it would have blocked two exits. No building is perfect but ours was very nearly so. We had made certain of two great fundamental requirements. A large auditorium and a large foyer which need never be changed or found to be inadequate.

The size of the auditorium, to seat approximately 1,340 people, has made the whole proposition commercially viable and the large foyer enables people of all incomes and ages to mix in a social atmosphere, regardless of the price of the seats which they are going to occupy. Not like the nineteenth century theatres which one writer said were designed to supply each social class with a separate part of the house to sit in with separate entrances and exits so that they could not mix.

These initial ingredients have been our greatest assets and whilst the concrete auditorium cannot be enlarged, and we have proved that this is not necessary, the foyer could, and has been increased in size with a new bar area and box office department.

I am convinced that if the audience is in one huge sweep of seats, instead of being chopped up into sections, there is incentive for it to react into mass laughter and emotion. Even though we have two balconies, one on either side, they mould into the centre and everyone can feel they are part of the whole and can see the rest of the audience. I have so often experienced the feeling of isolation created in some far-off circle or gallery of other theatres. On my second visit to the Stratford Ontario theatre, I regretted the circle balcony which whilst it had increased the audience to about 2,000, and may have been necessary for financial reasons, it had somewhat destroyed a lot of the well publicised intimacy between audience and stage.

I argued this point with Guthrie when he showed me the designs for the Minneapolis Theatre which was about to be built and which I later visited. He had advocated sections of the audience to be partitioned off. The same idea has been carried out at the Olivier Theatre in the National Theatre complex and at Plymouth. I have sat in one of these, on occasion, in all three theatres and felt as if I was in some sort of concentration camp. It was uncomfortable to see the rest of the audience looking at us as though we were a lot of VIPs. At least in all these theatres, except Plymouth where I hear there are complaints of sight lines for some people in the stalls, there are no pillars or other obstructions and everyone, as in ours, gets a splendid uninterrupted view of the stage.

The other requirement I have always wished for was that we could cut off the sides of the auditorium temporarily for more intimate events such as chamber concerts, recitals etc. This has been achieved wonderfully at Plymouth where a section of the roof can be lowered, by machinery, to cut off the upper circle. Whilst this does create other difficulties it must be conceded that it is a great advantage.

I know Olivier rather wished our auditorium had been more like a cockpit with all the seats in a steep gradient. I think our arrangement of one half being an easier gradient than the rest is better than having seats at the back so steep that you feel you are overbalancing on the edge of a precipice. I shall never forget the experience when, in my early youth, I sat at the top of the Scala Theatre to see a feature film starring the Gish sisters in *The Orphans of the Storm*: I felt all the time I would soon fall over into the stalls which seemed miles below. After all, you do not view life's pageant from a first floor window looking at the top of people's heads.

We only have two rows, M and B (reminiscent of a famous drug), which are not quite so good for sighting. Row B is on the same level as row A (for the aforementioned reason of provision for an orchestra) and, when we have the money to spend, we hope to alter this row in height so that it will be midway between the levels of A and C.* It seems peculiar that all the people who get seats in row B seem to be small people and all those in row A seem to be tall ones.

Over the years there have been many amusing descriptions applied to the look of the building. Correspondents have vied with one another in their inventiveness and the following are some of the examples:–

An enormous home plate in a tight little ball pitch.
A merry-go-round outside and a circus inside.
The roof is like an inverted radio telescope.
A concrete lozenge in a rolling Sussex field.
Erupting starkly like a brown and white concrete mushroom-shaped atom cloud from the tree-lined Oaklands Park. (Sally K. Marks)

A disquieting theatre because the soaring roof hangs too low above the saucer of the auditorium. It is like attending festivities inside an oyster. (Bamber Gasgoine).
This theatre sees the start of a bloodless revolution in British Theatre. The theatre at Chichester is revolutionary. It is mushroom-shaped, audiences sit in the top of the mushroom while below in the stalk are dressing rooms, offices and other facilities. (British Travel Association July 1962).

Perhaps we should have promoted a competition for the most exotic or outlandish definition of the theatre's appearance.

One of the most pleasant features of this theatre-in-a-park was its setting within a ring of magnificent elm trees. Alas, they fell victim to the elm disease which ravaged the countryside in 1969. The Trust was very conscious of beautifying the whole area and a scheme of tree planting was quickly devised, but it will take a long time before the same effect is produced with chestnut and flowering trees. Perhaps this was a better fate than

*(This was achieved in 1985.)

Macbeth, *1966 (John Timbers)*

that which other theatres have suffered, such as the National, where proposed skyscrapers can be built around it dwarfing it instead of it appearing to be a tall building on the skyline.

I enjoyed entertaining Denys Lasdun when he came down to Chichester to see the theatre at a time when he was preparing his plans for the National. We were able to discuss the pros and cons of an amphitheatre stage but I could not draw any conclusion as to whether he favoured the idea. He was just exploring all the possibilities and weighing them against the arguments of Olivier's experience at Chichester and the more orthodox urging of other directors.

As it turned out the Olivier Theatre was constructed with a wide open and somewhat thrust stage, leaving the Lyttleton as the proscenium one. These two alternatives plus the flexible Cottesloe small theatre gave the National all that it could possibly be given to suit all tastes and all plays.

The original principle of creating our theatre in phases, as money became available, has proved extremely successful. When Michael Langham came to Chichester in 1963 with the Stratford, Ontario Company, he spoke somewhat disparagingly about Chichester having been built on a shoestring. Whilst admitting that our lighting system was a thousand times better than theirs, he said the theatre was faulty in many ways because no one of the theatre world had been involved in the plans when it was being built. He had completely forgotten that Tyrone Guthrie had advised me from the very beginning and that Philip Powell and Partners had gone to see him, thoroughly discussed the preliminary sketches and had adopted his suggestions. Guthrie enthusiastically approved the final construction and when Olivier came in during the actual building he asked for only a few minor modifications of the stage area and these were made.

Langham had also forgotten that Stratford, Ontario had wisely started in a tent, with very few facilities, in order to see whether the adventure could be a success. This was one of my trinity of principles copied from their experiences which I had admired so much. I was determined we would act cautiously in the same way except that we started off with a permanent building as a nucleus around which improvements could be made.

One of our early experiences had been the use of a hut, at the rear of the theatre, to be used as dressing rooms for 'extras'. There was also a ramp so that scenery could be unloaded from the pantechnicons which housed the scenery for each alternate play. All this was accepted in great spirit by the acting profession in their co-operation in getting the first season off to a flying start. We were as keen to remove these temporary structures as were some of the members of the City Council who took the opportunity to moan about the appearance of the park. One even complained in open Council that he had seen some empty milk bottles at the back which were making the park untidy. I think there were six bottles in all!

On the whole, however, we have always had excellent relations with all three authorities. The planning committees (reckoned to be amongst the most difficult in the country) and officials, the local panel of architects and the building inspectors have been exceedingly helpful. I think this is probably due to our careful, tactful approaches, willingness to see their point of view when it seemed reasonable, and the fact that we never asked for grants.

The early difficulties with the magistrates have not been repeated and the fire authorities have been able to assess the special conditions necessary for an amphitheatre stage. Their requirements have generally been logical and have been carried out to the letter. We have, of course, suffered, like all institutions, from the frequent changes of officers which means that each new one appointed in charge of the local unit imposes new restrictions which he has gleaned from the theoretical teaching at the Fire Department colleges and which are individually irrefutable. It is the natural wish of each to impose his own authority in his area and whilst this can sometimes cause frustration it is quite possible to deal with it by reasoned debate if this can be achieved before a report is made.

Over the years the theatre, like Topsy, has grown and most of the additions have been shown during the planning stage to Philip Powell, and approved by him, to ensure that none of them would spoil his original concept. Once the main building had been finished he was unable to remain as our architect as he and his firm were involved in massive projects elsewhere.

It is quite amazing to realise now that since the first building cost of £120,000 in 1961/62 another £439,000 has been spent on additions. The way in which this money has been found I will deal with in the chapter on Finance. The building is now insured for £3,000,000.

The first major addition came about at the beginning of John Clements' reign. With his belief in London West End proscenium types of production, the back stage area became impossible because of the quantities of scenery. A large scene dock with a large scenery lift was constructed making it possible to provide below it a new set of dressing rooms with showers, rooms for heads of backstage departments and a small laundry etc.

I had always advocated that this sort of theatre should pioneer, in Britain, the proper use of the auditorium stage which would concentrate on the finest acting supported by unique and exciting lighting effects, superb quality dressing, and few props rather than elaborate pretty scenery. Therefore this need for, and use of, the scenery dock was a disappointment to me. I had hoped that concentration of the audiences' attention would be on the acting, rather than the surrounds on the stage, as such productions could be seen in all the other theatres.

The next important addition was the installation of air conditioning. Until then, that is for the first four years, we had been able to open the theatre only for the summer season with the addition of a month or so in the late spring and early autumn.

The first Christmas carol concerts necessitated the audiences coming prepared to wear overcoats, blankets and possibly some discreetly disguised hot water bottles. And yet they came filling the theatre rather than miss the joy of meeting together in the fellowship which had its own warmth. The foyer had underfloor heating but this was very expensive to run. We had always hoped to cover the foyer floor with carpeting but in those days suitable safe carpeting had rubber backing which would have been unpleasant with the heating below it. It was therefore decided to postpone this. What a difference the cost would be now. The vinyl flooring has proved wonderfully resistant to wear though cold in appearance.

A few letters in the local newspapers appeared complaining of the theatre standing empty and desolate for part of the year but they did not realise that we had to progress slowly until money was available to install the air conditioning.

At last we were able to go ahead and now it is possible for us to proclaim it as a theatre for all seasons. The greatest worry about installing air conditioning was to eliminate any reverberations from the necessary machinery, which would utterly ruin some performances. We insisted that whatever system was used it must be proof from any noise whatsoever.

This was splendidly effected by placing the motors in a separate building with the result that there is not the slightest noise from it. When it was first installed I was appalled at the sight of the huge aluminium ducts running round the base of the roof completely ruining the look of the auditorium. But by the time these ducts were painted the same colours as the walls they became inconspicuous and I doubt if many of the audience know they are there.

Sometimes down draughts are felt and I am one of the unlucky ones in the seats I usually occupy (my only privilege in the theatre is that I am always able to book the same seats). It seems impossible with the changing of air to eliminate entirely this slight difficulty but this disadvantage is little compared with the huge advantage everyone feels by being cool in summer and warm in winter whatever extremes of temperature there are in the park. I understand that at the time when we installed this only one or two of the London theatres had air conditioning, and some are stifling hot in summer even now. Glyndebourne has always been troubled in this way; especially is this difficult when sitting under the balcony after having had wine during the interval meal.

Machinery for air conditioning is not infallible but we have been lucky on the few occasions failure has occurred that it has not been on an extremely cold or hot day. The National Theatre was unlucky in that this occurred during their first year on the hottest day of the year.

We were especially lucky that the first year after we installed it there happened to be one of the very hottest summers (1969) and our troubles without the cooling system would have been immense. Here I would like to pay tribute to the wonderful voluntary help we get from the Red Cross and the St. John Ambulance people who have attended every one of our performances and given such valuable assistance in the few cases where there has been fainting or other sudden illness of members of the audience. On one occasion during a performance of *Terra Nova* (1980) a member of the audience had an epileptic fit and the show had to be stopped for a while. The cast continued after a pause as though nothing had happened and there were tributes in the press to them for the way in which they had carried on afterwards.

Before we installed the air conditioning in 1967 we suffered from the nuisance of people fanning themselves with programmes. This is particularly distracting in an open auditorium. The only time this occurs now is when people have indulged in drinking before the performance or at the interval. This sort of body central heating and that of those who take certain pills such as heart pills causes them to blame the atmosphere in the theatre. A little while ago I sat near a lady who, without ceasing, fanned herself with the pretty fan she had brought with her. When I mentioned it to her at the interval, explaining that it was very distracting, she apologised and ceased to do it. She had not realised we had fresh air blowing through the theatre all the time.

Air conditioning can be a disadvantage in certain circumstances as when *Miss Julie* was first designed. Four hundred and sixteen ounces of lilac toilet water were bought with the idea of spraying the auditorium to give realism to the lilac tree on stage. The designer had not realised that with the air movement all the scent went out to the park and none to the audience. It was reported that many people walking their dogs in the park wasted a lot of time hunting for a lilac tree!

During the summer the concrete building retains the heat for a long time but on the other hand it takes at least a day prior to an event in winter for it to be warmed up. This means that the cost of hiring the theatre for any isolated charity is considerably increased and organisers wonder why the cost of this, plus cleaning, employment of front of house staff, electricians etc, runs into a few hundred pounds.

The conical roof has had its problems. The main difficulty at first was the build up of heat inside and this was cured when in 1966 we lifted the apex to allow heat to escape. The main trouble was the fact that on occasions there can be a sun-drenched south side with a cold north wind blowing on the north side. Expansion and contraction causes gaps in the covering felt and metal.

Eventually this was cured by means of a system of sliding panels which overlapped and allowed for the changes in temperature.

Heavy rain or hail and external noises, such as over-loud speakers at football matches nearby, can be heard by the audiences. This latter nuisance only occurs at matinees and generally not during the festival season.

The cathedral bells can be heard faintly when it is a southerly wind and this has been appropriate in some dramas and sometimes it has been incongruous. All these are minor and very isolated occasions and I understand many other buildings such as the Festival Hall and the Albert Hall in London have the same disadvantages. Stratford Ontario had great difficulty when it was a tent. Whistles from the nearby trains in large shunting yards could interrupt a programme.

One day I read in the newspapers there was a scare about the use of calcium chloride mixed into concrete to preserve it from the effects of frost during building operations. This was reckoned to, in time, make the concrete crumble. I spent a sleepless night imagining the theatre crumbling into dust. I should have known that such a reputable architect, and the builders McAlpine, would not take such a risk, so all was well. This has been confirmed by them and by the several meticulous surveys that we have had over the years and there is no fear for the future.

The first major addition to the building was the provision of the scene dock, scene lift, extra dressing rooms with showers and rooms for the chiefs of backstage departments such as the engineer, electricians, carpenters and wardrobe. Extra space for properties, large and small, was indeed necessary and it was also a matter of keeping faith with our landlords, the City Council, that the hut should be removed as soon as possible.

John Clements' productions nearly always depended on scenery. Even Olivier was tempted by Roger Furze to have scenery for *The Broken Heart*, in the first season, which stretched from stage floor to the roof. To me this all seemed a step away from the original idea of an auditorium thrust stage presentation.

Lord Chandos in an interview by Robert Harling (*The Sunday Times* 10 March 1963) said:–

> 'We have learnt a lot from Chichester whilst considering the building of the National Theatre. We learnt nothing from the Mermaid as that was a conversion. I think that a panel of theatre experts, such as we have with Laurence Olivier, Peter Hall, Roger Furze, Tania Moisewitsch, should settle the requirements rather than bring in an outside architect-engineer-designer to take an entirely new fresh look at the problem.'

That we made mistakes was inevitable, but very few fundamental ones were made so both arguments are valid in their own particular context. When Lord Chandos was asked if such a building committee as he envisaged might not impose too many restrictions on an architect before he begins, he replied:–

> 'Not at all. We're back on a right relationship between patron and architect. The building committee is not only the patron, so to speak, they are artists in their own right. They will talk the same language.'

I have never stopped thanking my lucky stars for the conviction I had that our particular theatre needed someone from outside who never before had designed a theatre, but who, having had an inspiration, did consult and accept theatre advice. Anything orthodox would have failed in this area as it was already well supplied with such proscenium theatres.

In 1967 we extended the foyer at one end to make another bar and at the other end to make a box-office area, thus relieving the foyer of queues for booking. This created a cloakroom and sweet sales counter in the foyer. A new bar was given to us by Messrs Brickwoods.

In 1972 we added a 'green room' for the members of the companies and all members of the staff. Leading from this is a garden wall secluded enough for them all to relax away from the public gaze. This was one of those instant 'one morning it was a pile of builders left-overs' and by the afternoon it was a fully stocked garden with lawn and flowers.

A scheme for an addition to the box office to house a room for the Society was turned down at the last minute by the Society just when it was to be approved by the Trust. This was the abortive work of one architect. Then came the big scheme divided into three phases to get rid of the temporary buildings of the restaurant and administration offices.

Phase 1 was to be the administration buildings so that the ground opposite the main entrance to the theatre could be cleared for phase 2. This would be a two-storied building to house the restaurant and the Society room. Phase 3 was to have a fully equipped studio theatre adjoining the other building with common facilities.

Plans drawn up by Mr Paul White for all three phases were just ready to go for planning permission when he most unfortunately died. This was a great loss as he was an excellent architect and we negotiated well with him. This meant a loss of all the fees, including those of surveyors etc. Even though we obtained from his executors the agreement that we could use the plans, the next architect refused to use them as he wanted to create his own.

We built the new administration block attached to the south side of the main building, but no one on the Trust, or the Society Committee, approved his plans for the phase 2 building. It was necessary by now to find a new rehearsal area as our lease on the Minerva Studios (formerly the Unicorn Hotel) in Eastgate Square, had finished. His designs included a central space for trees and greenery which, whilst it would have been an attraction for the restaurant, would also have involved the Society room and this precluded the possibility of having a space for rehearsal wide enough to encompass the width of the theatre stage. Estimates also suddenly soared so it was decided to start all over again for the two final phases.

These most unfortunate delays have not only cost us large sums of money in abortive work, they have increased costs because of inflation. Now that planning permission has been granted for phase 2 (see Controversies chapter) we are starting, once again, on a big effort to get the money.

One last comment on the design of the theatre building. Overheard in the box office area. A couple studying the plan of the auditorium said 'The Greek pattern, it's based on the Greek pattern isn't it?' To which came the reply, 'Yes, the Greek pattern. You'd think they could have thought of something more up-to-date, wouldn't you?'!

CHAPTER 4
Use of Stage

When Sybil Thorndike opened the University of Southampton's new theatre she said:–

> 'As long as there are human beings the theatre remains the bulkhead for all sorts of questions, races, colours and peoples and it is the widest of arts. Music teaches us to hear, the painter sees more than the ordinary eye. The sculptor feels the great masses more than anyone else, but the theatre goes deeper.
>
> It shows what the creature is and how every creature is part of one another. The more we come to understand the theatre the richer we are as people. Others are following on close behind but we are in the forefront of this successful study, of human beings in all their problems. The theatre is a study of human beings in all sorts of atmospheres and problems. It is almost like a microscope.'

I hope it will always be remembered that when I first suggested how the Chichester Theatre should be designed on the same principle as that of the Stratford, Ontario Theatre, namely an auditorium or thrust stage, it was because I believed the finest reply that could be made by live theatre to the flat screens of cinema and television, was to promote the 3D dimension with which only live theatre could at that time, and even now, enthrall the public.

When considering the intense battle that has been fought ever since about our stage it should also be remembered that I never advocated that its style should replace the proscenium presentations. I have always said it should be promoted alongside as an alternative challenge to actors, directors, playwrights and designers.

It was the first permanent building for the auditorium stage in Europe, and whilst I am glad to see that similar ones have been built, such as the Sheffield Crucible and the Olivier Theatre at the National, much is still to be learnt of its use.

Tyrone Guthrie, who was the great exponent of this type of production, helped me throughout and I have paid tribute to him in my first book as well as emphasising my appreciation of the example of the Stratford, Ontario pioneers. I also mentioned the parts played by the theatre-in-the-round at the Pembroke Hall, Croydon, Stephen Joseph's Victoria Stoke-on-Trent theatre, and the open stage of the Mermaid.

The Mermaid, started in 1959 in the City of London, was the first example of a wide open stage unhampered by a proscenium, but still with the audience seated centrally. Everybody could see well and hear well and the brick walls stressed the exciting conversion from a riverside wharf.

It is very sad that following its rebuilding it has had the bad luck to be forced to compete with the huge Barbican complex housing the Royal Shakespeare Company financed by the City and millions of pounds from the Arts Council. The Mermaid's future is uncertain and everyone must feel sympathy for Bernard Miles (first knighted and then made Lord) when at the end of his career it was not possible to keep his cherished creation where he had been using his talents for acting and producing.

Labels and definitions are not always possible to put into black and white and so there will always be differences of opinion as to the correct description of our type of stage. Thrust, auditorium, or arena. Certainly not apron or in-the-round as it is so often called.

In January 1961 (whilst our theatre was being built) I wrote to Dr Richard Southern deploring the statement attributed to him that the proposed Southampton University Theatre would be 'the first twentieth-century theatre, except for one in Ontario, to be specifically designed for the open stage.' This led to a friendly exchange of correspondence in which he rightly pointed out that he had advocated the use of open stages in his book *The Open Stage* as far back as 1953.

What transpired from this correspondence was the confusion of terms. He felt that the Southampton project did have people on all three sides but to my way of thinking this was to a very minor degree, according to the plans, compared with the great protrusion of our stage, and that in Ontario, into the audience.

I quote his definition of 'open stage' and his belief that the word 'arena' was incorrect:–

> 'An arena must be, by definition, a full circle since it is the central part of an amphitheatre' (O.E.D.). Thus the only form of theatre to which the word is applicable correctly is the "Theatre in the Round". This whole terminology is loosely handled at present. Thus it is not abundantly clear to an outsider that your theatre is a pure open-stage theatre.
>
> Your phrase an "arena-stage" must be a contradiction in terms (since an arena cannot be a stage). It is my most firm belief that the techniques both of designing and playing in open stage theatres are fundamentally different from these techniques in theatre-in-the-round.'

Whilst I heartily agree with this last statement I still think, and I replied to this effect, that the use of the word arena is not so wrong despite the dictionary definition. Events at places like Olympia and the White City in London, have one wall where the performers have their entrances and exits with the other three walls peopled with an audience, even though the 'stage' extends much deeper than in our theatre. These seem to be called,

An Italian Straw Hat, *1967 (Zoe Dominic)*

by common usage, arenas. Surely 'in-the-round' means exactly that. The audience is all round the stage and not on three sides such as ours.

If I concede his academic definition then the labels 'thrust stage' or more properly, 'amphitheatre' seem more descriptive. 'Apron stage' means adding a mere platform extension, which many theatres have tried as a compromise to get out of prosceniums. So it is that, in this record of our theatre, I have alternately used the phrases 'thrust' or 'auditorium'. Dr Southern's preference for 'open stage' theatres portrays to me those theatres which have stages the whole width of the theatre without a proscenium, such as the Mermaid. This does not differentiate between those who have the audience in serried rows in a somewhat rectangular hall, perhaps with a few people at the side, and those, like ours, where the stage juts right out into the audience with people on three sides giving the 3D effect which gives suitable plays such an added dramatic impact. This I believe is the secret of our popularity with our audiences.

I am pleased that other theatres have been built with the auditorium stage concept since we began in 1962. The National Theatre's Olivier auditorium was influenced by Olivier's experience with us. Civic theatres such as Nottingham Playhouse and Sheffields Crucible followed our pattern and the new Plymouth Theatre has a fairly thrust stage appearance.

The National Theatre Company and the nucleus of their costume department came from our theatre. We naturally take pride in these facts as well as being the first permanent building for our kind of stage in Europe. It is therefore a little disappointing that some of the ones mentioned do not acknowledge these facts in their propoganda when they state they were the first, but these things happen when memory is blurred by the passage of time. We were very pleased to entertain representatives from Nottingham and Sheffield when they were contemplating construction of their theatres and we willingly helped them to investigate our construction and management.

We have always been ready to give advice on money-raising efforts to the new theatres and many were encouraged by our success such as the Yvonne Arnaud at Guildford and the Redgrave at Farnham. Whether they adopted our ideas, or not, does not matter but it is good for everyone if the theatre communities help one another. One of the virtues I admire in the farming world is where individual farmers keenly exchange their knowledge and skills rather than live in secretive competition.

I had always hoped there would be more of our kind of theatre so that experience by all concerned would lead to exchanges of ideas and plays suitable to our presentations without proscenium conditions. Since Nottingham opened I have heard they had considerable adverse debates in their local newspapers when the plans were first revealed, regarding the amphitheatre stage but, luckily in consultation with Tyrone Guthrie, and with the success of our theatre, they persisted. I doubt whether they have ever regretted their decision. I wish I had known of their controversy, I would have enjoyed joining in.

In 1964 the Stratford, Ontario Company made a special visit, at our invitation, and performed three plays from their repertoire. Namely *Timon of Athens*, *Love's Labour's Lost* and *Le Bourgeois Gentilhomme*. They expertly illustrated how such a stage can be fully utilised as a result of their many years' experience. It is significant that the many hundreds of people who saw those productions, vividly remember the excellent effects they demonstrated. Each of the productions showed how with little scenery, good lighting and almost ballet form grouping and movement, the stage was used to the full enjoyment of the audience on all three sides.

Olivier had only one stage step above the surrounding level but he increased this to two in the second year. The Ontario people immediately added one more step in keeping with their own permanent stage in Canada. The increased height, which made a great difference, has been kept ever since as it serves well for all sight lines.

The fixed balcony at the rear of the stage was altered by Clements and this again gave far more flexibility for various arrangements of scenery and background.

There have been over the years fierce battles over the merits, and mistakes, of using such a stage as ours and this is what I expected and hoped for. It is therefore with pleasure that I record both the favourable and the unfavourable reviews which have been written over the years. I will mix them as some contradict one another.

Here are some examples:–

Peter Roberts, *Plays and Players*, September 1963, reviewing the production of *Uncle Vanya*:–

> 'Whenever a production is staged on a new open stage such as Chichester's, is unsuccessful, it is the open stage that is blamed. When it is stunningly right like this year's *Uncle Vanya*, which now certainly does not need picture frame support, we are told that it, of course, would be just as good behind a proscenium arch. So, with the Old Guard, you just cannot win. But I'd say this production is a far more eloquent vindication of the open stage than any of the noisy and aggressive proclamations of its disciples.'

Peter Foster, *Sunday Telegraph*, 1963, says of the same play:–

> 'A pity it had to be played on the trot in that horrid arena.'

Olivier in a BBC interview at Christmas 1963 said:–

> 'Every lounge has a proscenium arch in the corner with the advent of TV. The theatre should offer something different. But what? The architect of the National Theatre has discovered that the over-forties hope for a proscenium type theatre whereas the under-forties hope for an amphitheatre.'

(Author's note: I started contemplating the idea of a theatre for Chichester at the age of 56.)

Michael Langham, artistic director of the Stratford, Ontario Theatre said:–

> 'Acting on an amphitheatre stage is like on a quicksand. We are on to something exciting and we want other countries to take part in the experiment. Theatre has to work from year to year, always on quicksands, always taking risks and adventuring. Only in that way can it keep alive.'

John Clements at a Theatre Society dinner said his job was a frightening thing to do and it presented immense difficulties and immense problems.

Alan Brien, *The Sunday Times*, November 1965, *Border Line Case*, said:–

> 'Chichester's vast open flight deck stage under its towering wooden big-top has its performers tumbling, cavorting into sight from under your feet and the backwash of lights painting the faces of the audience with great splodges of reflected colour seems designed for sport or circus rather than a play. It only needs the sweet stink of roasted peanuts, drifting chiffon veils of

cloudy cigar smoke, the monkeyish twittering and tweeting of young children and the occasional bobbing of an escaped balloon to become the kind of pop arena for which Brecht once yearned as the show place for his epic theatre. It is not surprising that the most successful productions here should be those which have some of the character of a wrestling match, a tournament, a political rally, a high wire act or even a public execution.'

(Author's note: for example, *Enemy of the People* 1975 had a political rally, *The Devil's Disciple* 1979 and *Armstrong's Last Good Night* had executions, and *As You Like It* 1983 had a wrestling match.)

Alan Brien goes on to say:–

'What seems native to this many tiered grandstand is the wide screened drama which John Osborne, Peter Shaffer and John Arden have recently returned to the stage. It demands physical spectacular action set, if not in jungles and battlefields, at least in parliaments and palaces. The language which best bounces back from the sounding boards is athletic and oratorical rather than the intimate and conversational. Domestic naturalism becomes oddly artificial and strained while ritual, mime dances, and duels receive some of their ancient power and significance. Chichester's authors must write for the public eye even more than for the private ear.'

Darlington, who many times enjoyed and praised the productions, said in an article in the *Daily Telegraph* entitled 'Fine step forward in bold excitement':–

'As the successful summer seasons succeed one another at the Chichester Theatre, and it becomes clear that a tradition has established itself, I find my own attitude towards this bold experiment changing slightly but steadily.

The chief question in my mind now, as I board the train for Chichester, is not what sort of performance I am going to see but how well will this performance fit the rigid requirements of the open stage.

In the earlier seasons I confess I was not so objective. I was full of admiration, and still am, for the courage which made the experiment possible and for the enterprise which financed it. I wanted it to succeed. I said what could be said of the advantages of the open stage production and kept a reflective eye on its drawbacks hoping they would be surmounted. They haven't been and now I think they can't be. Experience so far has been that picture stage plays inevitably suffer loss by being transferred to the open stage conditions.

Uncle Vanya and *St. Joan* did famously at Chichester but not until they came to the Old Vic did we see these productions in their full glory. Last night we took another step forward in this most valuable series of experiments.

How could a two-character play like Strindberg's *Miss Julie*, written, if ever a play was, for a small intimate stage but generating explosive force stand up to the transfer? It stands up very strongly indeed. I have never seen this play better done, and if it were not for the inexplicable tailing off and loss of power towards the close I should now be exploring my vocabulary for superlatives to do this performance justice.'

Tynan finishes his first article on the theatre:–

'I will postpone judgement on Chichester's open stage until I have seen its virtues better tested. It is not every day or decade that a new playhouse is baptised by a great actor. Therefore book soon and 'he that flinches' to give Fletcher the last word 'May he lye lowzie in a ditch.'

(We did not find any Cicestrians in any ditches or the Lavant stream.) It was Bernard Levin who first started talking about 'the vast open stretches of the wide open stage' at Chichester and we have been plagued with this phrase ever since. In actual fact the width of the stage itself is 30ft ½in actual stage width and 38ft ½in including steps; this is no wider than many London stages but it is the wide gangway around it, dividing it from the audience, that adds up to the wide aperture. This gangway is seldom acted upon but the surrounding steps of the stage are frequently used to great effect.

I would rather have this arrangement than one where the people are sitting right up to the stage, almost with their noses on the stage like children looking over a table that is too tall for them. This happens at the Sheffield Crucible.

Alan Brien called our theatre an aircraft-carrier stage, Fergus Cashin said 'Here on this half-threepenny-bit open stage' and Kenneth Tynan 'a broad-bladed-dagger thrust into the audience's heart'.

Just as interesting have been the comments of some of the stars who have appeared on our stage. Generally speaking it has been those of the older generations who have disliked it and who feel almost unsafe with no proscenium and with no wings at the sides to encompass them. It was not surprising that at a press conference before the play in which Edith Evans was appearing at Chichester (*Dear Antoine*, 1971,) she very forcibly (how else?) said:–

'I am not a devotee of the "apron stage". I like more illusion in the theatre and I am not madly in love with audience participation. I like to keep them in their places and hold them there. If they come up on the stage and interfere it is like holding a painter's arm. I am a rebel but I can adapt.'

She was only able to do a few performances and as she had to be helped with her exits by John Clements, her visit was not very helpful to our theatre.

Maggie Smith, who gave some splendid performances over the years, said of the stage: 'It is absolute agony for the first week and then suddenly it becomes great fun.'

Frank Finlay is reported as saying 'I find it frightening, it took a fortnight to get used to it. Now I adore it, I love it. It's the excitement of something new.'

Joan Plowright in an interview said:–

> 'It is essential to know about arena stages. Everybody's building them and not only in the USA. Enquiries are piling in from quite small countries to Larry. They *may* be the way theatres are going and it may not, but we've got to find out just because we can't be sure.'

Fenella Fielding said:–

> 'I think you can't cheat as much. I don't think actors' backs are all that boring if they are doing it properly.'

What cannot be denied is the great popularity of our three dimensional presentations which like great magnets draw back the people from distant areas, year after year. A considerable percentage of them can boast of having seen every production since they first started coming. Surveys demonstrate the long distances some travel to Chichester.

Many, at their first sight of the interior, are dismayed at the stark appearance of the bare lighting system in an undistinguished roof and the dark colouring of the surrounding walls. In fact the revealing of the lighting system is not in itself a disadvantage as it panders to the love people have of wanting to see how it all works, as shown by the fascination people have of seeing backstage when we run the various tours of inspection of the whole building.

As soon as the play begins they realise everything is related to the stage and what is happening there, without any distraction of gilded semi-nude cherubs and angels and draped curtains.

Beautifully decorated interiors of some theatres are, of course, no bad thing and some are glorious to look at as museum places. They live, as all beautiful things do, long in the memory. I vividly remember in detail those in Malta, Munich, Vienna, Venice and some in England. They did not, in themselves, necessarily enhance the plays or operas I saw in them but they did increase the sense of occasion.

Our playhouse is a place for the finest acting. The concentration on the players is the secret of the great popularity of the auditorium stage though many people may not be actually conscious of why they appreciate coming to our theatre, apart from the social gathering and the excellence of the plays. The excited talk in the foyer at the intervals is proof of the audience's reactions, and enjoyment, of having been involved in the drama or comedy.

Milton Shulman, calling our theatre 'the enormous cavernous reaches of the open stage', brings to mind the acoustics.

It would not be correct to say that the interior of the theatre has been free from criticism. The acoustics were difficult in the first season, one of the reasons being the low stage with only one step. The installation in 1963 of baffle boards, three on each side of the stage projecting from the walls at various angles, partially remedied the difficulties. The acoustics had been monitored before we opened by the usual methods of pistol firing and general conglomeration of sounds. We learnt a lesson with *The Broken Heart* scenery which had deep tunnels for entrances of performers. These caused sound to be lost by absorption backstage. Since then this aspect of the designing of scenery has been carefully watched.

Some of the acoustic anomalies must also be attributed to the players who were not familiar with the use of this kind of stage, and who did not know the need for projecting their voices to the wide swept audience. I know some authorities on speech-usage say it is not projection of voice but it is the easiest way to describe it in this case.

Criticisms always continue from members of the audience who do not concentrate on the spoken word. There are some who have a psychological 'block' to the words. I have experienced this myself and it is a fact that, if you are vitally interested in the play, or the personality of a player, you can hear, but if you are disinterested deafness seems to increase.

It reminds me of the story of a village yokel who, when accused by a questioner of being deaf, replied that he wasn't deaf except 'when he wasn't listening'! When talking to a drama club about acoustics I said 'There is a lot of truth in saying that bad acoustics are sometimes the fault of the actors . . . as well as of the audience. Many of us have been so 'deafened' by the microphones used by 'pop' singers that we find it difficult to adjust to the normal speaking on the stage. When an actor at Chichester turns his back some members of the audience immediately say they cannot hear him, but they can, and once you tell them they can, they do'.

Our box office officials have always done their best to place deaf people near the front providing they have knowledge of their impediment, and we have a special part of the booking form asking members if they have any special difficulty such as deafness, or a right or left leg which, through injury, needs an appropriate seat on an aisle.

People with one deaf ear, such as I have, do not get the advantage of dual focussing of sound and this is a disadvantage if values are low. It is an advantage sometimes when rock groups are belting out the sound. I find it a help when there are thunderstorms at night, or in the days of the war when there were air raids, to be able to turn over and blot the sound out. It is also useful when chairing committees to be able to ignore unhelpful interruptions from the opposition.

To prove that it can sometimes be the fault of the players, rather than the acoustics of the building, one has only to remember how Sybil Thorndike was able to whisper in our theatre and was heard distinctly by everyone. I have just been listening to Alec McCowen delivering his performance of 'Kipling' and every word came over distinctly, without effort, even when he turned his back; so it can be done.

I look forward to the time when we can afford a teacher for speech, and singing, such as the Royal Shakespeare had with the late Denne Gilkes whom I met on that famous occasion of my first meeting with Tyrone Guthrie at her flat in Stratford-upon-Avon.

Air conditioning does not help acoustics with currents of cold or warm air careering around the auditorium. Several conductors of orchestras and recital soloists have declared their intention to 'walk out' at rehearsals because of the lack of reverberation, or 'feed back' in the empty auditorium. Having been persuaded that all would be well at the actual performance their relief was very apparent at the beginning of the concert when they realised what a difference there could be when the place was filled with bodies.

The acoustics are certainly 'dry' and this has been especially commented on by some famous conductors. The spoken word, single instruments and light string orchestras do best. Large orchestras with heavy wind sections, brass bands and large choirs do not, in my opinion, do so well.

Regarding acoustics Mr Max Reese of the *Farnham and Haslemere Herald*, 23 July 1965, said in a review of *Trelawney of the Wells*:–

> 'As one left the theatre one suddenly remembered in *Armstrong's Last Good Night* about Chichester's acoustics. Regular visitors had come to believe that no play presented there could be consistently audible. And one suddenly realised that in *Trelawney* one had heard every word. Several of the lines are softly spoken and every actor always had his back or side to some part of the audience. Yet it did not seem that a line was lost in any part of the theatre. Why was that?'

Antal Dorati at his last concert especially came round to see me, in the Green Room afterwards, to beseech me to do something about the 'dryness'. I look forward to the time when we could have some experiments with wood surroundings on the walls etc, but this will cost a great deal of money and we shall hope to do this when we have finished the other priorities of new buildings so necessary for the use of the staff and the comfort of the audience.

A local correspondent writing about the visit of the Hallé Orchestra to Chichester in May 1963 remarked that 'the acoustics of the theatre were not as dry as he had expected. The building had resonance without reverberation and the sound overall was not so bleak as that of the orchestra seems in the London Festival Hall.'

Finally to return to comments on the use of the stage: John Barber, *Daily Telegraph*, September 1975, 'Apron Stage in Search of Wearers' writes:–

> 'I can also imagine a style of acting somewhat like the spectacularly visual technique of the silent film stars which would exploit the actor's whole body and radiate energy in all directions . . . The talking film killed off an art that must be resuscitated if stages like Chichester's are to be properly exploited.'

To sum up the possibilities of our stage, the *Mid Sussex Times* 'Theatre dream comes true', 18 August 1963, says:–

> 'The West Sussex Theatre where like Glyndebourne, at the other end of the county, the business on stage sometimes matches the beauty of the surrounding setting. When that happens you are truly blessed with a great night at the theatre.'

CHAPTER 5

Use of Theatre

After the first season I wrote to Olivier:–

'On my business diary for 3 July (opening day of our theatre 1962) there is this quotation:–

'I have then with pleasure concluded with Solomon
"Everything is beautiful in his Season"
WALTON.'

Please, for Solomon, read Olivier.'

Regarding the overall policy of using the theatre as a whole Olivier in one interview said:–

'I used to be afraid it just might not work to have the audience on three sides of the stage.'

On another occasion he said:–

'This is a bid for communication in a world in which the lack of it is the ostensible source of so much complaint and disappointment. Exchange of emotion, which conveyed in laughter, sympathy or silent understanding, is the communion through which the theatre may live and breathe.'

After the season I was asked for my reactions. I said:–

'Of course there has been controversy over the theatre, and undoubtedly we shall be the centre of controversy for some time to come. Whenever there is fresh air there are always complaints about draughts.'

A writer in *The Times*, 4 May 1962, recorded:–

'To walk round Chichester Festival Theatre is to have the feeling that when it opens Sir Laurence Olivier's Company will enter from one side and the audience from another, to meet, as friends do, and to spend the evening together, as friends do, while the play lasts.'

Alastair Sim in The Magistrate, *1969*

So many civic authorities have made the mistake of being too frightened to put up large enough theatres because they calculated the possible attendance compared with the repertory theatres they were replacing. These had been working in poor surroundings with, in some instances, mediocre companies. They forgot there was possibly a huge new public who would be enticed to the theatre in modern conditions and with performances of high degree made possible by the larger income from a larger theatre.

An extract from *Harpers* magazine in 1962 (author unknown) said:–

> 'If Parkinson's Law applies to the theatre (the building only appearing long after the vital need for it is passed) then Sir Laurence's new theatre at Chichester is a dying swan awaiting the cruel huntsman. But maybe the British genius for museumification, that talent for institutionalising the avant-garde into Subsection B, clause I, paragraph 3, that supreme ability to transmogrify the passé into the wildly new and adventurous, will once more conquer all. No doubt Olivier's magnetism and very real star quality will yet again triumph. At least it is the one theatre being opened and not being shut.'

On the other hand Elvira of the *Bromley Times*, 9 August 1963, in an article entitled 'Elm Trees grow tall at Chichester' said, after her visit to see *The Workhouse Donkey*, 'there was nothing she liked of the theatre or its use. She did not like seeing all the working parts like the lighting etc. She says when someone visits your house you do not start by showing them the drains.'

She owned she was the squarest of squares. She missed the raising of the curtain and the illusion it gives, she disliked the actors coming in by the many entrances like rabbits emerging from their holes to congregate like nibbling groups on the pastures.

Well, that's one point of view and maybe why I understand the Bromley Theatre, built much later, was on more conventional lines. I wonder if they are able to draw capacity audiences in the same way as ours and similar ones in America and Canada?

At Chichester, unlike so many provincial theatres which just take in touring companies with their packaged touring, four plays are created and produced for the season after five weeks rehearsal for each play. This means months of work for the artistic director deciding on the plays and balancing the whole programme to ensure a variety of appeal.

The main difficulty is that a play transferring to the West End has often to be reconstructed for a proscenium stage. The other difficulty is that even after four or five weeks' rehearsal the first night for the press is not in such good form as many plays would be after touring for weeks before the critics saw it. So many modifications and improvements can be made whilst touring and in our case the plays are often somewhat better after the first week.

Touring, on the other hand, is no substitute for adequate time spent in rehearsal. I remember forty years ago when the Mary Brough, Ralph Lynn,

Tom Walls and Robertson Hare Company toured Southsea and Brighton with their unique comedies, *Rookery Nook* etc. They were badly under-rehearsed at times and the comedy was often held up by necessary prompts and impromptu actions. Such performances were almost insulting to the provincial audiences as if to say 'anything would do for them'. Such low standards have never been seen at Chichester.

During the first few years it was our custom to have, on the Sunday night of each new production, a dress rehearsal with an invited audience mainly of friends of the cast. The Monday night was considered the night when Society members went and the press night was on the Tuesday.

Olivier was persuaded, after the first year, to introduce a schools' night on the Monday with the Society night on Tuesday and press first night on the Wednesday.

Persuasion is the right word regarding Olivier's agreement to the schools' night. At first he was dead against the idea and related many incidents of horrible interruptions and bad behaviour by children at the Old Vic and elsewhere.

On the first occasion when the schools came, with masters in control, there was intense interest and concentration by the children and no interruptions. In fact they pointed the moments of audience reaction that confirmed the interpretation intended by the performers. Olivier was converted. The main reason for this success was because all the children paid for their seats, albeit a very reduced amount, and this seemed to persuade them to have their money's worth.

It is a peculiar thing that people who come in free are more prejudiced against the event than those who have paid. On the one or two occasions when the TV companies have had an invited audience for a recording, members of the audience have expressed dissatisfaction more strongly than at other times.

The *Worthing Gazette*, 5 August 1966, commenting on the performance of *Macbeth* for the schools, said:–

> 'The final duel between our evil hero and Macduff is tremendously staged with real swords of heavy steel striking sparks from the walls and steps. I am told that the packed audience of schoolchildren who were allowed to watch Monday's dress rehearsal stood and cheered on the antagonists with an uninhibited glee one had thought had vanished with the coming of the blasé James Bond era of nonchalant violence.'

We can always reckon that the majority of critics will say that transfers of our plays to London are better there than they were at Chichester. The reason for this is often just prejudice against our stage or the lack of time needed for a play to be 'run in'. But sometimes this point of view is true and that is because the play was not one that should have been played on an auditorium stage.

One critic said of *The Chances* in 1962 that too often the actors showed the uneasy nervousness and lonely security of a council house family billeted in the Albert Hall.

In the same way Robert Muller in the *Daily Mail* said of *Uncle Vanya* that the entire production came across 'runny as an egg too lightly boiled'.

It is fascinating to compare this summing up with many others who, in contrast, praised the two productions in an entirely different way.

There were many adverse ones which were founded on a dislike of the openness of the stage compared with the closed-in cosiness of proscenium productions where it can all be rationalised, labelled and packaged.

On one occasion Harold Hobson wrote:–

> 'The Chichester Festival Theatre does, I think, effectively make out a case for the arena stage . . . It is not a question of whether the arena stage is better or worse than the proscenium arch. A sane man, if he gets the chance, uses both a Rolls Royce and his own feet according to the purpose he has in mind.'

That sums up the reasons why I wanted our theatre to be different from the surrounding ones in the south of England. To have conformed in the type of stage and in the orthodox style of building would have been fatal.

Sight lines have always been exceptionally good as I have recorded before. Alan Brien once described his visit to the Criterion Theatre in London:–

> 'I could not see as much of the production as I was pretending I could. My seat, as a critic, was impressively placed three in from the left hand aisle in Row C. And yet there was a triangular slice of the stage that I could only glimpse by extending my neck like a telescope. In this awkwardness the Criterion is by no means unique among London theatres. But the fact that it forced itself upon my attention suggests that all stages have disadvantages which we have simply forgotten to notice.'

He found the sight lines at Chichester very good. W. A. Darlington, *Daily Telegraph*, wrote in an article entitled 'Chichester and Around' whilst remarking that critics like himself were always given the best seats:–

> 'Occasionally, then, I and my like, (critics) are better off in the Old Vic theatre but equally the worst spectator at Chichester is better off than someone in a remote seat at any of the conventional theatres. The advantage, presumably, of the circular auditorium is nobody can get a very bad seat or be so far away from the stage that he can't even hope to hear what the actors say.
>
> Perhaps you remember my story of the girl on the bus who was overheard telling her friend how she had enjoyed *My Fair Lady* and added 'of course it would have been nice to hear what Rex Harrison was saying but what can you expect for five bob.' That surely could not happen at Chichester.

> The conclusion to which all this leads me is that whilst the theatre in, or nearly in, the round may very well satisfy the ordinary playgoer who is out for entertainment, and does not greatly care if the finer points of that entertainment are missed, it is bound to leave the connoisseur dissatisfied unless the play happens to have been especially written for its special requirements.'

Many directors have beautifully contrived the various ways in which scenery changes take place in full view of the audiences during the play and the intervals, eliminating those dreadful curtain drops and weary pauses which kill the continuity and flow of drama. The lights being dimmed an army of stage hands invade the stage dressed in dark boiler suits, or in some cases, in period costumes to blend with the dating of the play. Each has his allotted task in the removing and the setting of props or turning scenery around or bringing in furniture. In many cases it has been choreographed into ballet form and perfectly rehearsed to the delight and appreciation of the audience. Sometimes very special effects have been introduced. One or two remain in one's memory such as the one in *Old Heads & Young Hearts* (1980) when after all is set, and the scene seems ready to start, suddenly a stage hand dashes onto the stage and hauls up a Union Jack on the flagpole as though it was just an afterthought.

Chandeliers are lowered from the roof where, until then, they had been quite inconspicuous, carpets are rolled into long rolls for two to carry off, chairs and settees are carried away, or brought on, without hesitation, and with precision, so that they do not impede any other stage hand. Finally the lights go right out and actors move into their positions, often aided by pen torches, and when the lights go up they are seen standing or seated. Thus the drama or comedy is sustained, the audience has been entertained throughout, and the illusion of a new scene is revealed. The audience has not been cut off as though what happened behind a curtain were private manipulations of scenery and props by shirt-sleeved, sometimes short-tempered workmen. Surely the magic of scene-changing of an open stage replaces the magic of the rising curtain which so many enjoy in orthodox theatres. At the interval a fair proportion of the audience purposely stays in its seats fascinated to see the changes ready for the next act. Before the play begins the incoming audience is sometimes entertained by a solo accordionist, pianist or just characters assembling in a courtyard etc, and this is a favourite ploy at many other theatres where the curtain is not in evidence. Nowadays the emphasis is on entertainment from the moment you enter the theatre. Whilst we use quartets, the city band etc on first nights, I envy the large areas of the National Theatre which make possible real subsidiary entertainment by groups.

A theatre which is commercially minded might prefer not to have the audience staying in their seats at the interval, but would rather drive them into the foyer and bars. This is easily achieved with proscenium arches by lowering a very depressing safety curtain (required by the safety regulations) some of which curtains are plastered with advertisements. I remember one which had a large central advertisement such as 'Oh my poor feet' showing two feet immersed in a bath. Well, I suppose, if you cannot get the extra money from drinks (and this is an important source of revenue) then you should get it by advertisements. We prefer to give as much entertainment as possible and hope to get some revenue from ices and soft drinks, especially as so many people now have to remember not to drink if they are driving.

In the text of *A Patriot For Me* (1983) there are twenty-three scenes and these were woven into a whole pattern in an extremely clever way. In our pantomime of Christmas 1982 the changes were contrived by turning over the pages of a huge scenic book at the back of the stage, and this was stunningly effective.

Robert Selbie tells the story which I will leave in his own words:–

> 'The scene changes in *The Magistrate* (1969) were very elaborate and very fast. They were done by sixteen stage hands in very dim lighting. At the end of Act 3 the magistrate's room at the courthouse has to change rapidly to the drawing room of the house. Act 3 ends with the magistrate . . . Alistair Sim . . . collapsed on a chair in the middle of the stage.
>
> At the technical rehearsal the lights went down, the stage hands leapt on to the stage and the lights went up to reveal Alistair still fumbling his way off stage surrounded by stage hands, whirling furniture and scenery. He complained to John Clements that it was impossible for him to get off before the stage hands came on, and if they waited for him it would hold up the change too long.
>
> After a very short pause for thought Clements told Alistair to stay collapsed in the chair and the scenery would be changed around him. Right at the end of the change the crew picked up the chair, still with Alistair in it and carried it off to a huge roar of applause.'

On one occasion Maggie Smith, talking of the exciting presentation of productions on our kind of stage and the general atmosphere of the theatre, called it 'the unfathomable magic of Chichester which pulls back stars for only £75 a week which was a drop of £550 per week for me.'

Topol called it a theatre where you can reach the people, where you can talk to the audience. Peter Shaffer on several occasions said that he loved the Chichester theatre and was delighted to have his plays performed in it.

In *Horizon*, a magazine of the arts, 1959, in an article entitled 'The Theatre breaks out of Belsco's Box' the author (name unknown) writes of the Canadian Shakespeare theatre at Ontario:–

> 'Though we were aware of a vast blur of faces across the platform from us, the presence of our fellow men was not so much distracting as enlivening. We were, all of us, players and playgoers alike, at last in the same building. The actors were doing most of the work, as usual, but we were engaged in a

communal and reciprocal experience, candidly acknowledging each other's presence, sharing the field on which battle was to be done, engaged and involved in a meeting that could not help but straighten our spines, alert our ears, and heighten every capacity of response. Being thoroughly present and not merely eavesdropping, we longed to participate, and savoured the sense of being permitted to. The circus shape had now expanded to full size, and the big booming plays seemed bigger and richer for being able to exhale.'

In summing up all the accounts I have quoted, both for and against our theatre, I hope many will agree with J. C. Trewin when he wrote:–

'I can imagine there will be various kinds of opposition. Any adventure on such a scale as this must expect it. There will be the usual jealousies and the usual cynicism. But when the last gossip has faded, and the last of the sour grapes has been squeezed, the Chichester Festival Theatre remains, very simply, a triumph.'

Having been at one time an ardent amateur actor I regret that it has not been possible for amateurs to use the theatre. I should have realised, I suppose, that by creating a thrust stage theatre it would be difficult when nearly all amateur societies are trained, and experienced in proscenium atmospheres. They would therefore not be able to adapt their productions to arena conditions any more than the professional touring companies are able to do so.

Also, of course, the size of our theatre was a great disadvantage for them. The real fun of amateur acting is to play for several nights. The actors generally rehearse for weeks in their spare time in the evenings, having pursued their own vocations during the daytime. Our capacity would absorb all their potential audiences in one night. There would be no fun in that.

All members of professions are not inclined to accept amateurs and this is, after all, natural when people have qualified by extreme hard work to perfect their own calling and have to live by it alone. It is not easy to combine different standards of excellence as between professionals and amateurs. On the other hand I have found there is plenty of goodwill by the professionals to help if the occasion arises.

A further disappointment is the attitude of amateurs not taking advantage of the experience of the professional actors 'on the doorstep'. I would have thought they would be eager to learn from those who had been under the influence of the drama school teachers, and of the finest directors, from whom all actors learn a great deal. Many of the middle grade of actors would be only too willing to supplement their earnings by modest fees for lecturing or demonstrating. Somehow the amateurs have not taken advantage of these excellent chances to improve their techniques but seem, in the main, to adopt an attitude of 'knowing it all'. When I started the

Chichester Players in 1934 we did have actors such as Bransby Williams and Gordon Harker to lecture to us, and they were very helpful.

I look forward to the day when we can build our studio theatre designed for about a 300 audience. This would be a tremendous asset to the county as a whole, as well as to us. It would enable amateur groups of West Sussex and touring companies to promote their productions as well as being the right size for recitals, chamber concerts etc which are unable to fill the main building. If there is anyone generous enough to help this idea in a big way we should be very ready to name the building accordingly! Who wouldn't? Such a person would be making an important contribution to the cultural environment of the south of England.

Chichester is not well endowed with hotels and this has been an important factor in our not being able to get medium sized conferences. The thrust stage is ideal for such meetings and one of the joys of having it in the locality has been when a school's speech day brings all the parents and pupils together as there is no other place, such as school halls, that can hold so many people. It can be a very rewarding occasion for the staffs of the schools and the parents to be all in one social gathering and must do a great deal for the morale of the school as a whole.

Fashion shows are particularly successful when they use the many exits and entrances available, and the all-round plastic squash court has enabled international squash tournaments to be played to large audiences instead of the limit of one hundred spectators in local clubs. Over one half of our 1,400 audience can easily see the keyboard in piano recitals and in the playing of piano concertos.

Every year since we began there has been a schools' music festival, nearly always presented for two evenings. On one occasion there were 1,000 performers of varying ages from thirteen schools plus, 350 members of youth clubs, together with their parents. It presents a marvellous sight. Meticulously rehearsed and extremely well disciplined the children troop on and off the stage to form recorder, string or brass bands. It is refreshing to see the dedication and concentration by youth and it renews one's faith in the future. These occasions make the whole theatre creation worthwhile.

CHAPTER 6

Artistic Directors and Actors

It is true that this theatre must rely upon getting well known stars for it to survive because of its size and its locality. But it is even truer to say it also survives by its artistic directors.

John Barber wrote in an article entitled 'The Day of the Director', 1966:–

> Not all plays demand directors of quality. A popular star who always gives the same performance, anyway, only requires a functionary to see that the lights are on, centre stage. A knockabout farce may only need a referee, a thriller only a cabinet maker. But serious authors need interpreters and the best of these are artists who can turn a mess into a masterpiece. In the history of theatre ours may yet be remembered as The Age of the Director.'

From the beginning it has been the tradition of this theatre to consider changing artistic directors after varying periods. The thinking behind this is that having to devise programmes of four plays a year for three or four years can become a strain and can mean that many directors will have drained, at least for a while, the reservoir of their inventive talent. I know that this policy is controversial and many could argue knowledgeably against it. But we have found that it can, on the whole, work to the advantage of this theatre at least.

If we had been heavily subsidised with millions of pounds like the National Theatre, or the Royal Shakespeare Company, we could have then had plenty of associate directors, together with literary advisers, to take some of the burden. Then we could have had marvellous programmes of a multitude of plays all the year round.

The changing of directors every few years did not work quite like this for the reigns of Olivier and Clements. Olivier did four years, two entirely for us and two in conjunction with his National Theatre Company. On the very night of 3 July 1962, when we opened, it was officially announced in the evening papers that a definite decision had been made by the Government in conjunction with the Greater London Council, to build a National Theatre.

All of us, at that moment, knew that Olivier would most likely be appointed its artistic director and therefore his stay with us would be limited. The principal members of the National Theatre Board have never acknowledged that this announcement, at a time when a new theatre was

Vivat Vivat Regina, *Mary (John Timbers)*

born, was politically timed, and we should be considered presumptuous to even hope that we were that significant. Anyway it was a pleasant thought for us to harbour. At a meeting in the House of Lords a little while ago Lord Cottisloe told me he did think it was sheer coincidence.

It would have been marvellous to have had Olivier for a longer period but the nation needed him and that was of paramount importance. It was in the August of that year that it was announced he would be the director and I immediately wrote to him expressing my congratulations.

During the first two seasons our casts became very unsettled as the choosing of the future National Theatre Company took place and each of the members wondered if they were to be included in Olivier's choice. Some were appointed and some were not. There was much heart-burning.

The whole of our costume department was taken, with our consent, (how could we do otherwise?) together with the machines. Naturally the whole outfit went under the leadership of Ivan Alderman. It was all friendly and we felt some pride in having been the means of helping to lay the foundations of the National Theatre. It has been acknowledged on several occasions that it was formed in Chichester, though I expect it will all be forgotten in the passage of time.

I very much regret we did not reform our costume department and keep the machines. It would have saved us a great deal of money and I think we would have benefitted by better quality costumes, having learnt some of the unique skills from Ivan Alderman to pass on to new workpeople.

The relations between ourselves and the National for the third and fourth years was a matter of great concern to us. On 7 March 1963 I went with Pieter Rogers to a meeting at Grosvenor Place (at that time the headquarters of the Electrical Industries) and there met Olivier, Lord Chandos, Kenneth Rae and Stephen Arlen.

It was agreed that for the seasons 1964/65 the National and Chichester would work together with Olivier dividing his time between the two. I had misgivings for Chichester in this respect though I would rely on Olivier's undoubted loyalty to us to pull us through. The greatest difficulty was regarding the question as to whether or not it should be announced as 'an association' of the two or 'co-operation'. It was obvious that the National officials were nervous about too close an association. It was also obvious to me that Lord Chandos did not feel Chichester was of much importance to them and I could understand this when they felt they were creating something greater than anything yet achieved.

I was also very concerned that Chichester should not appear to be financed by them and so lose its independence by seeming to be a subsidiary company. However it was agreed, in the most friendly of ways, to publish a very early announcement setting out the basis of co-operation and this would take the form of a chairman to chairman letter from Lord Chandos.

The statement that was agreed to be published was:–

> 'It was agreed that an approach should be made to the Chichester Festival Theatre regarding the 1964 Festival offering the Chichester Festival an eight weeks' season of plays to be agreed. The Festival would be conducted under the auspices of the National Theatre on billing arrangements to be discussed. The terms would be negotiated on a similar basis to those which would appertain to a normal provincial season, either by way of a minimum guarantee to the Chichester Festival to cover their overheads, or a straight percentage. It was proposed that the National Theatre should take over the responsibility for providing costumes, scenery etc. It was considered that only by a scheme of this sort could the collaboration between the Chichester Festival and the National Theatre organisation, including its Director, be continued satisfactorily to both parties.'

This was confirmed by our Board but I was disappointed to hear very soon afterwards that the National had had second thoughts on the wording and on the timing of the announcement. Whilst Lord Chandos over-ruled them regarding the main wording he did feel that it would be best if it was not announced until near the end of our season.

Naturally Olivier, at that time, was deeply involved in so much organisation that it was impossible for him to come to discuss these matters with the Board. There were very long letters between us and Lord Chandos. The main worry of the National officials was the misinterpretation that the press might make of the statement. Such as, 'It might lead to a series of questions on detail which neither Chichester nor the National Theatre would find easy to answer.' Or, 'Can Chichester tell the National Theatre what to do?' Or, 'Imperialistic National Theatre swallows up Chichester', or again, 'Can Chichester dismiss the National Theatre?'

Whilst I suppose any of these distortions could have taken place, I really think the real nervousness of the National officials was that the National Theatre might be belittled by the restrictions placed upon it by reason of its association with us.

Lord Chandos assured me that 'they were giving the future the thorough and proper consideration which it deserves and striving hard to find a solution to technical, legal and public relations problems.'

Eventually it was agreed to leave the announcements to the end of our season in August. It said in accordance with the proposal contained in a letter from Lord Chandos to me:–

1. An eight week season under terms to be arranged for three plays, two of the plays to be productions originating in Chichester and the third a successful play originating from the National Theatre's own repertory to be accepted.
2. There to be overall direction by Sir Laurence Olivier of all plays.
3. This arrangement to be for the 1964 Festival.
4. The plays to be decided by the Director.

When Olivier failed to get a very long detailed letter from me I sent a copy, to which he replied in detail and there was an amusing postscript. 'I have tried in vain to discover how your first letter never achieved delivery. I am so sorry about this. Had it been addressed here I would have guessed it had been "posted" by my son down the lift shaft. If I'm not as quick as a cat this happens to a lot of my mail not to mention other valuables.'

When speaking at the Theatre Society dinner that year I laid emphasis on the fact that when the National left we should be independent in the same way as when we had started. That whilst the National Theatre were with us we were only in co-operation with them and were not a 'second company'.

Doubts were expressed in the local press as to what we should do when the National Theatre left us and the usual doubters crept out of the wood again with their wishful thinking of doom and disaster. Olivier remained a stalwart supporter of our theatre and whilst heavily burdened with the two directorships he fought several battles for our independence with his National Theatre associates.

One of these occasions was when William Gaskill, who was directing *Armstrong's Last Goodnight*, wanted the opening postponed by three matinees due to under-rehearsing. I was at my practice in Jersey at the time and it so happened I had been asked to attend an interview for the BBC *News Round Up* with M. Vickers. This was on 3 July , three years to the day from when we had started. I was in their studio high up above the quay at St. Helier when an urgent telephone call dramatically interrupted the interview. It was Mr Gaskill pleading with me to agree to the postponement.

I was horrified that all the press announcements and the bookings already made by the public should be so easily cancelled, thus reflecting badly on the efficiency of our theatre. I knew that it was not unprecedented for such a thing to happen in the theatre world but it seemed unnecessary in this case. I could understand it if it had been due to the ill-health of one of the stars or some untoward event such as a grave illness, or death of royalty, something that would have been outside our influence.

As I was adamant in refusing, another official of the National Theatre rang up soon after to persuade me, causing another interruption of my interview. I think it was Kenneth Tynan but I pointed out that Olivier was the artistic director of our theatre and so it must be his decision as the artistic direction was under his full control. I wondered why he had not made the decision on his own, and had not telephoned me himself.

Later he confirmed that it was necessary to postpone and I then accepted the situation though I felt, deeply, that the public had been 'let down'. The recorded interview then proceeded, Mr Vickers having shown great patience and understanding. I was later, much delayed, able to get back to my practice.

I am not ashamed to say that I hero-worshipped both Guthrie and Olivier. In the brittle clinical atmosphere of the present day hero-worship and patriotism are supposed to be the 'hush puppies' of the older generation. I therefore have the utmost contempt for those who seek to make their living by writing character assassinations of famous people. Unable to do anything themselves, courageous or heroic, they can only tap away at their typewriters delving into the weaknesses which everyone has at some time of their lives.

I have told before of the inspiration I received from Guthrie and my admiration for him as a person, a giant in more ways than just his physical height. I have also written of the early days with Olivier when, during the first four years, we had many a tussle. After twenty years I have increased my appreciation of him and count myself fortunate to have been a friend of his. I have kept in touch with him and Joan Plowright over the succeeding years. Such friendships with members of the theatrical profession cannot be as completely deep as they can be in the outside world.

I have come to understand over the years that really deep friendships in the world of theatre are only possible between members of the theatrical profession. These are based on the true brotherhood of those who are bound together by the bond of having to earn their living in the theatre. The youngest assistant stage manager will receive more warmth of lasting comradeship than anyone outside the profession; it is a closely guarded world. Who could criticise this when life is so precarious in a profession where so few can achieve full employment or fame?

Actors and actresses play opposite one another for several months, and then probably never meet again for years and then in a different part of the world. It is not always easy to remember one another's name. I am told that is the reason for the lavish use of all those 'dears' and 'darlings' which cover up the temporary loss of memory. They are not the insincere blandishments the public believe them to be.

Carol and I were invited to be at the National Theatre the night it was opened by Her Majesty the Queen and we prize the memory of that night especially the moment when Olivier came onto the bare stage alone, to make his bow to tremendous and sustained applause. It was an historic moment for him, and for the National Theatre after so many years' gestation.

I felt that perhaps we had influenced a little the decisions that had been taken in the designs for the stages that had been built. We had definitely helped the nation by pushing forward the resurgence of theatre buildings. Perhaps the fact that ours had begun from 'the grass roots' of an audience wanting a theatre to be built was not a bad thing.

Olivier was extremely anxious for the future of Chichester in that it should have a worthy successor when he went to the National. In those days I was able to have private discussions with the drama director of the Arts Council on such vital matters as the appointment of artistic directors and other officials. Mr J. L. Hodgkinson and later Mr 'Dick' Linklater were always ready to see me and were helpful in every way.

As usual I also consulted Guthrie on the people most likely to be the best to succeed Olivier and he sent me his usual caustic but helpful comments on the various directors who could fill the special needs of Chichester.

When, on two occasions, I was invited over to Brighton to discuss the matter with the Oliviers, I found they were completely convinced that John Clements was the one person we should have and, if we accepted him, they would give their full and considerable support to him and to us. Guthrie had not thought so, looking as he did from the needs of the special outlook and direction of plays on our kind of stage, and the need for a younger forward-looking evolution of our work.

The Board readily fell in with Olivier's ideas and though I had some doubts, I was asked to approach Clements. Knowing that Olivier had

Vivat Vivat Regina, *Elizabeth (John Timbers)*

already hinted to him about the possibility of his directorship of Chichester, I invited Clements and his wife Katie Hammond to come over for lunch one Sunday so that we could talk over the possibilities and see the theatre by ourselves without the interruptions of everyday occupation by the staff. I also wanted to keep the matter of our conversations private in case they did not come to anything.

He had seen one or two of our productions from amongst the audience, but when he and I went onto the stage in the empty auditorium he said, with a great sigh, 'Oh dear!' He was obviously deeply depressed and so was I. I felt ready to advise the Board against his appointment.

Carol joined us, with Katie, for lunch at the Ship Hotel and it was a dismal affair. Both he and I felt it was not going to work and I was appalled at his lack of enthusiasm.

It would seem that Olivier overcame his worries after further discussions and, as the Board were still enthusiastic, negotiations began. The contract became involved and difficult as with his background of family connections with the law, and his experience as an actor-manager, he examined every comma and full stop. Finally, one day, I motored to Brighton and met Clements at his house at 11 o'clock at night to finalise the contract.

After minute word-by-word analysis of the contract document I had at last to say, 'What does this all really matter? If the Board and you do not get on together all the words are meaningless for we should just have to part and that would be that.' So all was agreed at last and I left for Chichester well after midnight, motoring home with mixed feelings. In the end his term of three years was twice extended and after that he was with us for a further two years, making eight in all, until we thought it was time for a change. A very successful directorship from many people's point of view.

He was one of the last great actor-managers and he managed the theatre excellently. He very soon accepted the challenge in a happier spirit, especially once he had persuaded Doreen Dixon to leave the Royal Court to work with him once again. The two of them ruled the theatre with rigid economic efficiency even though most of the staff found him remote and lordly. He reminded me of one of the early barons. One member of the staff remarked on one occasion that she thought he actually knew her name after six years.

In those days when we had to watch finances meticulously he never allowed any of the directors of the various plays, or designers, to go beyond their budgets, no matter what excuses were tried, and this gave the Board a very comfortable ride during his stay. Doreen Dixon was completely and utterly loyal to all his wishes and she was a tremendous force in keeping the staff together.

I think that after that first day, when he stood on the stage and after talking to Olivier, he decided he would have to convert the theatre to as near as possible the West End theatre style with which he was most familiar.

When he was appointed he was asked about the stage and he replied 'There may be room for experiment, I will have to study the problem.' Clements never, in my opinion, really liked the open stage. He converted it to a duplication of West End productions with pretty scenery, and many of the sets were said to be measured to within an inch so that they were easy to transfer to a particular London stage.

Transference of plays to London is a very good thing for our finances and he did a great deal towards Chichester being known in the London scene. It is good as long as the plays are not specifically chosen just to be tailored for that purpose. It must be the other way round for the preservation of the Chichester image.

To my mind, in relation to the original idea of promoting the special techniques of the open stage, the influence of Clements was ultimately not a good thing for us. Many of our present audience would not have agreed with me on this as they slid into a comfortable programme of revivals, and well known plays, almost entirely played in the orthodox way.

I had envisaged, and many of the critics had expected, that Chichester's thrust stage would open up a new era in Britain where the advantages of such a stage could be learnt and practised. New plays could be written for it and there would be many courageous experiments.

I think therefore that Clements unwittingly did a disservice to Chichester however pleasant the audience found it. The Board were certainly delighted with the box office receipts.

During the reign of Olivier we not only had his attempts to come to terms with the stage, though he would be the first to admit they were not one hundred percent successful: we had at least one play *The Royal Hunt of the Sun* which was written for such a thrust presentation and we had the visit of the Stratford, Ontario Company whose excellent use of the stage I have already mentioned.

Standards of acting were kept unquestionably high during Clements' directorship and, whether it was his own directing or another's, there was always a very polished, fully rehearsed, production. He was always able to cajole, on a friendly basis, the highest rank of stars and this was due to his own image of confident leadership of the top hierarchy. Stars, rightly jealous of their reputations, must have confidence that they will be successfully directed in first class presentations.

His personal knowledge of the famous actors and actresses made it easier for him to persuade them to come to Chichester for small fees and many performers wished, at that time, to include Chichester in the history of their careers.

Since most of them have now played on our stage it is more a question of inflation difficulties that make some of them more reluctant to come just for the reputation. The directors of later seasons have had more difficulty in this respect.

Clements said in a *Plays and Players* interview with Ronald Hastings, *Daily Telegraph* 1972:–

> 'There comes a point around about November when I stare at the wall and say "Ladies and Gentlemen my next trick is impossible". Then when somehow I feel like Pearl White tied to the railway tracks I begin to move. Planning a season at Chichester is becoming more difficult. I do not believe in being hamstrung by a 'policy' for Chichester. I do what I want to do and what I know a lot of people want me to do. There is no such thing as the public, there are several publics. There is a public for greyhound racing and a public for Mozart, and only a small overlap and I try not to restrict myself to one public. If I have a policy for Chichester it is to put the weight on actors.'

Whilst he maintained his principle of promoting the finest acting the audience became accustomed to an appreciation of artificial scenes and pretty surrounds. Use of props, expert symbolic lighting (he always seemed to favour golden sunshine) seemed to be absent on most occasions. It has taken a long time to start a return to our original conception. Olivier certainly achieved an excellent use of our stage with *St. Joan*, and the background scenery of *Uncle Vanya* was very simple and adaptive.

Returning to our original aims and beliefs would now upset a large number of people but such a change would also bring back a number of drama-dedicated people who would appreciate it. The Royal Shakespeare Company, when they were desperately short of money, succeeded on many occasions with symbolic surrounds and lighting in focussing the concentration of the audience on the fine acting.

I am sure that Olivier, if he ever reads this book, would now be looking at me disapprovingly, as he does in the Hailstone portrait of himself which is above me as I write. He would have the look he often gave me, as much as to say 'What right has this fellow to give opinions when he is not one of us'. However, I do think that members of the audience do have a point of view. After all it is all done for their appreciation and analysis (even if sometimes ill-informed) and it can always be ignored by those of the theatrical profession who, as a result of their training and experience, feel they know better.

Katie Clements was loved by all at Chichester and I think we were all pleased to feel that in her last years she did so enjoy sitting in John Clements' office meeting everyone in the theatre. The staff made a small garden next to the office where she could sit in the fine weather, watching all that went on and giving her opinion on all that happened. Sadness showed often in her eyes but her great courage and indomitable spirit overcame it all.

The policy of changing directors every three or four years now came into being. There were great misgivings by some members of the Board as to whether we should ever get anyone to replace Clements but fifteen of the top directors wished to be considered and we saw all of them.

Many were too committed for some time ahead to fit into our programme, a few withdrew, others seemed too academic for our theatre and some seemed too unusual in their outlook.

Finally, having known Keith Michell by his acting and acknowledging his undoubted artistic talent in various branches of the arts besides theatre, we appointed him for the usual term of three years which eventually was extended to a fourth year.

Both Olivier and Clements found their first season the most difficult of all until they got the 'feel' of the Chichester audiences and Clements, particularly, seemed to find his last season the most difficult of all after selecting twenty-eight plays. This has been the pattern for all our directors especially regarding the first season. It could be one of the arguments against the constant changing of directors.

Unfortunately from the very start of Michell's appointment he was assailed with the criticism that he had never 'managed' a theatre and whilst his talent as a fine actor and his artistic successes as a painter were most noteworthy, this was supposed to be not enough.

This theme, to this very day, is still repeated in parrot fashion without due reference to the successes he had during his four years. Undoubtedly he did well despite his failures. What director does not have his failures? Whereas some have only their successes remembered, people mentioned the failures and omitted to mention Michell's successes because the criticism was so often repeated. Such are the penalties of public life when those who are supposed to be knowledgeable pronounce a verdict without relation to the facts. I would like to deal with the actual plays in a further chapter to prove my point.

One superior headmistress inferred to me that I had no right to an opinion as she, and all the people who really knew about such things, had decided that Michell had failed.

Keith and his wife, Jeannette Sterke, gave their warm friendship unsparingly to all of us and this has only been matched since by Patrick Garland and his wife, Alexandra Bastedo, and John Gale and his wife Lisel. This is an essential factor in a caring community such as Chichester where the Board, the artistic director and the permanent staff all work together as a friendly team, a fact which is remarked upon by everyone who comes to work at the theatre.

Michell listened to other people's points of view and, like Garland, had a great love of Chichester and all it stood for. He was not easy in discussion, sometimes taking a long time to pronounce his opinion. This was due mainly to his artistic values, as he would only settle for what he considered the highest standard of artistic result. At least he listened, and was not averse to changing his point of view. This made it easy to accept his ruling without resentment, if any of us had a different point of view.

After four years Peter Dews was appointed as we had known him as a successful director of several of our plays. His record was mostly of the 'live' theatre and we were sure he was a vital personality who would manage the theatre in the way we wanted. His only condition was that he must be supported by an administrator to take away the day-to-day routine of financial and staff direction. This was agreed at a meeting between the chairman, Dews and myself when he showed himself as completely enthusiastic and eager to make a great success of his term of office. We both felt the Board had made a wise decision.

Unfortunately within a month or so of his appointment he suffered a slight stroke and his whole attitude through no fault of his own seemed to change. In all fairness I can only attribute his resentment of the Board to his illness. After he had consulted specialists, the Board generously decided to carry on with his contract and appointed Patrick Garland to support him as an associate director for the first year. They had always been friends and the combination worked well until the second and third years when Dews was on his own.

He still remains an excellent director of individual plays and has directed one play for us since his time as artistic director.

It was the unanimous wish of the Board to appoint Patrick Garland as our next director after the help he had given us with Dews and because of his reputation. A very popular appointment which was hailed by the critics and the public.

His first act, before he started his first season, was to marry Alexandra Bastedo in Chichester Cathedral on 17 December 1980. All the members of the Board, and the staff, have enjoyed their real friendship during his three years and the addition of the fourth was never in doubt of being granted.

He, too, required to have the managerial work taken off his hands so that he could concentrate on the choice and direction of the seasons. An administrator was appointed and this combination of artistic director and administrator would appear to be a satisfactory arrangement provided the two can work sympathetically together. We have gone through the regimes of Olivier with Pieter Rogers who did tremendous work in the evolution of the theatre from the very beginning; Clements with Doreen Dixon who were a perfect combination for management; Michell with Robert Selbie who was promoted from production manager to administrator, a happy relationship; and then to the dual appointment of Keith Green with Patrick Garland until the arrival of John Gale as executive producer alongside Garland.

John Gale, impresario of many record-breaking West End successes and chairman of the West End Theatre managements, felt he wanted a change of scene and was very willing to work with Garland as their friendship had lasted many years. This brought a much needed 'lift' to the whole theatre after a run of twenty years. A new authoritative outlook, born from a wide experience, means that someone is surveying the whole scene from the outside making sure the theatre does not remain in a 'rut'. I forecast many battles in the future but this should be stimulating and diversifying.

Much as I dislike dual appointments, this has worked exceedingly well at present, as the two are in tune with one another and both are dedicated to the ideals of Chichester.

Patrick Garland brought a scholarly approach to our direction and choice of plays as well as a sympathetic understanding of the needs of the actors, audiences and staff.

The huge majority of actors who come, and those who provide the concerts, enjoy their stay at Chichester. The interest in their welfare shown by the staff, and the people of Chichester itself, together with the feeling that they are in pleasant surroundings, is the magic Maggie Smith spoke about when describing her feelings for our theatre.

I always wanted Chichester to be unique in many ways, and I think it is, though many other theatres will have their own particular attractions. We must not think we are unusually special, but it is right to try to be so.

John Gielgud in Caesar and Cleopatra, *1971 (John Timbers)*

The thorny question of how the theatre is to be managed still remains to be solved. There is no formula that will encompass the diverse and changing personalities involved. The blending of artistic aspirations and financial considerations will always be difficult and a sympathetic but strong Board is necessary to handle such recurring problems.

It is amusing to look back on the various directors' attitude to the Board. I think, in the main, all of them would naturally have preferred not to be controlled, or hampered, according to which way they viewed it. If they had acted like a dictator, and I am sure in most cases it would have been as a benevolent one, they could have wielded power and had their own way. It must be very obvious to anyone reading this book that I, also, would have liked to have been in that position. However, to be just, I could not forget, or discard, all those who had so unselfishly helped in every way to bring the idea of the theatre to fruition, so I have accepted the rulings of a democratic Board, however much it irked at times. Members of the Board, besides their work at the beginning, have given invaluable advice throughout the twenty years and for that I am deeply grateful. If they were an 'awkward squad' at times, so was I an awkward member.

Olivier accepted the presence of the Board after some heart-burnings on both sides and I am sure he began to find great amusement from studying the varying personalities. It would have been great fun to know what he said to Joan after some of the meetings. He took it all in good part as he felt, quite rightly, that he was in at the beginning and that he had helped not only the building but the character of it. That was why he refused to accept the first season's fee we had offered but reduced it so that he was part of the crusade.

If Guthrie had been with us at that time he would have studied all the members of the Board, noted their idiosyncracies and used them in his productions as character parts, probably in the crowd scenes.

Clements accepted the situation with gentlemanly aloofness and, I think, irritation which was mostly obscured. Michell certainly found it very entertaining and treated it with friendly aplomb, never appearing ruffled but never being conquered by it.

Dews seemed to enjoy having a war with the Board as if we were the enemy of directors. I think this was uncharacteristic of him as we had not seen any signs of it when he directed plays before this appointment. This was an unhappy period for us all. Garland was exceedingly friendly with all the members but he did not lose his authority because of it.

One thing is certain and that is that the original demand for an administrator over the whole of the theatre, including the artistic director, would never have worked especially if he had had no previous knowledge of theatres. Infusion of new blood can cause congealing if not compatible with the existing system. There are many theatre traditions which are good, and some which are bad, but it takes great tact and much diplomacy to remove the bad ones.

CHAPTER 7
Audiences

Miss M. L. Walsh, a writer on theatre for many years, wrote:–

> 'Chichester Festival Theatre has a lure of its own. You get the feel of a beckoning as soon as you set out. When the day happens to be one of brilliant sunshine for your first visit of the season, nothing anywhere, not even in Sussex, commands a more adventurous sense of occasion.'

It is true that our theatre has created a vast new playgoing public in this part of England. The proportion of retired elderly people is greater here, in the south, than in any other part of the British Isles. The rest of the population, of all ages, have also been attracted to the plays and concerts which otherwise would not have been available to them. The cost of a visit to a play in London is considerable. Travelling expenses, and possibly a hotel for the night, makes the cost impossible for those with fixed incomes and some of the others would rather accept the convenience of seeing the finest acting 'on their doorstep' than journeying up to London.

During a season of approximately twenty-two weeks there are normally eight performances a week in a theatre capable of holding 1,340. This, together with a Christmas show, various visiting productions lasting a week at a time, and concerts, means there are over half a million visits to our theatre.

Many do not realise how large the theatre is when they see the building from the outside for the first time. This is because the seating reaches right out to the limits of the building whereas most theatre buildings have corridors and offices built around the auditorium making the buildings look more massive. Philip Powell very cleverly tucked such offices, and dressing rooms, underneath the auditorium but new buildings have since been erected at the back and some unobtrusive ones at the sides. This leaves the main hexagonal in its original exciting form.

From the very beginning our audiences have been criticised for being smart and elegant. Critics and newspaper reporters love to mention the words middle class as though it was something beneath their own status in life. Surely most of them have been of that origin themselves and personally I am proud of being of that middle class or 'yeoman' breed.

How some people love to divide the populace into classes. Sectionalising into tribes is, of course, as old as the world and happens in every nation. Prejudice thrives on it and feuds destroy what would otherwise be a peaceful existence.

Those who indulge in the practice of class warfare seem to be mostly burdened by inferiority complexes or 'chips on their shoulders'. At the present time the amazing social revolution that has taken place in the 1980s means that the label 'working class' presupposes no one else works. The 'upper classes' are no longer only the aristocrats and land owners, but can include anyone who has made money, by whatever means. It is a pity that the film *Intolerance* by D. W. Griffiths is not shown again with its stupendous message to those who would divide people by the old-fashioned prejudices.

What is wrong with people who dress well according to their ability and resources? Making the best of themselves, instead of being neglectful of their appearance, is not vanity but self respect and often self discipline. Especially does this apply to a theatre-going public where the players are honouring the audiences by making the best of their talents and the audiences are honouring the players by their presence.

It is always a pity to see well dressed ladies, whether they are dressed by Marks & Spencer or by leading couturiers, being let down by their escorts in open neck shirts and scruffy jeans. Our audiences are cosmopolitan, and what is wrong with them enjoying themselves on a social occasion? A gathering together of people is always an occasion.

A writer in the *Drama Theatre Quarterly*, August 1981, wrote:–

> 'Though the annual Chichester Festival has been just about the major theatre success of the last two decades, its success can hardly be attributed to the press.
>
> The theatre's audiences have been criticised by some reviewers who automatically disdain a congregation among whom tidy hair, clean shirts and smart frocks predominate. What can you expect of a theatre, these critics ask, that has to pander to the effete tastes of the West Sussex 'stockbroker belt'?
>
> This awful inverted snobbery would be amusing if it were not so tedious and unfair.'

An article in the *Evening Standard* 22 July 1964 said:–

> 'If dinner-jacketed Glyndebourne reminds one of the country house-party and open-necked Stratford of a riverside picnic, Chichester has the pleasantly alfresco atmosphere of a school's sports day. Munching slightly over-exposed open sandwiches amid pale-eyed girls in summer dresses in what looks like an avant-garde pavilion set down on the edge of a playing field one almost expects to hear starting guns and distant applause.
>
> With such brilliant theatre in such a superb setting it seems churlish to complain about the catering. But for those who go down by train, the eight-and-a-half hours between leaving and returning to Victoria is rather long on nothing more substantial than Smorgasborg in the theatre's restaurant.'

John Barber in 'High Days and Holidays', *Daily Telegraph* August 1981, wrote:–

'A visit to the theatre is still an occasion. The cost of tickets alone sees to that. I do not know of a woman who does not dress up a little, if not a lot, and at the very least a man will wear a suit. I would happily wear a black tie if other people would . . . There are some who strongly object to the fuss. I have an earnest friend who insists on frequenting the stalls in open neck shirt, sports jacket and jeans. For him the theatre should be considered a natural relaxed activity, like going to the pub. What I would call a kind of insult he intends as a sort of compliment.

And I think he is dead wrong. Like the medieval feast, it is an occasion for rejoicing, one shared by the community to celebrate the suspension of gravity and a break in routine. But you don't just go to laugh, you go to be there, to be part of a holiday crowd. The same thing happens to a degree when a party of a score of people get together for a grand night out for a birthday, or an anniversary, and a visit to the theatre seems the only possible choice.'

As to the dinner-jacketed Glyndebourne audiences referred to above, I well remember, at the opening season, receiving a letter from the managing director of Moss Bros deploring the fact that we had not made dinner jackets compulsory. Actually at Glyndebourne they are not compulsory but the 'You are advised to wear' note works well. That is the correct approach to an audience in such a place as Glyndebourne, where it is only the occasional visitor, generally from abroad, who does not comply and thereby stands out almost apologetically.

To have made it 'the thing' at Chichester with its audiences of all ages (thank goodness) in a theatre of 1,340 seats would have been impossible. Moss Bros can be pleased however that on first nights there is a fair proportion of dinner jackets to honour those special occasions, even if, as one correspondent described the scene, they stand out like dominoes.

Another writer described us as:–

'Chichester has become the last great house-party, as comfortable and as dead as any social event ever held at the stately homes nearby. Drinks are served on the lawn, and we need only a few croquet hoops and Gwen Ffrangcon-Davies announcing that 'a play is served' to complete the illusion.

Chichester's audience must be one of the richest and conservative in the land. What price a new play? Better to give the customers what they all too clearly want, even if that does seem to be a re-creation of 1959 from which year comes half of this season's productions.'

Does the National Theatre really pride itself on the proportion of its audiences who appear scruffy, and who seem to have drifted in still wearing their workclothes? Does it really like to demonstrate that their theatre is a sort of 'free for all to wander in' like some amusement arcade? I think the very high standards of their productions warrant a better recognition from those members of their audiences who indulge in such slackness.

John Rosseli in *The Guardian* said:–

> 'It seems a lot of unnecessary hard work for a lot of Londoners to traipse off to the South Downs for a play but *Uncle Vanya* was worth it.
>
> I daresay the same was said when Glyndebourne was started but they came, and so it has been throughout our history. Not large numbers from London but always a proportion of the audience, in the same way as those from abroad.'

In a survey when questionnaires were distributed amongst the audiences 4,228 were returned, being three times higher than the average polls conducted by professional organisations on public issues, including politics; 7 per cent came from Chichester city, 53.7 per cent from the Chichester district (reckoned as anything up to half-an-hour's car ride), 13.5 per cent for one hour's car ride and 19.1 per cent for anything from one to two hours and this included London. See Appendix VII for another survey.

In the first year the best seats were 25 shillings (and we debated at the time as to whether that was too dear!) and they are now £8, and this is a sombre thought. One person complained in the local paper the first year (1962) that he had stayed at an hotel who charged the best part of £3 for dinner, bed and breakfast. The dining room did not open in time to have a meal before the theatre and was closed when he returned. What was more the management refused to make any reduction for the dinner he was never able to get!

When we started I promised there would always be a section of cheap seats which could be purchased on the day, a policy that is in line with most other theatres. This was primarily intended for students and people visiting Chichester for the day. On one occasion I found these had been eliminated by one of the directors but they were soon restored by the Board. These seat concessions have been the cause of many debates, like so many other well worn topics that seem to raise their ugly heads every year so tediously. Searches for new methods of increasing revenue become more insistent each year, as things get more difficult. It is always a fight to keep seat prices down, as well as bar and programme charges, in order to prevent members of the audience feeling they are being drained of money as soon as they enter the building.

The facilities of all public buildings are open to criticism especially during the time when they are evolving phase by phase. Harold Hobson in one of his rare outbursts of indignation criticised our toilet arrangements. His censure of the men's was unwarranted but that of the ladies' highlighted a real problem. Whilst admitting there was more provision than in London theatres, he wrote of the embarrassing queues stretching into the foyer from the two areas provided. What had not been fully realised, when

Julian Somers, David Henry, Sue Jones Davies and Donald Sinden in Enemy of the People, *1975 (Reg Wilson)*

the plans were made, was that the main traffic of people coming to the theatre would come by car and this meant that there was need for these facilities after a long car drive.

To provide enough space was a difficult proposition but we built a large addition which is discreetly hidden out of the way of the main foyer. Americans would call it a 'comfort station'. Despite the notices in the other toilets, and prominent signs in the foyer, it has taken years to get people out of the habit of queuing and it is still not used by the majority who seem to prefer being embarrassed rather than read the notices or see the photos of the new area which everyone who goes there says is superbly arranged.

One other occasion was when Harold Hobson spent a good proportion of his critic's notice of a play by berating us for not letting latecomers into the auditorium. He mentioned the difficulty of getting through the traffic, especially at Goodwood racing time, and felt sure there were times during the performance of, for instance, *Miss Julie*, when they could have been let in. In the same article he mentioned the difficulty of being seated behind pillars at the Royal Court or the Aldwych. He forgot to mention that this difficulty can never be experienced at Chichester where everyone has a complete view of not only the stage but the rest of the auditorium audience. He concluded his article by praising the courtesy of our staff which he himself had experienced and advised people by all means to go to Chichester but please to arrive early.

Because of the wide sweep of the auditorium, and the reflected light from the stage, any entrance of latecomers can easily be seen and is very disturbing. This is much more difficult than when people are arranged in serried rows in an oblong hall. It also makes empty seats much more visible and we hear remarks that the theatre is not full when only a few seats here and there are not filled. If the back of an ordinary theatre is empty no one notices it.

The restrictions regarding the letting-in of latecomers is controlled, in the main, by the director of the play and who can blame such directors from wanting to prevent tense moments from being so easily destroyed. It is in the interests of the players and the members of the audience who have taken care to arrive on time. But there can be hold-ups and diversions due to road accidents and the staff always try to filter people in at opportune times; their job is not an enviable one when some people fail to be reasonable.

I vividly remember one occasion when we left Chichester at 2pm to get to Glyndebourne easily in time for a leisurely tea before the performance at 5.15pm. It was only an hour-and-a-half's journey. Just outside Chichester we were diverted by the police at a road block and heard afterwards it was because a tanker had overturned on the Arundel road spilling dangerous chemicals. We had to take the Bognor–Littlehampton road where there was extreme congestion due to the holiday traffic and to the diversion.

We entered Lewes at 5.15pm so I gave up hope and stopped hurrying as I knew their strict rule not to let anyone in after the curtain had risen. However, when we arrived at the entrance two stewards rushed over to the car shouting to me to give them the keys of the car and they then unceremoniously bundled us in and almost threw us into our seats in front of a glowering angry audience. The lights went out immediately and the performance began half-an-hour late. I can only presume many others had been delayed and the management had heard of the unusual circumstances. Rules in some instances have to be broken and it is an excellent management when it can be so sympathetically flexible.

Courtesy of the staff was one of the principles I laid down at the onset in order to make the place of entertainment a pleasant and friendly place to enter. On one occasion the Russian Ambassador was so impressed with the friendliness of the staff that later he sent some bottles of vodka and some miniature dolls to be distributed to the front of house staff.

Fashion writers have, on occasion, enjoyed writing about our audiences, and one advised ladies to wear turquoise, soft gold or the dustiest of pinks to blend with the carpet of olive green nylon and the deep purple seats. Short dresses with bare backs or half shoulder. Ladies were advised not to wear orange and to have a stole or evening jacket in which to stroll outside. This was in 1962.

In the years to come many will be amused at the fashion notes for the charity performance of *St. Joan* in 1963 when Princess Margaret and Lord Snowdon came to the theatre:–

> 'Brocades in vividly contrasting colours . . . that was the fashion story at the gala performance. Variations of deep brown and copper, midnight blue and electric blue, gold and coffee, and candy pink and black were among the colour combinations chosen.
>
> Full short skirts were mostly worn by the younger women while others favoured the simple elegance of straight or long skirts. Fur wraps and stoles were well to the fore for the chilly gusty weather and they accentuated the effect that brown in many shades was a popular choice of colour.
>
> There were several gowns in velvet, and here the colours were often deep red or plain black. An interesting choice, which followed Paris's latest evening wear, was a short circular skirted dress of ginger and chocolate brown chiffon.
>
> Pastel shades added splashes of colour to an otherwise dull day, and a novel evening coat was worn in a bright strawberry pink. This coat was of a loose design with the back piece cut completely as a square and a gathered skirt below this.
>
> Dresses worn on this occasion could well dictate the fashion in evening wear in Chichester this year for if the weather remains cold heavy materials such as brocade and velvet will be a must.'

In the first year we had many royal visits. Princess Margaret and Lord Snowdon viewed the theatre whilst it was being built. Princess Marina, accompanied by Lady Rachael Pepys, saw many of the plays during the latter years of her life and always seemed to enjoy herself thoroughly mainly because she liked the visits to be comfortably informal. The only concession she accepted was sandwiches in the Green Room during the interval.

Lavinia, Duchess of Norfolk, our Patron, sees nearly all the plays and enjoys bringing parties with her. Her Grace, one of the loveliest of people, regardless of the little time she has to spare from her multitude of charity functions, still finds time for any special occasions at the theatre and her presence increases the importance of such events. The only trouble is one is anxious not to add to her heavy self-imposed burden of charitable works.

Many notable people, from all walks of life, regularly visit the theatre and amongst those who came, for instance, in the second season were, besides the ones already mentioned:–

> The Duke of Norfolk, Alan Bates, Dora Bryan, Tom Courtenay, Lord Chandos, Lady Diana Duff-Cooper, George Devine, Kenneth Horne, General Sir Brian and Lady Horrocks, Nicholas Hannen, Jocelyn Herbert, Wendy Hiller, Kenneth Haigh, Miriam Karlin, Robert Morley, Joan Greenwood, Andre Morrell, Yehudi Menuhin, Paula Tennent, Peter O'Toole, Anthony Quinn, Dame Flora Robson, Antony Quayle, Artur Rubinstein, Athene Seyler, Lord and Lady Thorneycroft, Arnold Wesker,

Peter Wyngarde, Elsie and Doris Waters, John Clements, Neville Blond, Albert Finney, Margaret Johnston, James Mason, Geraldine Page, Rip Torn, Elizabeth Welch, Jerome Kilty, Michael Trubshaw, Lesley Storm, Gloria Swanson and many others.

A late night train used to leave Chichester at 10.15pm which meant a worrying scramble for the bus waiting outside the theatre to get the people to the station. It was a slow train stopping at many stations on the way and getting to Victoria at midnight.

British Rail discontinued this train after a while as it meant far too many staff were being kept on all the way up the line and there was never a very large crowd of people using it. Now that we start at 7.30pm instead of at 7pm (at the request of the majority of people as expressed in a survey which we undertook), it would be impossible to expect to have the facility of a late train, especially as nearly all the people from London come by car or stop overnight in the city.

When the train did run one correspondent in the *Daily Mail* wrote:–

'If you don't like people who start conversations with strangers in trains, take my advice and don't come back from Sir Laurence's productions at the Chichester Festival Theatre by Dr Beeching's late night theatre special.

It is the chattiest most un-British train that British Rail run. Of course everyone on the train has something in common. They can all discuss the play they have just seen. But there's more to it than that. It's a trainload of men and women (mostly women) without anything to read. For as the Nigerian gentleman said "Somehow it isn't done to take a book to the theatre so we don't". The chatter went on non-stop to Three Bridges. Then, anyway in my compartment, conversation flagged momentarily and a tweedy blue-rinsed lady in flat heels said "All this silence spoils the evening, doesn't it. Shall we sing?" We just avoided that.'

The 7.30pm opening does give much more time for people from afar to get home from business, pick up the family, and drive through the traffic in comfort though it does involve the theatre and restaurant in more expensive overtime. For the locals who live nearby it creates the awful choice of whether to have a meal before or very late afterwards, but then these problems are everywhere, especially if you go to a restaurant and the service is slow. Late night in London is especially a worry these days when the streets, buses and suburban trains are not the safest of places to be in. One of the pleasant features of life has gone now that one is unable, in a carefree way, to stroll through the streets, after the theatre, shop-gazing whether it is in England or abroad.

When Olivier started our theatre he wanted to put in the programme a 'code of behaviour' for the audience and my contentions with him are dealt with in my other book. The one item I did heartily agree with him was his request that applause should be limited to the end of each act. A habit has since grown up, which I deplore, for the first entrance of famous actors and actresses to be applauded and this is sometimes repeated for their exits. Many of the older members of the profession love this adulation but, to me and to many others, it breaks up the illusion of the play especially in the intense dramas. It happens more in provincial theatres than in London.

Luckily it is a tradition in our theatre not to have speeches from the stage, except in very special circumstances, as it is always pathetic to see members of the cast looking self-conscious in their costumes hanging around listening to the speech just after they have made a vivid impact in their own particular role.

It has also been a tradition to have only three bows to the applause at the end and these are generally stage managed to act like a continuity of the action of the play or musical, skilfully enacted so as to include all sections of the audience on the three sides.

Darlington, in the *Daily Telegraph* 1969, in an article entitled 'We all go to enjoy ourselves' wrote:–

> 'The ordinary playgoer should be able to tell, from the reviews, whether or not he would be able to enjoy the play or whether it would be one he detests. Meanwhile if he won't take my word for it that there are thousands and thousands of uncommitted playgoers who get pleasant outings at the kind of play he detests he has only to go to the Chichester Festival Theatre any night.
>
> He won't enjoy himself, of course. One of the plays this year (*The Caucasian Chalk Circle*) has, God help us, a very "marked" message and the other (*Antony and Cleopatra*) is, Heaven save us, in verse. But he won't be able to deny the spontaneous enjoyment of those about him; and if he tries to make out that these people are not as normal as himself he is not the intelligent man I take him for.
>
> If he can get in, that is, because it is always crammed. It is crammed at matinees too, as I have ocular proof of this myself four times this summer.'

The loyalty of our audiences is tremendous as shown by their continual financial support of our various building projects. I will deal with this more specifically in the chapter on Finance.

The large car park belonging to the District Council which adjoins the theatre holds approximately seven hundred cars and this has been an amenity enjoyed by the theatre's audiences. It was formerly a grass field used entirely for the holding of the Bishop's Fair or the Sloe Field Fair which has rights to use it as a fairground once a year on 20 October (or the nearest weekday) since 1107. It was named after an ancient sloe tree in Oaklands Park. It was Dr Thomas Sharp who in his report on Chichester (commissioned by the City Council in 1948) pointed out that it should be used as a peripheral car park for the city. It was later asphalted over and this was a tremendous boon to the fair, which had previously been a sea of mud on some occasions, and for the use as a car park. It is now commonly known as the theatre car park and there must be many who, not knowing its history, believe it was made especially for the theatre.

A great many attempts have been made to make it a paying, instead of a free, car park especially by a few city councillors who saw this move as a chance to limit the popularity of the theatre. Now it is the officials of the District Council who might increase the financial resources of the council in the easiest possible way regardless of the damage it would do to the welcoming attitude of a city to its visitors.

Officials know that, however many times they are defeated, they will get their way in the end by wearing down the opposition with the persistent initiation of debates. I daresay by the time this book is read they will have succeeded, but it will do more harm than good to the city.

The theatre is opposed to it not because of the extra payment their audiences will have to make but because the congestion before the performances will be great, and illicit parking in the streets around will be a waste of police and warden manpower. People, in the main, arrive during the twenty or so minutes before a performance, and whatever system is adopted, payment at the gates or pay machines, will cause long queues and late arrivals at the theatre.

It is a peculiar thing that people seem to be over-anxious to get away from any function anywhere, regardless of the time the function ends. Even if it finishes a quarter of an hour earlier than expected there seems to be a panic to get out first and away. Some will even spoil the end of a play by disturbing everyone to get out first. Another peculiar trait is when the semi-infirm try to get out first and this holds up the easy flow of other patrons who are more mobile, whereas if they waited a little they themselves would have an easier way out.

As it is, one correspondent wrote:–

> 'Some modern Debussy might find material for a tone poem depicting the evil passions evinced in the desire to get out first in the car park after a performance. Several bars scored for motor horns and percussion might be devoted to the lady who tried to force me out of my line to oblivion.'

Two visitors to the theatre I shall never forget. In July 1962 I was hurriedly summoned to the theatre to entertain Vivien Leigh. This was a delicate situation since the object of the exercise was to distract her from meeting Olivier at the interval which would have been embarrassing.

The other was when Lord Beaverbrook came to see the building just before we opened in 1962. Olivier reluctantly agreed to meet him but because of previous incidents they only greeted one another coolly. Later he enquired whether we were a registered charity and although I was able to assure him we were, I do not think he ever donated to the theatre. Yet another great exponent of private enterprise who failed when his beliefs came to the test.

CHAPTER 8

Finances

This theatre has been built and successfully maintained for twenty-one years by donations from the public, whilst heavily subsidised theatres, attracting Arts Council grants and local rate support, are mostly floundering because of their financial position. It is indeed a miracle that Chichester almost alone is unsubsidised in this way and yet it is almost able to pay its way.

Whilst the finances must be divided into those of the Trust and the Productions Company, there is an overlap inasmuch as there is a rent paid by the Productions Company for use of the theatre, and this helps the finances of the Trust to build and maintain the theatre and ancillary buildings. This rent must come from the box office and general incomes of the productions.

The original theatre building and all furnishings together with the temporary buildings of the restaurant and administration offices were built in 1962 at a cost of approximately £130,000; this for a theatre holding 1,340.

By comparison the original Mermaid in 1959 cost £120,000 for 498 seats; Belgrade, Coventry, cost £310,000 for 911 seats; Nottingham £370,000 for 750 seats; Leeds cost £200,000 for 750 seats; Yvonne Arnaud in 1966 cost £240,000 for 570 seats.

Undoubtedly we built at the right moment not only for the building industry but also before inflation made such buildings so much more expensive. A comparison of the seating capacities will emphasise my reasoning that the smaller the theatre the more it starts off with debts that can never be recovered. The income can never provide for the best productions to attract the large incomes which are necessary.

Glyndebourne succeeded without Arts Council support for its own particular reasons of high priced seats for opera and prestige sponsorships cleverly promoted. Norwich boasts that it is the only theatre in the United Kingdom which is self-supporting without Arts Council help but it does have a large subsidy from the rates. Chichester has so far had nothing from local authorities and only a few grants from the Arts Council. For many years it has been self-supporting, and even on occasions made a profit, with the invaluable help of sponsorship from Martini and Rossi for the Productions Company from 1978 to 1983. With great enthusiasm and generosity, Nissan U.K. Ltd are now sponsoring the theatre seasons for five years.

The Trust during twenty-one years has only received £47,500 from the

Arts Council towards the building or equipment. This is an infinitesimal amount compared with that awarded to other theatres in general. In fact, it is equivalent to what many other theatres get in one year whilst ours was spread over twenty-one years.

In the beginning we received praise from the Arts Council for having built the theatre without any appeal to them for financial support. Lord Cottisloe, Nigel Abercrombie and J. L. Hodgkinson were shown over the theatre and entertained by us to lunch. At the station, when they were leaving, they remarked what a joy it had been to see something which had not entailed them in being begged for money. A complete change of experience for them.

I must take responsibility for my dislike of being dependent on grants from any authorities. I was convinced from the beginning, and I still am, that such theatres as ours can, and should, be self-supporting. I felt that being supported from resources that some feel are inexhaustible, leads to extravagance and 'feather bedding'. Conditions have changed drastically since we started and rampant inflation makes life more difficult; therefore it is more necessary now to seek help from sponsorships.

But whilst we were able to exist without financial help I felt it was wrong to drain away the resources of the Arts Council which could mean life or death to many repertory companies. I trusted the British sense of justice that when we got into difficulties, through no fault of our own, the fact that we had resisted the temptation to ask for grants, when we could work without them, would be taken into consideration. Instead we have been told that we were unceremoniously, and without consultation, 'taken off their list' and could not be considered for any help. When a conference was called of all the theatres in the United Kingdom in 1983 to inform them of the new Arts Council policies, we were excluded. This, to my mind, is unjust and un-British. We have saved the Arts Council many hundreds of thousands of pounds over the years.

On the other hand we have kept our independence, though this should not be at the expense of higher priced seats or low salaries for the artistes. At one time we were urged by one of their representatives to increase our top prices from £3.50 to £5 in order to make such a price seem favourable by comparison with the National Theatre. When I asked why we had been crossed off their so-called 'list' I was asked whether or not we had declined to raise our seat prices. This persuasion I thought was appalling advice from a Government sponsored body when every effort was to be made nationally to keep down inflation.

On another occasion one of our delegations was told 'The Arts Council would frankly be far more worried if a repertory theatre, such as one, say, in Bolton foundered than if the Chichester Festival Theatre foundered.' I leave the reader's imagination to recognise what I felt were the reasons behind such a statement.

No one could deny the extreme difficulties which face the Council in parcelling out grants to all and sundry. It would require a Solomon to do this fairly. Some people look upon the Council, in the prestigious building in Piccadilly, as some sort of Aladdin's cave and do not consider there is any virtue in a theatre such as ours which strives to pay its way. Perhaps it would have been a good idea to have one or two representatives of theatres which independently are financially successful, on the Drama Advisory Board.

The Arts Council works increasingly through its regional Arts Associations and expects County Councils and District Councils to give annual grants to these bodies. It is now Arts Council policy that no main grants will be given to the performing arts unless there is an equivalent or proportionate grant from the local rates.

We are particularly unfortunate in West Sussex in that the County Council is not culturally minded in this respect, though it does help the various musical education schemes for schoolchildren. This unenlightened attitude seems peculiar in an area of the south of England.

In 1982/83 the West Sussex Council gave only £2,500 to the Southern Arts Association, the regional body of the Arts Council. Hampshire gave £51,400, the Isle of Wight gave £4,060, Wiltshire gave £15,400, Dorset £4,000, Berkshire £15,000, Oxfordshire £11,805. In direct aid to the arts West Sussex is also bottom of the league.*

Since the initial raising of the £130,000 our public have donated £400,000 and this together with the rent over twenty-one years totalling £260,000 and large donations from the Society has enabled us to maintain the buildings and create the additions. All improvements have been paid for and there are no outstanding debts. As a result of appeals a reserve fund is being built up by the Trust and by the Society to pay for the building of phase 2 in the latest scheme.

Additions to the main building cost £299,707 and the new administration building cost £140,000. Repairs and maintenance costs £39,818.

Because audiences see almost capacity attendances most of the time, they tend to think we are doing so well we need not appeal for money. They do not realise the Trust only has the rent from the Production Company to help with maintenance and new additions, and the Trust is therefore on its own to find the extra money for these. We have always believed in the principle that we would never start a new project until we had at least two-thirds of the money in our balances. This saves having the worries and burdens of debts which can dampen any progress.

I do not think applying for grants for capital schemes is relevant to the arguments I have stated regarding the ability of a theatre to stand on its own box office receipts from attractive productions. The Trust in provid-

*In 1985 the West Sussex County Council increased its contribution to the Southern Arts Association from £2,500 to £20,000 to be increased to £30,000 in the succeeding year.

ing buildings in which actors can be employed is giving a service for the whole profession, especially in these days of unemployment, and as such should have the wholehearted support of the profession.

On one occasion I wrote around to many actors and designers hoping they would find some interesting theatrical souvenir for our 'new building appeal' auction. One actor replied that it was 'disgraceful for anyone to ask actors to help with building theatres'.

One of our difficulties in raising funds has been the shortage of very big industrial firms in this district. The area is mainly devoted to small light industries and it is therefore a problem how to involve such possible help. The late Philip Whitehead, when he was a member of the Board, solved the difficulty by forming a yearly patron list of firms. We promise to publish their name on every piece of our literature such as programmes, cast lists etc, so that the fee they pay can justly be counted as advertising in the balance sheets.

The fee is now £300 for which they receive £150 worth of tickets which they find extremely useful for staff and for the entertaining of business visitors from abroad. The other £150 goes to the building fund and this has been a great success.

Another scheme which I thought up with David Goodman was called 'The Thousand Club'. Anyone subscribing £100 or more, either by direct donation, or by seven year covenants, became a member of the Club. They received no privileges, except a possible social event once in a while, but they did have a silver plated name plate on a seat in the auditorium. With 'tongue in cheek' we said it would be limited to 1,000 even though we never believed it could reach such a large number. However the latest recruit, at the time of writing, is number 792 and many of the original members have renewed their covenants once or twice. The total amount of this scheme is approximately £115,000.

The best part of all these schemes is the fact that almost everyone, when sending their donations or patron fees, write letters saying how much they, their families and friends, enjoy the theatre. They all say they are only too pleased to support us. Such tremendous goodwill is amazing but it lays a big responsibility on the management to sustain it.

A typical letter was the one we received from a Major John Bower, Persian scholar and ex-Indian Army officer, who made over the royalties from his book *The Golden Pomegranate*, a translation of Persian poems, so that he could endow a seat in the theatre. He wrote, 'I wanted to put back into the Arts something in return for what I have got out of them.'

It will be seen that the Trust depends on the Production Company and vice versa. The Productions must rely on the box office receipts, front of house takings and rents from restaurant and bars. Incomes from these have got to be watched almost day by day and budgets must be devised and kept.

Since Mr John McKerchar joined the Board he has revised and brought up to date all the accounting systems so that with the co-operation of Mr

Rex Harrison in Monsieur Perrichon's Travels, *1976*

David Bartleet, our accountant, the Board is kept fully aware of the month to month situation. This is an enormous help to everyone especially those who fix the budgets and those who have to keep to them. The Board is alerted by warning signs if expectations are not being fulfilled and this is where entertainment projects cannot be compared with industrial concerns. It is impossible to guess what the takings will be for any particular play; so often the play that is expected to be the winner of the season turns out to have the lowest box office appeal. So budgets, as regards receipts, have to contain many 'guess' factors. Fixed expenditures on staff and other overheads can be estimated correctly and production costs once agreed can be kept if thoroughly supervised.

The greatest danger of budgeting is the unreliability of any guest directors or designers if they do not accept, from the beginning of their engagement, the 'facts of life' in running a theatre such as ours, which does not have access to limitless subsidies. There have to be continuous debates and confrontations.

Directors and designers naturally have their reputations to mind all the time. The finished article reflects their artistic judgements. Our Board has had to lay down a strict rule from the beginning, even with Olivier who accepted the control, that once the budget is fixed there can be no excuses to alter it at the whim of someone who has made a mistake. Such instances can occur where, for example, a designer suddenly dislikes the effect of the kind of shoes that have been specially made either because of colour or fashion. We have said he must put up with the mistake unless he can find some other economy to balance the extra cost.

Any supplementary budget is a death knell to strict financial control. It is always easy to spend other people's money whether in this atmosphere of entertainment, local authorities or charitable institutions.

Once it is known that supplementary budgets are possible they will soon be reckoned upon to get people out of difficulties. Unfortunately there will always at times be catastrophies which cannot be avoided such as performances cancelled, or postponed, due to the death of royalty, or illness of stars causing ticket refunds to be made. Costumes can be burnt in a fire or destroyed in a flood. All our costumes for *The Circle* were burnt in a furniture van on the way to London. Insurance against such mishaps and the building up of reserves are the responsibility of the Board of Management.

Perhaps the word 'festival' was not such a good choice at the beginning, though it did signify the aim of this theatre to skim the cream of the inflated population which occurs in this district during the summer invasion of tourists. Certainly the Arts Council has thrown it at us as an excuse that we are not a full-time theatre. However, since we have air conditioning to warm the theatre in the winter time, we are open for nearly forty weeks of the year. As we have nearly full capacity audiences of 1,340 this supplies a greater need than many other theatres which are open the whole year with smaller capacities and smaller attendance percentages. The closed months are necessary for rehearsal periods as we create our own plays. At least 'festival' does indicate the 'festive' atmosphere we try to portray.

Sponsorship is the necessary substitute for subsidies. Whilst the Southern Television Company was in being we received a yearly donation of £1,000 and we were very grateful for this support. The Television South which succeeded it has just decided to grant us a sponsorship, from the TVS Charitable Trust, of £20,000 for the year 1984 and we are deeply thankful for this. Some of the banks and other institutions have sponsored some concerts but the rest of the sponsorship for the years 1978–83 came from Martini and Rossi.

They have been a colossal help to us, not only have they maintained throughout an extremely friendly relationship, they have added to their main contribution by extra help on special occasions. We have kept faith by agreeing to all their modest demands for advertising in the programmes and bars. They have also benefitted by the sale of their products which amounted to an estimated £25,000 each year, so it is not just a one-way benefit. Sponsors cannot be expected to go on for ever as their advertising values have to be widespread all the time.

Members of the Theatre Society have worked magnificently raising money for the various building projects and amenities, especially in the early years. Every conceivable method of persuading people to give money has been tried with varying success.

Particularly gratifying was the response to their appeal for money to build a lift and special toilets for the disabled. Within two or three weeks the money had been subscribed (approximately £16,000) and letters poured in approving of the idea. The attendance of the disabled at the theatre has increased tenfold and it has been a joy to everyone, especially the attendants who look after them, to know how much the facilities have been appreciated. Before the lift was installed the disabled were carried into the lower auditorium by our attendants but this was a somewhat nerve-racking experience for some however well it was done.

Norman Siviter, as secretary of the Society, and I attended a reception on 8 December 1981, given by the Royal Association for Disability and Rehabilitation when HRH The Duke of Gloucester presented us with a certificate in recognition of the theatre's help in providing special facilities for the disabled.

The Society has over many years invited the public to viewings of the theatre both front of house and backstage. These have been efficiently organised by the voluntary members of the committee and on most occasions it has been necessary to have two sessions during which parties are conducted by guides followed by demonstrations of the lighting and sound equipment and talks by directors and technicians. Queues extended far into the park waiting for admission.

Once a year, in the spring, the members are invited to a 'forum' to hear from the artistic director the details of the forthcoming season, and lively discussions take place between the director and the audience. I never go to these as I like to have the dramatic surprise on the first night rather than being influenced by a previous analysis given in the form of a lecture; but hundreds do like to know all they can about a play before they see it. Plays can be taken too seriously and I know some who even take the text with them to the play to check the accuracy of the presentation. The majority of plays are written in order that they may be seen. If you are looking at the text you might just as well be at home and hear the words on the radio.

I remember once when I was in the upper circle of the Kings Theatre at Southsea for a performance of a Gilbert and Sullivan opera. The surrounding audience were obviously from a teaching college and many were studying the score most of the time. They were treating the light opera as though it was a religious observance and when there was laughter at any time they looked up annoyed and actually 'shushed' us. Fanaticism comes in many forms, but then so does the use of wit.

The Society also helped us to organise the great auction of antiques in October 1981 when Sotheby (King and Chasemore) led by Mr Leslie Weller and Mrs Sophie Shalit raised £19,000 for our Development Fund. Amongst the few souvenirs donated by the profession was a pullover from Rex Harrison which he had worn in *My Fair Lady* and seven hats which Kathleen Harrison had worn in a television series.

Besides garden parties at Stansted, home of Lord and Lady Bessborough, during one of which 'The Mitford Girls' gave a cabaret, there were the 'Elizabethean Revels' which are best described in the words of the poster advertising the event:–

> 'Venison from Woburn; 3 guineas, as much food and drink as capacity. Mead Punch, and other brews, for swilling gussling and carousing. Ye shall witness divers princely entertainments such as the like never performed by any society in England. Whereto will be employed the best wits and skillfulest artisans in devising and composing many ingenious speeches, delicate devices, melodious music, pleasant games and pastimes for your sport and great delight.
>
> Present will be many famous names from the theatres at Stratford, the National Theatre and Chichester. Rosemary Harris, Robert Stevens, Norman Rossiter, The Carl Dometsch Consort, Diana Poulton, Pearl Goodman and David Wood. Venison from Manchurian Silks and Chinese Water Deer supplied by the Duke of Bedford, Cumberland style wrestling and a 'wrong doer' pelted in the stocks. Also Billie Whitelaw, Tom Courtenay, Maggie Smith and Robert Lang. Traditional music will be by Chappie d'Amato and his Elizabeadles with a 20th century 'Tudor Rock' session. Herbert Menges, master of the Musick Richard Seal and the gentlemen of the Chichester Cathedral choir.'

It was all good fun and a great success despite the fact that the food soon disappeared leaving none for late-comers, and many found the mead stronger than they had anticipated.

The Society ran many of the usual fund-raising events such as coffee mornings, barbecues, races at Fontwell Park, a reception and ball on board the liner *Windsor Castle* and jumble sales. At one of the collecting points for jumble a hundred-year-old 'Bishop's Cross' was given in anonymously. When this was taken to a local jeweller for valuation the manager demanded that it should be taken out of the shop as he declared it was associated with 'black magic'. It embodied the figures of a scarab beetle and the devil on a swivelling centre piece. No one divulged where it went to after that.

CHAPTER 9

Critics

A word or two about the critics. Many learned articles have been written about the use and abuse of drama critics and one can only have some sympathy for them in the dilemma they must so often find themselves involved in when criticising the work of artistic people.

The love-hate relationship which most actors must have for the critics, according to whether they get good or bad notices, is felt just as much by the directors and managements of the theatres. Many a time I have felt, as other theatres have felt, that the critics should be banned when they seem to have unjustly besmirched the work of the actors and others engaged in a production.

It is always flattering for a theatre such as ours to have them coming down here at some inconvenience instead of just going round the corner to a London theatre. Since nothing is worse than being ignored we can do no other than welcome them, provide them with all the facilities they need, and put up with them when they give bad notices.

To see them rush off as the final applause commences to their newspapers to transmit what appears to be a spot 'summing up' seems a poor way of passing judgement. One should however remember that they have probably already read the play, or seen it many times before, and have already written up most of the criticism of the play itself, leaving space for comments on individual players.

Actors and actresses who, having worked hard for months to perfect their parts and give of their best, though this is not often displayed on first nights, can have their reputations affected by a few words or by being ignored. It is difficult to believe any of them who say they are not affected by the notices. Even if they don't read them I am quite sure they have them read to them or at least they know all about them from other people's comments.

Respect must also be felt for the critics. What a way to earn a living by sitting calmly, or in many cases in a state of irritation, night after night watching plays with, I daresay, just the faint hope that sometime, somewhere, they will have the thrill of a great dramatic experience.

As to their notices I suppose, for the sake of the uninformed reader, they must detail the plot of the play even if this takes up the main part of their article. The contents of such articles can easily be forecast especially when they make an obvious heading such as *The Sleeping Prince* being commented on by 'A pity they woke him up'; or *A Broken Heart* and 'It broke my heart'.

The only guide the public can have, since all reviewers have their own way of judging plays, is to follow the critic who seems to coincide with one's own particular attitude to the plays that are enjoyed or disliked.

Chichester audiences seem to be affected in the first week by the reviews but soon after make their own judgements by 'word of mouth'. This is a trait of any fairly closed community in the smaller cities and towns as compared with any large metropolis like London. I often think Chichester survives despite the critics, a sort of 'be damned to the critics' attitude.

On the whole, for a great many years, our theatre suffered from an extraordinary prejudice that seemed common to all the critics. First of all we had adverse criticisms during Olivier's time when they were trying to teach him what they would expect from him as the ordained National Theatre artistic director. Then came a softening during Clements' time except from those who wanted to see the full potentialities of the thrust stage.

Next came the prejudices against Michell, then a reaction to sympathy during Dews' directorship, finishing up with the genuine acceptance of Garland. What did puzzle me was the lack of acknowledgement, except from Darlington and Hobson, of the uniqueness of our enterprise. Here was a theatre built by an audience because they wanted one. One that was not a heavily subsidised or commercial West End theatre, but one which was out to give the best of drama and help the revival of 'live' theatre. One where if any profits were made they would be ploughed back into the theatre, not squandered or paid out to company directors and shareholders.

Why were the notices almost consistently deprecative? Naturally some of them were thoroughly deserved and we knew which those were, but standards were higher than in most other theatres throughout the country. Whilst Hobson was helpful, it was Darlington who really saw behind the adventure the true meaning of why this theatre was ever created. All we expected was understanding, not sympathy, and we accepted criticism when it was obviously deserved but we did not accept the hint of prejudice that seemed to pervade most reviews.

One of our difficulties has always been the fact that, unlike most other theatres in the provinces, we create our own productions and do not just rely on touring companies. I exclude theatres like Nottingham, Theatre Royal Manchester, Bristol Old Vic, etc which probably have the same difficulty. So the critics see the plays after only two or three performances, and these are more or less previews. Time and time again, predictably, whenever one of our plays was transferred to the West End the same statement was made that 'it was far better in London'. Of course it was after two months 'running in' at Chichester. So often it is even better within a week when cuts and modifications have been made and the cast gets into the

Clive Francis and Susan Hampshire in The Circle, *1976 (John Timbers)*

rhythm of the action. I have always felt that the critics should not be invited for at least a week and on one occasion this was tried; the mistake was the decision to make it the Monday following the start. This made the cast nervous all the weekend and continuity was destroyed. So it was back to the original Wednesday and the same criticisms appeared disregarding the difficulties of a new-born creation.

Another difficulty which I believe is forgotten is that because we run two plays in tandem there is always the cast of the other play at a first night. These members of the profession are somewhat over-keen to give a response to their fellow actors on the stage, to impress the critics of the worthiness of the play. This is seen in the early stages of the play but a rather more normal audience reaction takes over after a while. Perhaps the critics take this as a typical Chichester audience reaction but they would find it balanced and correctly evaluated later in the run.

I have often wondered whether the critics think I am 'standoffish' or aloof because I have never attempted to meet any of them. I should certainly not think it correct to intrude on their sacred domain, the press office, at the interval of a first night. My reason for not meeting them has been that I would hate them to think that by meeting them I was trying to gain good opinions or favours for our theatre. Also I suspect the professional press representatives of our organisation would think I was trespassing on their preserves. I would have enjoyed on many occasions the opportunity to meet the critics as a body to discuss with them their attitude to our theatre.

Edward Goring, writing in October 1967, 'Hobson's not so choice, or why have critics?' says:–

> 'They are comparatively useless, powerless and therefore harmless. Like so many dotty institutions they are tolerated on account of tradition.
>
> But now that anachronisms, such as the proscenium arch and the Lord Chamberlain's role as stage censor, are being swept away it is amazing that no one in the theatre has suggested getting rid of that other hangover of Hazlitt's day, the theatre critic.
>
> I have no axe to grind. I am a critic and as long as theatre managements continue to invite me to witness their latest attempts to get their money back I shall be happy to go along and tell them what I think of their chances.
>
> Yet the theatre welcomes its critics with a willingness that amounts to masochism. And we just don't deserve to be there.
>
> Is this kind of talk wise? Well, I am taking Alan Brien at his word. In this year's Chichester Festival Theatre's brochure he wrote, "It is only fair that the critics should be the most criticised people around the theatre. As we judge so should we be judged."
>
> I know that I shall scarcely be believed whan I report that some of my colleagues lay awake at night worrying about what they have written. And so he should. Bernard Levin, for instance, used to put the producers in a real dilemma. Naturally they were unhappy if he disliked a play. They were equally unhappy if he liked it. They felt this would frighten people away.'

This is not the medium in which to have a lengthy discussion on critics in general but only in regard to their attitude to our theatre. One day I hope they will drop what seems to be their prejudice against 'the open stage', the 'wide open spaces', and the self-respecting audiences. I hope they will give some encouragement to the unsubsidised theatres who try to make a theatre pay on its own merit and not by the clutching of begging bowls.

The critics I have the greatest sympathy for are those who write for the local papers. Their dilemma is acute, especially when they are criticising local amateur productions. If they give a bad, sometimes truthful review, they are apt to damage their own paper which then receives numerous indignant letters proclaiming 'I will never take your paper again'.

One example of what I felt was unfair criticism was when Hannah Gordon, who had appeared with great success at our theatre, was made to say in an episode of a television series called *Telford's Change* that, in effect, Chichester Theatre was not worthy of having any subsidy.

This offended a large number of the members of our audiences and I felt, for once, impelled to protest to the Director General of the BBC. He very graciously replied saying he understood our feelings and was sorry if we were disapproving of the remark.

He went on to say:–

> 'The remark was made by a character – Telford's Wife – who was later described as a 'Miltiades at Marathon'. In other words she was a fighter for the weaker side which in this instance was a 'tiny repertory company stuck away out in the sticks'. This was plainly a device by the author to establish his character's personality and role in the series. I do not believe it would have been interpreted in any other sense by the great majority of viewers. I appreciate the reasons for your concern but, from experience of similar incidents in other plays, which almost by definition will attract a predominantly thinking and reasonably informed audience, I think I can safely assure you that no harm will have been done.'

It just seems a pity that the playwright, for some reason best known to himself, chose to name our theatre, rather than use a fictional one, in such a derogatory manner.

In the meantime we will fight on to keep our standards, inviting the critics, whilst agreeing and disagreeing with them to keep 'the pot boiling' with healthy criticism. In fact there is nothing else we can do!

CHAPTER 10

Controversies

I enjoy controversies. They make you think and they stimulate your imagination. Not like the stilted rules of debate as practised by the ruling Government and the Opposition in the Houses of Parliament but by a free exchange of views with the possibilities of compromise and common agreement. If agreement is not possible then both sides are left with a satisfied feeling that they have at least displayed their 'strong views'.

During the twenty-one years of our existence many subjects continually emerge for discussion almost ad infinitum. I will, before telling of one or two major issues, briefly recount a few small affairs.

The National Anthem

From the very beginning I enjoyed the fact that this theatre kept to the playing of the National Anthem either before or at the end of each performance. It was a tradition until the start of Keith Michell's directorship.

Michell was immediately criticised by a large number of people, writing to me and to him, and this added to the bad publicity he had already received for his supposed lack of qualifications as a theatre manager. Actually the truth of the matter was that he had not realised it was played at each performance. It was not a deliberate alteration of our theatre procedures and certainly not, as some wanted to infer, an expression of disloyalty to the Crown because he was Australian. Amazing how some people's imagination can be stretched.

When, as the result of the adverse correspondence, the matter was discussed at the next Board meeting of the season, arguments were then put forward by the management to the effect that it was not played in any other theatre and not even at the Royal Opera House. Difficulties came, they said, if before the play began people had just got settled in and then had to stand and they said it stiffened the feelings of the audience before a comedy. If played at the end it killed the joyousness of a comedy or the impact of a drama.

I personally dismissed the argument about other theatres as I see no harm, only good, in our theatre being as unique as possible. That is what we had set out to be. A majority of the members of the Board agreed with the management and I was defeated.

It was therefore kept for royal occasions. In one case it was splendidly done by the Chichester Cathedral choir when the Queen was at a performance, and on another occasion when the Queen Mother was present for the Canadian performance of *Love's Labour's Lost* an actor came onto the stage and in candlelight played the anthem on a harpsichord.

It is, of course, wrong when it is played in some unusual, peculiar way which causes a ripple of laughter over the auditorium. This happened when the Queen opened the National Theatre and the brass ensemble played a specially written version of the anthem which finished with unsubdued laughter from the audience, completely spoiling the importance of the occasion for a while.

One correspondent writing about our theatre commented sarcastically:–

> 'Rising to its feet for the National Anthem before the evening has even begun (where else in England does that happen now save at horse trials and the Royal Tournament) the audience seem to affirm that it is there for a ritual artistic celebration rather than any kind of surprise.'

It was one of those debates I lost but it is still played at the first and last performances of the season as well as on royal occasions. It is significant that Garland gave way to the wave of patriotism that was felt during the Falklands conflict and the anthem was played at each performance and was greeted with enthusiasm.

The Red Army Choir

Concerts by the Red Army Choir on 12 & 13 April 1970 were criticised by letters to us, and in the local papers, protesting about their appearance at the theatre. Most of the letters, not a great number in all, stressed the fact that the choir were serving members of the Russian Army, wore army uniforms and sang patriotic songs. Memories of what had happened to Czechoslovakia were revived, and quoted, but there was general agreement that Russian culture and art should not in themselves be banned. It was the military aspect that offended and I could understand the objections.

As it happened both concerts were fully booked and an extra Sunday afternoon performance was given. The only protest at the time were a few young Liberals standing silently at the park gates. The cultural aspect would have been best served if the choir had not been a military one.

Free Programmes

One of the principles I laid down in the first days of the theatre was to create an atmosphere of welcoming entertainment: the friendly open box office without grills and glass partitions to sever the link between staff and customer. Also the friendly smiling usherettes handing out free programmes. The reason I like to see free programmes is because it shows that patrons, having once spent their money on tickets and travelling, are not being badgered for extra payments in the theatre. Furthermore it is pathetic to see men fumbling in their pockets, and waiting for change, whilst holding up others in the entrances or standing in humble queues near the stage whilst the usherettes scrabble for change. Myopic economists can only calculate and quote statistics of the money which is lost by not selling programmes. They cannot seem to appreciate the amount of goodwill free programmes create and they do not realise that it is one of the subtle reasons why our theatre is so popular. Unfortunately this matter has been urged almost every year and lately the Board have discarded my ideas because of the pressure of finances. I deeply regret it.

Leisure Centre in Oaklands Park

Rumours that a leisure centre, or youth sports centre, was to be built in the city circulated during the years 1982/3. Then suddenly the District Council inserted notices in the planning announcements proposing to build one either adjacent to the theatre on a site at present occupied by the Archery Club or on the ground of the Chichester Football Club farther south of the theatre.

The proposed two storey building would contain three squash courts, assembly hall, games room, social room and offices. It was obvious that this would not be sufficient eventually and that it would, in time, need a swimming pool, indoor tennis courts etc. It would become a large conglomerate construction.

Whilst the football ground would have been far enough away from the theatre the archery site would have completely ruined the aspect of the 'theatre in the park' and spoilt the whole look of the park.

All the societies interested in the environment objected strongly to the centre being in the park as there were better sites elsewhere in the city.

Members of the Board whilst applauding the need for such a centre instituted a massive campaign to object to the spoilation of the theatre, by means of letters pouring into the committees of the Council from trustees and influential people. Resolutions to proceed passed by the appropriate committees were finally overturned by 43–6 when the matter was discussed by the full Council.

One of the tricky aspects of this controversy was for us not to condemn any more buildings in Oaklands Park as our application for our phases 2 and 3 had been deferred by the Council whilst the leisure centre was being debated.

I have detailed in my previous book how at the very time we were building the theatre there was a sudden demand for a swimming pool in the city and this caused opposition to the theatre appeal. Now again, by coincidence, this sudden move to promote a leisure centre, a completely new concept, was being used to delay our permission for the replacement of the temporary administration and restaurant buildings.

Our plans had been known for over twenty years and it was unfortunate that it was at this moment that we were, at last, able to ask for planning permission after the many delays with various architects. At any other

Management staff 1976 1. Tom Alexander 2. Bill Green 3. Bill Donnison 4. Andy Neal 5. Colin Hedgecock 6. Stuart Tyler 7. Alan Cramsie 8. Adrian Whitaker 9. Paul Rogerson 10. Hugh Ryder 11. Michael Brennan 12. David Bartleet 13. Maureen Davis-Poynter 14. Elizabeth Redding 15. Joseph Dixon 16. Gypsy Madgin 17. Margaret Henderson 18. Keith Michell 19. Tim Oliver 20. Barbara Blay 21. Susan Dudley-Ward 22. Lynette Ogdon 23. Anna Sims 24. Jenny Wright 25. Jean Kemnitzer 26. Shirley Poland 27. Anne Hillier 28. Robert Selbie 29. Jeannette Sterke 30. Nancy Hotston 31. Pat Packham 32. Vanessa Lees

time the application would have gone through after the normal consultations and amendments.

I think our attitude to the whole controversy is best summed up by my letter in the *Chichester Observer* on 8 September 1983

> 'The Chichester Festival Theatre has never asked for grants from the County, District or City Councils. As far as it is known by us it is the only theatre of importance in the United Kingdom which does not have support from the rates.
>
> Many theatres get substantial grants, amounting to tens of thousands of pounds each year in some cases. We have always been proud of the fact that, up till now, we have not needed to do so because of commercial sponsorship and the strict business methods by which the theatre has been run.

The Arts Council, instead of appreciating the money it has been saved, has penalised this theatre because it is not subsidised by the rates.

Instead of being a burden on the ratepayers this theatre has actually contributed to them by paying rates on the three-and-a-half acres, ground which would not otherwise have been rateable. This has amounted to £75,000. It also gives tremendous pleasure and recreation to approximately 500,000 people each year on three-and-a-half acres, compared with the number of people using the other forty acres of the rest of Oaklands Park.

The Oaklands Park was bought for recreation. This includes recreation of the mind as well as the body, and this is rightly balanced at present.

The new building adjacent to the theatre, within the boundaries of the land leased to it, has been planned over twenty years to replace the temporary buildings and has been very carefully designed in relation to the unique theatre building to hide, somewhat, the rather ugly hospital laundry.

The Theatre Trust, which is a registered charity, has always been very keen on tree planting schemes and the trees which have been planted to replace the ill-fated elm trees, together with those which will be planned in the future, will gradually grow to enhance the whole area.

Personally, as a resident and ratepayer for fifty years in Chichester, I wholly support the idea of a leisure centre for Chichester providing it is for all ages where they can meet and enjoy each other's company whilst pursuing their own particular activities. It will help them to understand one another as they do, I believe, in the excellent Midhurst project.

The school campus at Kingsham Road, or a space adjoining the College of Technology, would seem to be the right places for easy access and car parking, and where there are already sporting facilities which are not fully used during the evenings, weekends and holidays. At least it would ensure the centre was used by students, as well, during term time.

There should certainly be a swimming pool but this time I hope it will be of competition length so that events of national importance can be held there. One day perhaps a skating rink could be added.

If the leisure centre could be done in phases, as money becomes available, and each phase is constructed in the best possible way, and not skimped because of expediency, the resulting centre could be a source of pride for the District Council and for the City of Chichester.'

Our plans for the new buildings were subsequently turned down by the Development Control Committee by eight votes to four even though they had previously agreed to them in principle in July 1982. However the Planning Committee and the full Council agreed to the plans later that month.

Such difficulties and debates take place in every small village, town and city and the only difference between a city such as ours and a large metropolis is that the individual issues, and people, are better known and therefore the general public are more aware of the issues. It is not because such places are narrow minded or petty.

Danny Kaye

When Clements announced his programme for 1967 he said it was to be 'a season of laughter'. Eden Philpotts *The Farmer's Wife*, George Farqhar's *The Beaux Stratagem*. Shaw's *Heartbreak House* and Carl Goldino's *The Servant of Two Masters*.

He also announced that Danny Kaye (aged fifty-four) was to play in the Goldino play and this was important news for the international press. He had not played on any stage for twenty years having confined himself to cinema, television and tours to help UNESCO. Instead of the usual press conference, which we generally held at the spectacular Martini Terrace at the top of New Zealand House, it was held this time at the Waldorf Hotel in Aldwych. I had vivid memories of the very first press conference we held there in February 1960 to launch the theatre. The drama that day was very fitting for the adventure we were then starting and here we were again seven years later.

Danny Kaye was present on this occasion and the world's press were there eager for some good quotes from a personality who was renowned for his quick repartee. It was reported that he had flown over the night before and that he had administered oxygen to a woman passenger in response to a request from the pilot who knew he had previously had some medical experience.

We found Danny Kaye very friendly and keen to play at our theatre. We did not get much opportunity to talk to him as he was surrounded all the time by the reporters.

At the conference he was asked what salary he would get at Chichester and he replied £75 per week. He had asked for £76 but 'that skinflint Clements would not agree' and when he found out that Olivier had played for us at £70 he agreed. He said his appearance would ruin Chichester off the map. He further quipped 'What shall I do with all that money?'

He was also asked why he had turned his back on television for a play in Chichester where the six weeks' salary would barely cover the cost of his London hotel suite for one day. He replied:–

> 'It is a new kind of challenge that will stimulate me as a performer. I may fall down in Chichester. I may be the biggest bomb ever. If I were going to do Hamlet I'd be a lot more concerned but this is out and out comedy, a Hoakey comedy, and I think I have some kind of acquaintance with that.'

Ronald Hastings, in *Plays and Players*, quoted Danny Kaye as saying he did not consider '*The Servant* as being called a classic. To keep on referring to it as a classic did not do it any good, it only put off the actors. This was not just a wisecrack, there was a lot of truth behind it which only a refreshing visitor from America could see.'

Later in the month he came down to the theatre with Clements. I think what he saw that day contributed to what happened later for it was a very dreary miserable February day. The theatre was deserted and looked most depressing. Also it must have seemed a long way from the centre of theatreland in London. In fact I rather believe it looked like one of the out-of-town theatres he was accustomed to in America and which I saw when I was in New York and Chicago. He certainly could not have gauged the status of our theatre.

He visited the Millstream Hotel at Bosham and reserved the whole of the top floor of a two-storied wing of the hotel not, as the papers said, for his entourage but, as he said later, to accommodate all the friends from all over the world who would want to visit him during the run of the play.

The first unfortunate happening was that during this year, of all years, the Piccolo Theatre of Milan was engaged by the Aldwych Royal Shakespeare Company to perform their version of the play, *The Servant of Two Masters*. Since this was the masterpiece of their repertoire they gave very polished performances which gave rise to splendid reviews and many articles in the press such as the one in the *Evening Standard* which was headed 'Oh! Danny, what a challenge' and said:–

> 'Now that we have seen the real thing heaven help you! As if to say 'Follow that' the Piccolo Theatre of Milan brought their renowned production of *The Servant of Two Masters* to the Aldwych last night . . . just three months ahead of the one you are to do at Chichester.
>
> This was not simply laying a theatrical flare-path; it was comic precision bombing devastating the very country over which you have to travel. The style of the acting, the beauty of the 18th century Venetian setting and the brilliant invention of Ferrucio Soleri in your part of the servant Arlecchino, is going to be very, very hard to follow.
>
> Though handicapped throughout by a black Commedia dell' Arte mask (I can't see you tolerating that) and dressed in a harlequin costume, this actor's display of acrobatics, semi-juggling and miming was a rare treat. Line for line you might well be funnier. You'll get laughs with pauses – those long quizzical looks of yours – where Soleri goes through it like a tornado.
>
> But what I can't imagine is where you are going to find a comparable wealth of obviously traditional business – the trapping of a fly, slapping of your hand while fondling a maidservant's bosom, disappearing into a clothes chest and popping up again like Punchinello.
>
> Well, Danny, have I put the wind up you? No sadism is intended. I can assure you no knives are being sharpened. We are all longing for you. But oh! you've got something to beat. Your great admirer, Felix Barker.'

The next unfortunate happening was the war that broke out between Israel and Egypt. Danny Kaye attended and spoke at a meeting in the Hollywood Bowl. He became highly emotional and declared he would go to Israel to entertain the troops and help the morale of the nation he loved so much. This was reminiscent of the time Topol was with us and we were always on tenter-hooks in case he was called up for military service in the, then, troubled Israeli situation. He was an enrolled member of the army reserve.

Danny Kaye's declaration meant that he was opting out of our contract. Actually the war was already over and many said he could have entertained all the Israeli troops in a matter of days. The news that he was breaking our contract was reported world wide and Peter Coe rushed over to America to see him but failed, after a long session, to convince him enough to change his mind.

On 13 June during an interview I said, 'My fighting spirit has been aroused, I hope we shall be able to make a victory out of a disappointment.'

He was thoroughly condemned by the theatrical profession for not keeping faith with the public and the sort of 'the show must go on' tradition. Wild statements, such as 'He must never be allowed to perform in the British Isles again' were made and Clements declared himself as being enraged. It was suggested in some quarters that he had become worried about a stage appearance in such a part after such a long absence from stage performances and that he did not feel adequate for it. A few wrote saying they could understand his loyalty to Israel and that it was in keeping with his charity work for the League of Nations, and his crusading for children all over the world. How quickly a world-loved person can fall from grace.

One paper said he was scouring Israel to find troops to entertain. Roderick Mann wrote:–

> 'Will Danny Kaye be stoned if he sets foot on British soil again? Will angry actors clobber him before he even gets through customs? Has that special relationship forged nineteen years ago with his never-to-be-forgotten Palladium appearance gone completely up the spout?'

Not only did Danny Kaye emphasise his wish to reimburse all the theatre's deficits, and the hotel he had booked at Bosham; he said he would come over several Sundays to give concerts for the benefit of the theatre. He complained that Clements never mentioned this fact publicly.

Collie Knox said:–

> 'We would be excused for thinking that an army whose deeds shook the world with admiration stands in no desperate need of morale boosting. Fortunate indeed is a country that can arouse such passionate loyalty in the son of its Faith. What would Solomon have done? It is right and proper that a man of principle should so order his life and act according to his conscience. What is apt to prove tricky is when two principles meet head on – the signed and sealed commitment involving a team, and the sudden emergency. In *Heartbreak House* Bernard Shaw makes the character say – "It is neither just nor right that we should be put to a lot of inconvenience to gratify your moral enthusiasm, my friend." '

Personally I felt it was a mixture of all the circumstances I have related, together with his possible reaction to the dismal visit he paid to Chichester which made him believe we were a minor out-of-town theatre of no great importance. The proof of this was when the international reputation of our theatre was revealed to him — he was staggered at the uproar his deletion had caused. I firmly believe, and understood, his emotional feeling that he would be a hero to Israel. I also believe he was feeling the usual nervousness all actors feel in the early stages of preparing a play, especially after the eulogistic notices of the Piccolo Theatre's visit to London.

He immediately said he would pay all Chichester's expenses which had been incurred by his non-appearance and this he did in full. Bookings for the play had already been heavy. A tremendous wave of sympathy for us was evident by the many offers of help we received from all directions. Danny Kaye paid for all the extra costs of reprinting tickets, literature and preliminary expenditure on production.

The hunt for a suitable star to replace him failed and it was hurriedly decided to do another play of similar content. *The Italian Straw Hat* was chosen, to be directed by Peter Coe. There were only two months left and in that time an excellent cast was formed and this resulted in a brilliant success which soon became fully booked. Very few people asked for their money to be refunded. In fact, only 22 out of 41,000.

One paper quoted the landlord of a local inn called 'The Nag's Head' as saying, 'If he [Danny Kaye] walked in here today I couldn't bring myself to serve him.' The paper further commented that 'greater love [for the theatre] hath no publican than that!'

The substitute play *The Italian Straw Hat* to my mind had the added ingredients for success by virtue of the challenge it gave to all concerned and the determination to show Danny Kaye that his absence was not, after all, fatal.

The design and direction were inspired and were allowed to remain in their first freshness without the toning down and modification of too many critics in rehearsal. It had the scintillating brilliance of a high velocity rocket compared with the laborious thunder of a canon shell.

All in all Danny's defection was a good thing for our theatre as the goodwill shown to us was greater than had ever been experienced before. It welded the profession and the audiences into a common bond of achievement and I, for one, was glad it had happened. Whilst I hate any question of contracts being broken I believed in Danny Kaye's sincerity on this occasion. Artistes would not be artistic if they were not emotional.

A Patriot For Me

On 8 March 1983 a press conference was scheduled to take place at the Martini Terrace in London at noon. A Board meeting was arranged to take place at the Royal Overseas League immediately afterwards.

It had been obvious to members of the Board that for some time Garland had been in great difficulties with his choice for the first play of the season. This had been caused by many disappointments in fixing stars to plays and in obtaining copyrights.

As far as any of us knew the play had still not been chosen as late as the Friday before the Tuesday conference. On the Monday evening Lord Bessborough rang me and asked if I knew that Garland was proposing to stage John Osborne's controversial play *A Patriot for Me*.

He remembered having seen it at the Royal Court Theatre in 1965 when it had been shown at a 'members only' occasion. It was staged at a 'private' session because the Lord Chamberlain, as censor, had mutilated the text so much that Osborne refused to consider any cuts at all.

Bessborough sketched out the story for me, with its homosexual content, and related the cuts of three scenes and many lines which had been ordered by the censor. These cuts are detailed at the back of the text of the play in the edition published by Faber and Faber.

Whilst Bessborough said he could not remember either he, or his wife Mary, being shocked at the time he did not think it was possibly suitable for our Chichester audiences. London would be a different matter with its huge population which could support a 'specialised' subject like this. I took particular notice of Bessborough's point of view as he is by no means 'narrow-minded'.

I rang the chairman, Henny Gestetner, and suggested she might persuade Garland and Gale to delete the play from the announcements at the conference so that the Board might have the opportunity to discuss this play which was the most controversial one ever proposed for our theatre. The two directors refused, however, to alter their plans and so the four plays were announced.

At the Board meeting the matter was debated but there was nothing that could be done and it was accepted. Bessborough hoped Garland would make some cuts but this proved impossible as Osborne refused any such idea. I said I would not make any more objections until I had actually read the play, but I deplored the fact that the notices for the press and the booking forms had already been printed the Friday before the conference without the Board knowing of the decision.

I read the play that evening and again the following evening and I was disappointed that such a play was to be performed on our stage. I found myself in total agreement with the censor's cutting of two of the scenes. One is where the main character is raped by other men and the other where he is seen first reviling and then endearing himself to the young man with whom he has obviously just been in bed.

The 'drag ball' scene (also cut by the censor) did not seem so important as such impersonations are seen in pantomime and by Danny la Rue and Hinge and Bracket on the modern stage. The only difference being that in this play the characters are serious in their masquerading whereas in the others I have mentioned it is done just for comedy.

I decided that, personally, I did not want to see the play because I should be bored and saw no point in wasting money to see it. Unfortunately having mentioned this to only one or two people that I should not go to the first night, or see any of the performances, it was 'leaked' to the press and I was bombarded by all the national papers, BBC TV and ITV and radio representatives asking why I was not going to the play.

I gave the same single answer to each of them that 'this was a personal matter' and gave no other explanation. This enraged some of the reporters who, frustrated from making an elaboration of the statement, headed their articles such as one 'An Angry Old Man'. This in itself was amusing as I was not angry, just disappointed that we were having such a play and I certainly never feel old!

I just happen to have deep convictions, right or wrong, on such matters and there is no law which says I must see every one of our plays. It seems a pity to me that the public has now been so 'brain-washed' by the violence and sex seen so much in the theatres and on television and cinema screens that it has lost its sense of what is right and what is wrong.

To use the word 'shocking' is to bring the discussion down to a low level and does not do justice to some people's well founded ideals. Those who excuse their tolerance of such plays as being 'modern and broad-minded' must accept some small responsibility for the deterioration in the nation's morality.

My next deep concern was that the description of the play in our brochures was misleading to the public and that many people would be going to the theatre unaware of its content and would be disappointed by what they saw. I felt it was the responsibility of the Board, and management, to make sure people knew what the play was about; they could then make up their minds whether they wanted to see it or not.

All that was said in the first brochure was:– 'An ambitious officer of the Imperial Army of the Austro-Hungary Empire, who is blackmailed into becoming a spy for Tsarist Russia. Spanning the years 1890–1914 the play reveals not only the tragedy of an individual but also the character of the institution in which he achieved his high rank.'

There was no mention of homosexuality and no warning that it was unsuitable for children. At least in the description of *Feasting with Panthers*, depicting the trial of Oscar Wilde, there had been such a warning about children.

After my protests that we had a responsibility to the public the wording of all other notices was altered and I was then satisfied that the public had the choice to see the play knowing its content.

The attendance at the play for the first few weeks was very high and I am told this was somewhat due to the publicity I had created but this was certainly not my intention. Later on the audiences fell off, when curiosity had been satisfied, and it only achieved a 69% total which is low for our theatre. It also did not do so well in London as expected.

On the other hand it was hailed by everyone who saw it as being a very splendid production with the finest acting and presentation. I do not think the theatrical profession has any licence or god-given right to portray any and everything that happens in life just because it happens. Where does it end?

Since I understand everything of the lowest perversions and malpractices has been exploited and seen on stages, one can only hope it will have been found in time to be utterly boring and deadening, and a revulsion will take place, but that is hardly likely in my lifetime.

What of the play itself? Whilst the first one-third is a normal story of almost Ruritanian romance, the two-thirds remaining are explicit. It is the story of a man who is in a highly responsible position of trust on behalf of his country, who finds he is homosexual, indulges in its mode of life and is thereby blackmailed into betraying his country and his friends.

He does not do it because he believes in the ideology of the enemy, he does not do it to keep faith with his friends or himself. He betrays all these ideals because he has over-indulged himself and has got heavily into debt. He does it simply for money. The play is supposed, nowadays, to be relevant to the exposures of traitors such as Burgess, Philby and Blunt, but at least they were supposed to have done it because they believed in the Soviet way of life.

When it was performed at the Royal Court it was hailed as a great play. I wondered why it took another twenty years for anyone to produce it again and why did the National Theatre give up its option to us? The actual life story, on which the play is based, shows that Redl was a most unpleasant rogue whose action caused the death of many of his friends.

Someone begged me to go to the play as otherwise Osborne would be most upset! I am quite sure he neither knew of me nor most certainly would he care whether I went or not, and rightly so.

Nicholas de Jongh writing in *The Guardian* on 10 May 1983 said:–

> 'A whiff of scandal is drifting through the prim cathedral city of Chichester. After years of living in the deep, safe recesses of the past dressing itself up in annual star-infested revivals of old favourites, Chichester Festival Theatre is about to meet up with the theatrical present, or at least the mid-1960s . . . Influential Chichester Festival people have been much opposed, especially Leslie Evershed-Martin, the theatre's powerful founder who has had his way with every Chichester Festival Board and Artistic Director since Laurence Olivier departed.
>
> Evershed-Martin is one of those affected. "I don't want to discuss it. It is a private matter," he told *The Guardian*. He had wanted to make sure the Board knew of the play's content and now that they did, he would say no more. But had he read the original reviews of the play? Did he know it was voted the play of the year for the Standard Drama Awards? But Mr Evershed-Martin declined to say anything more.'

I wish I had had the power Mr de Jongh assigned to me; it would have been fun. I have always accepted, sometimes most unwillingly, the democratic rulings of the Board. Let there be no mistake. My friendship with

Patrick Garland is as firm as ever and I consider him to be a fine director. We just have a difference of opinion on this particular matter.

The facts are quite clear. My objections to the staging of this particular play on our stage were based on deep-rooted convictions which I have every right to express as personal opinions and which need not be shared by other people. Whilst I wished to keep these much misunderstood opinions to myself during the run of the play, so that its chances once accepted by the Board should not be affected, I feel it is only right that I should express them now at a much later date.

Finally a comment on censorship made by Henry Fielding in an article entitled 'Over to you, Sir Laurence Olivier' in the *Daily Herald* when he was discussing the question of the censor's mauling of *The Workhouse Donkey* and John Arden's fury at his (the censor's) interference:–

> 'I would like to see something like a prosecution by the police. I would like to see Laurence Olivier in the dock with a playwright and a director charged with conspiracy to publish an obscene libel and I would like to see them plead guilty and offer no evidence in their defence . . . My idea is that such a plea would stymie the law and that something might be done to blow clean air through the theatre. If all censorship were removed, the Lord Chamberlain's office packed up overnight and at the same time possibility of police prosecution removed, the general effect would be for the better rather than for the worst . . . At first catchpenny managements might loll in lasciviousness but genuine artistic talent would eventually conquer it.'

CHAPTER 11

Anecdotes of Plays and Players

I do not propose to analyse critically the many plays we have produced during the past twenty-one years because there are always too many judgements that could be made varying from person to person. It would therefore not be of general interest to read of the reactions of one member of the audience.

On the other hand I do believe the ordinary playgoer has a point of view since play acting is not just for the pleasure, and livelihood, of the players. The plays are of little use, except sometimes as literary gems, if they are not set before an audience for their amusement and enlightenment.

The most interesting aspect of our theatre is the effect each director has made in his own way on its evolution. Changing every three or four years each director has stamped his own personality on our history by his choice of plays and this in itself is fascinating.

When I first saw the interview with Tyrone Guthrie, conducted by Huw Wheldon, on the *Monitor* television series I was most impressed by the extract of the film shown which depicted a battle scene from Guthrie's production at Stratford, Ontario, of Shakespeare's *Henry Vth.*

The realism of the battles showed the potential use of a thrust stage compared with that of a proscenium one. No more queues of soldiers 'marking time' to get onto the stage, no devices of men rushing around backstage to augment the battle wave of men from which they had just retreated. No false boards of spear heads carried behind a backcloth to represent advancing armies.

Here the warriors hurtled in from all sides, battling at the feet of the audience, with sound effects of further reinforcements apparently hidden in the depths below. This was truly 3D perspective.

So the idea of the thrust stage was especially for spectacular events rather than in competition with the more claustrophobic three walls picture frame of the proscenium theatres so necessary for certain plays.

This was the difference between the two styles of presentation which I thought could work 'alongside' one another, not one replacing the other.

The example of our theatre promoted the construction of the two stages at the National. We had demonstrated Guthrie's conviction on open stages and consequently the National's Olivier open stage was considered to be necessary, alongside the Lyttleton proscenium stage, so they had 'the best of both worlds'.

So far how have the various directors of our theatre, in my opinion, succeeded in exploiting the advantages and avoiding the disadvantages of open stages?

Olivier's four years, two of which were in association with the National Theatre Company, used the spectacular potentials by presenting *St Joan*, *The Royal Hunt of the Sun* and *Armstrong's Last Goodnight*. Obsessed, at first, with the need for movement his presentation of *The Chances*, as his very first play, was excessively fast-moving all over the stage at all levels and exits. It made for a joyous festive opening and the audience loved it. Many believe it could well be revived one day. Several scenes, such as in the trial in *St Joan*, were enhanced by the wide stage whilst some of the smaller scenes, such as on the banks of the Loire, needed a smaller stage.

The Royal Hunt of the Sun was exactly right as a spectacular production. We understood that Peter Shaffer had held his play hoping that at some time it would be played on such a stage as ours. It contains much symbolism of acting and scenery fully exploited by John Dexter, Desmond O'Donovan and Michael Annals.

The storing of the gold treasure scene and the final lament of the drooping masks were moments of great theatre.

> Mervyn Jones in the *Tribune* 10 July 1964 suggested it could easily be turned into a ballet. Since then it has been produced as an opera.

J. W. Lambert in the *Christian Science Monitor* said:–

> 'This personal drama is set in total theatre to a degree never attempted in the British theatre. John Dexter's production clearly opens and contracts the lens of the stage. Michaels' scenery and costumes are stark and stunningly sumptuous by turns. It is a joy to be able to salute an enterprise which strikes up from the tiny terrors of most contemporary plays to touch the hem of immensities.'

Peter Saffer wrote the play in 1959 and, so it is said, promptly lost it. After an 'unregal hunt' it was eventually recovered in a Euston Station telephone kiosk.

Bernard Levin called it 'the greatest play of our generation'.

I went to see it again in New York at the Anta theatre. Christopher Plummer played the part of Pizarro. I sat there determined to be unprejudiced as to its presentation on a wide open proscenium stage. Try as I might I missed some of the glorious moments we had had, such as the unrolling of the great blood-red nylon carpet which signified the massacre and the piling up of the gold booty and the sudden revelation of unfolding petals of gold high up stage.

I agreed with *Plays and Players*' (27 March 1966) comment that it lost, because of its new vast and restricted stage, a great deal of its atmospheric pageantry.

Royal opening of The National Theatre in the presence of HM The Queen and HRH Prince Phillip. Lord Olivier, 25 October 1976. Author and wife far left

J. H. Lambert in the *Christian Science Monitor* July 1964 said of the Chichester production:–

> 'The programme says "Movement by Claudia Chagrin" and indeed movement is used here in balletic exuberance which British players are ill-used to employing . . . though at Chichester they arise to the occasion pretty well.'

Because of illness I had to miss the first night on 7 July, so not being present on the first night of *A Patriot for Me* (1983) was not the only first night I had missed (see chapter 'Controversies').

My wife, Carol, had a nasty shock when during the afternoon of the *Royal Hunt* first night performance a reporter from a London national paper rang up and offered his sympathy to her about me and asked 'if under the tragic circumstances' she would be going to the play. After a muddled discussion it became obvious that all he had known was that I was in hospital and not that worse had befallen me. I was in the London clinic for a minor operation.

On the day of the *Royal Hunt* opening Buckingham Palace had arranged a garden party for the theatrical profession, the first of its kind. The party was to celebrate Shakespeare's birthday. Olivier declined the invitation because he felt his work at our theatre was more important. When I read in hospital the attack on Olivier in an article by Atticus in *The Sunday Times*, I was upset that our theatre had become embroiled in a refusal for a royal occasion.

I sent a telegram to Olivier on the 6 July saying 'Distressed by Atticus article in *The Sunday Times*. Our theatre cannot be associated with other people's cheap impertinent insults. Please could you go. Could you charter helicopter South Bank to Tangmere or Oaklands Park at Chichester's expense?'

He replied by letter, 'You and I are spending our lives trying to convince people that the theatre is serious work and not a hobby. I feel sure that the Palace would be the first to realise such work must come before social pleasures. Imagine my invidious position with press and public if I chose the second before the first. I don't think while Chichester is relentlessly pursuing the public for money it is proper for it to go round in helicopters. Worry not, no great harm done. Keep cheerful and get better.'

The Atticus article singled out those critics and members of the profession who were going and those who had refused for various reasons. Some of the playwrights were making derogatory remarks about the Crown.

I sent a letter to Her Majesty:

'I am distressed by the contents of *The Sunday Times* article regarding the clash of dates with our theatre tomorrow, and I hasten to be allowed to assure your Majesty of our loyalty and respect.

If I had known of this before, the Directors would have cancelled or delayed the performance, but I find this is impossible at this late stage as we are under contract with the National Theatre.

We disassociate ourselves completely from the contents of the article and beg to express again, to your Majesty, our devotion and delight in the interest you have shown in our theatre and the tremendous pleasure you have given to everyone when you have graciously visited it.'

The Lord Chamberlain replied that whilst Her Majesty appreciated the sentiments conveyed in the last paragraph of my letter the Chamberlain's office would not have wanted the dates of our opening to be changed causing inconvenience to us or the National Theatre. He further stated there had been very few refusals.

The whole incident underlined the very strict discipline which is traditional in the theatrical profession regarding rehearsal, punctuality and adherence to programming.

Plays and Players, January 1964, reporting on *St Joan* and *Uncle Vanya* said:–

> 'Theatre-goers are today more than ever schizophrenics. They respond to the reality of Shaw's or Chekhov's world whilst, at the same time, they

> enjoy the artificiality with which it is represented . . . and because the arena theatre enables more of the audience to indulge in this schizophrenia, arena theatre has probably in the end more to offer the modern theatre-goer. Certainly if your *Uncle Vanya* and *Saint Joan* have warts they won't be able to hide them from an arena audience . . . but then your arena audience wants them both warts and all.'

Some interesting facts emerged from the presentations of *St. Joan* and *Uncle Vanya*. Critics' notices about *St. Joan* were headed with such phrases as 'Splendour of Shaw and a magnificent Joan', '*St. Joan* is rich in fine playing', 'A maid who will be remembered', 'St Joan conquers the open stage', and 'If a miracle is something that creates faith, Joan's Joan is not far short of one.'

Several young actors who appeared in *St. Joan* are now amongst the first ranks of players. Especially Derek Jacobi who played the part of Brother Martin and Robert Stephens as the Dauphin.

Uncle Vanya was a 'one-off' example of Chekhov on our style of stage. With such a cast as Lewis Casson, Fay Compton, Laurence Olivier, Joan Plowright, Michael Redgrave and Sybil Thorndike it could not have failed even if it had been played on a field. Because of the necessary claustrophobic quality of Chekhov plays the fact that this *Uncle Vanya* was such a colossal success for two years led other directors to believe all his plays could be played on arena stages but many doubt this is a correct assumption. *A Month in the Country*, *The Seagull* and *The Cherry Orchard* have not necessarily succeeded in our theatre.

One particular moment in *Uncle Vanya* demonstrated the truth that actors or actresses can display emotions when they are turned away from the audience as well as when they are facing. It was at the end of the play when Joan Plowright realises, as Sofya, that she has no longer any chance of interesting Mihail, the doctor (Olivier), in her love for him. She sat with her back to the audience with hunched shoulders brilliantly depicting her abject dejection.

The trial scene made full use of the stage with its circle of priests all with their backs to relevant sections of the audience, even though one critic disliked it as being like 'animals crouching around their trainer who revolved slowly like some desultory water-sprinkler'. Joan Plowright received the 'Best Actress Award' for her performance.

The last night of *Uncle Vanya* at Chichester was extremely emotional after the two season's run. There was an all-night queue, the forerunner of many that we have had, and when I saw the people sleeping on the stone paving outside the theatre I arranged for them all to be admitted into the foyer with its underfloor heating.

The Workhouse Donkey and *Othello* displayed in certain scenes the advantage of two levels of stage and the flexibility of the many exits and entrances but, on occasion, the smaller cameos suffered.

As *The Workhouse Donkey* was a new play by John Arden I asked Olivier if I could read the text before it was produced. He replied:–

> 'I am delighted for you to read it. As even constant readers of many years standing would, I feel, have some difficulty in finding their way round, and through this one, I think I should assure you that in the first place three-quarters of an hour, at the very least, has to be removed from it, including some songs etc. In the second some considerable work is yet to be done on what then remains; and in the third, the censor's requirements will, of course, be carried out to the letter.
>
> I don't *think* you will recognize yourself among any of the Civic characters, though you may possibly find poetic indication regarding some of your old associates.'

I enjoyed Olivier's spark of wickedness but he appeared to be dismayed when I told him that up to that time, in Chichester, party politics had only just started, as hitherto it had been a Council made up entirely of 'Independents'. The petty conflict of party politics would therefore not be so topical for Chichester audiences.

This play was one of the last to receive the attention of the censor before the post was abolished. His cuts were many and whilst some of them were nonsensical, according to these days, to be recorded here one is, I think, worth mentioning to show the sensitivity of the censor. It was 'Stage Direction' four dancing girls, one pair dressed in balloons, the other pair in little bells. 'This must be explained what other dress besides balloons and bells the girls are wearing. Drawings of women's bodies must be submitted.'

At the end of the first year (1962) of Olivier's reign it had been announced that he would be the first director of the National Theatre and so he began to recruit members for his company from among the players at Chichester. Amongst the ones chosen were Max Adrian, Martin Boddy, Frank Finlay, Derek Jacobi, Robert Lang, Anthony Nicholls, Michael Redgrave, Robert Stevens and of course Joan Plowright.

There was naturally some unrest amongst the rest as they awaited 'the call' and the process of 'one for you and one for me' during our seond year.

In 1964 the changeover took place when the Chichester productions were in collaboration with the newly formed National Company for two years. When articles appeared headed 'Will Chichester become nationalised?' and 'What will happen to Chichester now that Olivier has gone?' I had to make statements to the press and emphasise in speeches that we should be reverting to being independent.

The Dutch Courtesan by contrast seemed brash and tawdry, but then I am prejudiced against such revivals. They seem so out of pace and time, and very seldom seem woth reviving nowadays. Many have lain buried for

Ingrid Bergman and Brian Spink in Waters of the Moon, *1977*

so long and it never surprises me that they have taken so long to be exhumed. The bawdiness has little effect, excused as it is as a portrayal of those days.

I liked the heading of a review by David Nathan in the *Daily Herald*, 'I've a word for my old dutch . . . Daft.' Another one was headed in the *Evening News*, by Felix Barker, 'This is ripe for Pulpit Protests'. He wrote:–

> 'It is pretty ripe stuff and unless the Church has lost its tongue of fire since the 17th century, the cathedral pulpit will surely be railing on Sunday against the 'lewd' entertainment of Sir Laurence's 'Venus Palace'. My lay pulpit has the job of suggesting that, interesting though the intention is, the piece does not merit having its bones rattled.'

As far as I know, nothing came from the cathedral pulpit and I am glad. The play hardly deserved such recognition. However, one does wish that the Church did still have its 'tongue of fire' or 'fire in its belly', whichever part of it should let the world know that it still stands unequivocally for its principles.

And again the *Daily Telegraph*, 19 July 1964 headed 'The Dutch Courtesan:–

> 'Like all plays written before the Censorship Act of 1737 this is exempt from the Lord Chamberlain's blue pencil. Prolonged exposure to its succession of lavatorial jest seems to suggest to me two conclusions. One. His Lordship is setting for us a very low level of tolerance for simple smut if he thinks we shall be corrupted by such colloquialisms. Two. Our daring dramatists are setting us an even lower level of shockability if they think we shall be excited by such naughtiness.'

Another correspondent reported:–

> 'If all the four letter words were laid end to end they would stretch all the way from the Chichester theatre to the office of the Lord Chamberlain who, if he could, would instantly ban them. Happily he can't. The play was written a good century before 1737 when the Lord Chamberlain's functions were defined.'

Pieter Rogers had hinted to me that Olivier was harbouring a notion that he would not play the name part in the forthcoming *Othello*. I therefore wrote what I hope was a tactful letter to Olivier saying how much we were all looking forward to his performance. Perhaps he had only been playing with the idea as he was overstretched with his work for both theatres and needed a respite. We heard no more of the idea and, thank goodness, he played it as scheduled.

I get tired of those who, with presumed superior knowledge, will always compare every important performance with some previous rendering in the past by some great actor or actress. Luckily I had seen only minor attempts of *Othello* and so I was able to enjoy what I felt was one of the greatest performances I had ever seen.

I did not care about the controversy as to whether the part should be portrayed as a Negro, as he did, or as a Moor. All I cared was, having decided to play it as a Negro, he had perfected every gesture, every intonation. Joan told me of how, after he had seen and listened to a Negro on the top of a bus one day, he had gone home and spent hours rehearsing the right intonation of the words he had heard. I went many times and enjoyed each performance more each time. I would have liked to have gone every night.

The best description that coincided with my feelings was related by Milton Shulman in the *Evening Standard*, 22 July 1964, on seeing it for a second time:–

> 'His periodic gusts of rage under Iago's promptings . . . the flailing arms, the metronome-like swaying of the body, the convulsing epileptic tremors . . . now achieve a crescendo of violence which give them a credibility even Shakespeare would have found surprising.
>
> And in his final plea for understanding, clutching the dead Desdemona in his arms, Olivier's soft, breaking voice grips the house with pity at such frailty and wonder at such love. There is no use asking you to go and see this great performance since every seat in the place is solidly sold.'

Othello, Bamber Gascoine in *The Guardian*:–

> 'The first amazement about Olivier is his physical transformation. To adapt the song, he walks like a Negro, talks like a Negro; from his hairless shins, drooping eyelids, the stipulated 'thick lips' of the text and a loose hip-rolling walk, which I thought at first might prove to be a caricature but which remains firmly real, to the uncanny inflections in his voice or the deep throated chuckle with which he parries Iago's preliminary thrusts.'

Darlington said of *Othello*:–

> 'I am not surprised that *Othello* was better on the auditorium stage at the National Theatre as each play is better on the stage it was originally written for.'

All seats for *Othello* were sold within eight hours of the opening of public booking and over 2,000 cheques were returned that day. It was one of those occasions when I was over-joyed that we had built the theatre.

21 July 1964 was the first night of *Othello* and whilst Joan Plowright was motoring from Brighton she burnt her dress with a cigarette. This was a sad dilemma for her as she was, naturally, anxious to be in good time for the beginning and to present Olivier with a rose for his performance. Instead she had to return to their home to get another dress and was therefore forced to miss the beginning of his special night. Olivier had to be content with 'prop' rose.

In the spring of 1964 we had the memorable visit of the Stratford, Ontario, Company. I had worked for many months, after my visit to them, to get this visit arranged and my only regret is that we have not been able to repeat such visits. It proved a very costly adventure for that company, but it was a resounding success for them and for us. I have mentioned before how their performances have remained in the memories of our audiences to this day. They displayed the artistry they had attained by their experience of our kind of stage especially in their beautiful 'ballet-like' presentation of *Love's Labour's Lost*.

Michael Langham immediately requested a higher stage and the use of up-stage balconies as they had been accustomed to with their own theatre designed by Tanya Moisewitsch. The production of *Timon of Athens* was excellently done though I found it difficult to reconcile some of the Canadian voices and especially the production being in an altered period which resembled the post Suez Middle East; I found myself all the time having to translate my thoughts back to the period of the original play. Such transferences of time periods please the vanity of producers, and are excused by the resemblance of the plot to modern times, but to me it is like using the language of *The Dutch Courtesan* implanted into a modern bedroom farce. It needs a translation of thought all the time for the audience. Music by Duke Ellington was an innovation.

Le Bourgeois Gentilhomme was the third play and was a new production for the company in preparation for their own season in Canada later. It was well praised by the critics.

The day the Canadians arrived was a bank holiday and it was a drizzly, miserably cold day. We had been told they would have already had a meal before they arrived, but to our consternation they told us they were cold and hungry and all looked disappointed at their reception in England.

This was a considerable problem as everything was closed for the bank holiday. Eventually we discovered someone in a small restaurant who rescued the whole situation by cooking a vast amount of beef casserole and in an hour-and-a-half all were feeding ravenously. Soon afterwards they were settled into the houses and flats allotted to them, in and around the city, and next morning the weather broke into the glorious spring weather that only England can unfold in such quick changes of weather.

The welcoming press conference soon had everyone wreathed in smiles and good fellowship and this atmosphere remained for the whole visit. We suddenly realised someone had forgotten to get a Canadian flag so a messenger was sent to Ontario House in London and they kindly gave us one.

There were numerous parties and receptions all the time they were in England, and especially notable were those given by Lord and Lady Bessborough, the Mayor of Chichester councillor Brookes, the High Commissioner for Canada and the Agent General for Ontario. Reciprocal invitations to parties came from the chairman and the fifteen governors who had accompanied the Canadian company.

The high point was, of course, when Queen Elizabeth the Queen Mother came to a Gala performance of *Love's Labour's Lost*. Her Majesty entranced everyone by the way she spoke to all and sundry, showing sincere interest in each one, not forgetting to speak to all the waitresses who lined the path to the marquee. Olivier had refused an invitation to receive an honorary doctorate at the Birmingham University on that day, saying his duty lay with the theatre for Her Majesty's visit.

On the last night the farewell party was given by the Chichester Theatre at which I made a personal gift of a silver 'loving cup' to cement the friendship between the 'mother' theatre in Stratford, Ontario, and the 'child' theatre in Chichester, England. In my speech I said it was a two-thirds turn of the wheel. The final third would be if ever our company performed in their theatre.

Olivier came and said:–

> 'We cannot let our friends from Canada leave our shores without a word of profound thanks for what they have brought us from across the Atlantic . . . we thank them for the new life they have given to our poet; for the skill in the direction of the three plays and the liveliness and depths and charms of their acting, for the breath of the New World in the body of the Old. For the joy of *Love's Labour's Lost*, the delight of *The Bourgeois Gentilhomme*, and for the dynamic version of the tragedy of Timon.
>
> The swans from another Avon have indeed flown into Chichester harbour and enchanted not only the people of Sussex but all those who have made their pilgrimage to this Cathedral city to see them. The ideals of Leslie Evershed-Martin have captured for us again the Canadian dream of Tom Paterson. You must forgive these few lame words before our friends leave us. The words of Mercury are indeed harsh after the songs of Apollo and it is very sad to say with Armado 'You that way and we this way.'

1965: the programme was announced on 28 January: *Armstrong's Last Goodnight*, *Trelawney of the Wells*, *Miss Julie* and *Black Comedy*.

Armstrong's Last Goodnight is probably one of the best but most misunderstood plays we have produced. Most people found it, as I did, very difficult to understand due to the use of Scottish Lowland speech. Many people put this down to the acoustics but as I have already related one correspondent asked why this was so when every word of the *Trelawney* was heard perfectly. I hoped that when I saw it a second time I would hear the words better but in fact the company, having got used to the play, became broader in the language and I found it even more difficult.

Gaskill was probably right to render it all in the correct period speech but the play was not appreciated in the way it should have been. Its story is full of dramatic moments and powerful in its intent. The acting was of the highest order, especially by Albert Finney, who got universal praise together with Robert Stevens.

One of the amusing incidents that occurred during the rehearsals for

Armstrong's Last Goodnight was when the players complained they could not hear each other's words, not because of the difficult dialect, but because Jimmy Wilson was rehearsing his bagpipes in the foyer. He was forthwith banished to the park much to the amusement, and possible enjoyment, of citizens walking their dogs in the park. What would he have done in the streets if it had been a London theatre?

Trelawney of the Wells was a delight in every sense of the word. Every change of scene was manoeuvred with great charm and panache which brought delighted applause from the audience and added to the sweetness of the story and the acting. Louise Purnell's portrayal of Rose particularly emphasised this aspect of the production by Desmond O'Donovan. The music arranged by Marc Wilkinson was based on the haunting melody from 'Ever of Thee' by Foley Hall.

One of our original supporters of the theatre was the late Major Clarke-Jervois of Petersfield in Hampshire. He was critical of many of our plays, especially the more modern ones. I was therefore very pleased for him when we had *Trelawney* in our repertoire as he had played in it himself at Canterbury as a young member of the 'Old Stagers'. But, alas, he came away angry and disappointed, saying that the audience and the cast had 'sent up' the play, especially the laughter which greeted the oft repeated saying 'If only Mother could see me now'. In the early days this was treated as serious sentimentalism. Different times, different interpretations! Whilst the sickly sentiment had gone there remained a love of beauty and romance.

Two plays in one evening was a new departure for us. What a contrast there was between Strindberg's *Miss Julie* and Shaffer's new play *Black Comedy*. The sweltering passion and tragedy portrayed brilliantly by Maggie Smith and Albert Finney plunged the audience into deep gloom at the interval. *Black Comedy* in the second half swept over the audience in a gale of hilarious laughter. Based on a Chinese traditional play of people acting in the light, but thinking they were in the dark, created a situation of constant comedy and I have never seen an audience so convulsed.

I shall never forget watching two people in the audience who could not even raise a smile whilst all their neighbours were doubled up with laughter. The spectacle of these two, who looked rather like a very prim brother and sister, fascinated me throughout even whilst I was as fully committed as the rest of the audience.

Millicent Martin was once reported as saying: 'I prefer laughter to applause. Clapping is something an audience DOES. Laughter is something they can't help doing.'

Graham Samuel, writing about *Black Comedy*, said:–

> 'In an ideal world this glorious farce would always be seen as we first saw it at Chichester. We knew nothing about it except its title and as the first bewilderment and then surprise and then pure pleasure broke over us at the

> wit and sheer inspiration of Peter Shaffer's idea, a feeling of delight pervaded the theatre like nothing I have experienced before. The audience laughed in all the right places when the humour hit it. The audience at the Old Vic, in a typically first-night way, insisted on showing itself with-it by laughing too much and too long and, what is unforgiveable, too early so that some of Shaffer's lovely lines were killed half way through.
>
> 'Appreciation is one thing, 'chi-chi' another and this curse of first nights slowed down the pace by a total, I am sure of fifteen minutes, giving the piece an occasional air of slowness which was not due to any failure of writing or performance.'

So ended Olivier's four years as director of Chichester. With the formation of the National Theatre Company for the last two years he had presented several very great plays, some new ones, and a feast of the finest acting. We had much to be grateful for and in a few cases the directors he had used, besides his own direction of some, showed what could be achieved on our stage. Many of the younger generation of actors and actresses became great stars at the National and other theatres later because they had shown their potential skills at Chichester. Would our reputation crumble now that he had gone? His oft repeated assertions of devotion and love of our theatre were proved when he took considerable trouble to persuade us to appoint his successor, John Clements, to ensure our success in the future years. He was convinced that Clements would continue to build on the firm foundation he had laid.

John Clements started his first season in 1966 with the announcement that he would extend the season to sixteen weeks. The programme was *The Clandestine Marriage* by George Coleman and David Garrick, *The Fighting Cock* by Anouilh, *The Cherry Orchard* by Chekhov, and *Macbeth* by Shakespeare.

The Clandestine Marriage introduced Alastair Sim to our stage for the first time and, of all the older generation, he enjoyed the full use of the stage. He was one of those amazing personalities who can act with every part of his body and this related to all sides of the audience even if at the same time they did miss some of his unique facial expressions.

He appeared in several other plays in the coming years and each time his appearance drew full houses, particularly when he was partnered with that wonderful comedy actress, Margaret Rutherford. Both of them were tremendous favourites in and around the theatre and the city, just as the Thorndikes had been. Many times we met Alistair Sim and his wife at the theatre restaurant and they were always ready to be friendly and natural. Both he and Margaret Rutherford enjoyed the special freedom of acting on alternate days, making the most of rest days which this arrangement offered.

Many reviewers aptly described Alistair Sim's acting. A typical example, which I liked, was one in the *Glasgow Herald* (June 1966), which said:–

'Sim's Lord Ogleby (*Clandestine Marriage*), all leers and palsy, kept going on pills and potions and the sight of pretty faces, is more of a buffoon strayed out of Molière than Garrick's eighteenth century elder fop but in every agonised step, each glittering fix of the eyes, a delicious performance. The evening lightened and gleamed every time he came upon the stage.'

Robert Selbie tells the story of the unique ability Alistair Sim always had of improvising his own antics by inventing them quietly at home and producing them at rehearsals to the astonishment of the cast. In this play at the final dress rehearsal he emerged from one of the doors on the balcony in the character of Lord Ogleby, wearing a nightshirt and slippers, and rushed for the stairs. He seemed to slip on one of the steps and slithered down the rest of the flight. Everybody was very concerned, because even then he was not young. It turned out to be a bit of business which he had worked out and kept it in with great effect for the whole of the run.

The Fighting Cock was remarkable in one respect, and that was to see Clements and John Standing in the same play, especially when in the text the son knocks his father down. Clements in his part of being an arrogant autocrat to this family, and to the world in general, was in fact humbled twice by being knocked down. This was a brave way to appear in his first part as a new artistic director of our theatre by appearing to be humbled. This was repeated later by Keith Michell when he was likewise derided and despised in his first appearance in the play *Tonight We Improvise*. In the case of Clements with his well-founded reputation as a celebrated actor-manager it had no undesirable effect, but with Michell it was unfortunate with the prejudice manifested against him.

The Cherry Orchard which everyone seems to produce everywhere 'at the drop of a hat', proved to me that our stage is not right for Chekhov. I suppose Clements felt that if *Uncle Vanya* was such a special success this would be the same, but the *Vanya* was unusually filled with some of the greatest stars of our time, playing parts equivalent to their own ages, and could not fail on any stage. This *Cherry Orchard*, though it had several fine actors and actresses, just did not seem to hold the audience, or the critics, to any extent.

Macbeth was a splendid triumph for Clements, praised by nearly all the critics as one of the finest renderings of the play and acclaiming Clements in the title part. Hobson called it 'one of the great *Macbeths* of our time'.

Michael Benthall used the stage to its fullest extent and the banquet scene was particularly spectacular. I am sure it will be considered heresy to say I do not much like Shakespeare's comedies, but I do love his tragedies and would see them all as many times as possible. Clement's *Macbeth* was one of the great moments in our history.

Margaret Johnson as Lady Macbeth was an unusual portrayal, and it

Helen Ryan and Hywel Bennett in Terra Nova, *1980 (Zoe Dominic)*

took some time to adapt to it, but as the play progressed the sincerity of her acting rose to an impressive performance. The cutting of the witches' cauldron scene at the beginning was a shock but many critics praised the substitution of placing them in different parts of the upper stage.

One of the actresses who played the part of a witch was terrified of heights and when asked to play one scene on a platform cantilevered out from the top level she insisted on a safety belt. A leather belt was wrapped round her waist and this was attached to a chain bolted to the concrete floor.

Zena Walker as Lady Macduff earned unanimous praise for her poignant acting in the scene where she is murdered with her son.

One critic said of the production of *Macbeth*:–

> 'Certainly one could find no more perfect setting for the most stirring and passionate tragedy ever written in the English language. The arena stage provided the ideal platform for this magnificent drama and at the end the applause seemed more for the theatre than the players.
>
> This was ultimate vindication for the Festival Theatre, the complete answer to the cynics and doubting Thomases who questioned its design and purpose. As the action flowed to and fro across the three cornered stage, the audience was drawn into the centre of the whirlpool of human greed, lust and hatred, savouring as never before the play's cataclysmic passions. The whole theatre company and audience caught up in the excitement and horrible fascination of the macabre story.'

The play lived up to its reputation of being the most unlucky play in the business, though it is generally top box office. Michael Benthall, the director, was very ill all through the time of the rehearsals, one of the actors playing the part of a thane committed suicide, Margaret Johnson broke two ribs and Clements lost his voice. During a rehearsal of the duel between Macbeth and Macduff, Clements and Ray McAnally, using bamboo canes in place of swords, became unco-ordinated in their movements. McAnally ducked too slowly with the result that Clements' sword hit him across the bridge of the nose, causing a broken nose and two black eyes. That night he appeared as Lopakhin in *The Cherry Orchard* stitched and covered in plastic skin.

At the end of his first season Clements said: 'It has been a greater success than I hoped for even in my wildest dreams.'

On 17 February of that year I was invited to take part in *Getting a Word in Edgeways* on BBC radio. I think it was at the suggestion of John English of the Birmingham Youth Centre, with whom I had been on friendly terms since the opening of our theatre. The broadcast was a disaster. Unfortunately English's voice sounded like mine, so no one could make out which of us was talking; we got saddled with each other's mistakes or unpopular opinions. I, at least, am not a person very used to public discussions of this sort though I have done many interviews on television and radio. We were sat in a circle on uncomfortable chairs, looking at one another, and subjects were shot at us with little time to think about them. It is always fine for practised broadcasters, such as politicians, who have expounded their views on subjects with which they are familiar many times before in public or in private.

But what really killed the atmosphere from the beginning was the fact that a distinguished lady was one of the three, and on occasion after occasion said she could not possibly speak on the subject proposed as either she, as a prominent chairman of a County Council committee, or her husband in his political office, would be embarrassed in their positions if she spoke. She was probably right to be careful. So many of the interesting subjects were deleted and the atmosphere became more frustrated. When the question of censorship came up it was met with stilted answers and I heard the producer say 'cut it all out'. The rest was broadcast two days later but I, for one, found no pride in it.

1967: *The Farmer's Wife* by Eden Philpotts, *The Beaux Stratagem* by George Farquhar, *Heartbreak House* by Bernard Shaw, and *The Italian Straw Hat* by Labiche and Marc-Michel in place of the proposed *The Servant of Two Masters* in which Danny Kaye was to have acted.

The Farmer's Wife was a delightful romp to start off the season and we have found it important, from priority booking point of view, to have a good popular play to open up each season. Several players soon became favourites with our audiences, such as Bill Fraser, Michael Aldridge, Fenella Fielding, Sarah Badel and John Standing. It almost became like a repertory company as Clements used his favourites in the four plays.

Some critics said our audience in Sussex enjoyed this play because they felt they were seeing their Devon neighbours in similar circumstances. That simile was over-stretched. It was the play itself, and the acting, that made it such a success.

The Beaux Stratagem was obviously chosen by Clements as a reminder of the great success he had with his wife, Kay Hammond, in 1949 when it became a record breaker for a long running classic. Superbly dressed and well acted it did not, however, get unanimous praise from the critics. Probably some were comparing it with Clements' earlier triumph or, perhaps like me, they were getting tired of these revivals. One felt great compassion for Katie at this time; how she and he must have longed to be on that stage acting it again.

Fenella Fielding distinguished herself by missing the train at Victoria and arriving in the park by helicopter just in time to appear on stage. She was applauded by a very relieved cast as she landed with a great Fenella spectacular entrance.

Heartbreak House was, as usual, a Shaw controversial presentation. It was powerfully played and directed by Clements with a fine performance by Irene Worth for which she was awarded 'Best Actress of the Year'. The play itself was dissected and diagnosed probably far beyond Shaw's original intention, but unlike some of his plays, it was considered by most to be outdated. One critic said: 'it was pouring out a sparkling torrent of non-stop human pathos, shrewd observation, biting satire, withering scorn and much else'.

Sound effects at our theatre have always been extremely good. The Zeppelin roar and the anti-aircraft gunfire brought back to me such raids when I was a schoolboy in Croydon. The family, with an hysterical servant, sitting in the hall until the cyclist went by blowing a whistle for the all-clear. And one evening, my eldest brother, home from the trenches, revolting and saying 'if this is how I am going to spend my leave I don't think much of it.' The next evening he took me up to London to see George Robey and Alfred Lester in *The Bing Boys are Here*. All these memories flooded back to me, but I wondered, with many others, why Shaw had suddenly introduced this into a play where there had previously been no sense of a war going on.

The final flourish of the season was *The Italian Straw Hat*. I have related in the chapter 'Controversies' the story of Danny Kaye's deletion from *The Servant of Two Masters*. Thrown into confusion only two months before the start of the fourth play Clements, after thinking of replacing him in the play, decided to abandon it and substitute it with a somewhat similar play. He and Peter Coe wisely picked a hilarious comedy with a splendid cast. It was a roaring success being heralded by banner headlines in the national press saying 'Danny, we didn't miss you' etc. Brilliantly lit and superbly played, it was sunshine and gaiety all through. Challenged, the cast was determined to win through, and the result was uproarious. A few dull moments but they were few and far apart. The rest was sparkling and I have thought how much better it was, given inspired direction such as Peter Coe gave it, that it did not suffer from the lack of time but gained from it; nor was the sparkle deadened by advice from outside directors and managers. Peter Rice designed thirty-five lovely dresses in two-and-a-half days and the whole set was like a wedding cake.

Startling moments abounded, such as the band arriving one by one at the top of the staging to produce a jaunty brass melody throughout; Fenella Fielding appearing from under a supper table saying she had been tossing a salad and was looking for a radish; Sarah Badel as the bride with jerky wooden doll action throughout and with the family twitch displayed every now and then; Anton Rodgers, stupidly vacant chasing around, and the auditorium filled with the wedding party, gendarmes etc.

There was an all night queue for the last night which ended in a riot of balloons and the whole cast mingling with the audience in a frenzy of embraces and kissing. How often does a theatre see such a scene of gaiety. It was only possible in an auditorium such as ours (*Hellzoppin* and the Crazy Gang shows excepted).

1968: *The Unknown Soldier and his Wife*, *The Cocktail Party*, *The Tempest*, *The Skin of our Teeth*. An unbalanced programme with two almost allegorical plays, one at the beginning and one at the end of the season. This can easily happen to any director by the time all the plays have been settled after many changes in the engagement of players. Plays have to be abandoned to suit the availability of stars who suddenly retract when they have a spectacular offer of television, or film parts, which they cannot refuse either for the sake of their reputation or the difference in money to what we are offering.

I enjoyed *The Unknown Soldier and his Wife* mainly because of the fascinating personality of Peter Ustinov both on the stage and off it. I remember him holding court in our cellar at one of our parties, brimming over with stories from his journeys in all parts of the world, spiced with satire and wit. Acting a part all the time but changing chameleon-like with his impersonations. In the play he gave a wicked portrayal of all that was worst in various religious phases throughout the many historical periods of the play with many logical, and illogical, comments on humanity's inhuman manipulation of the common man. There were memorable performances by a very young Simon Ward and the ever pregnant (play acting) Prunella Scales.

He called the play 'two acts of war separated by a truce for refreshment'. This was the first British production. It gave food for thought and yet portrayed the great Ustinov sense of theatrical entertainment.

The Cocktail Party brought Alec Guinness to our theatre. I had my wish fulfilled that in two seasons we had him and Irene Worth, the two who had so valiantly started off the Stratford, Ontario, theatre. His performances, always well worth studying, showed a perfection equivalent to that of Olivier. Directed by him the play was meticulously arranged for our stage but somehow it was compared a little unfavourably by the critics with his original presentation in Edinburgh in 1949. Peter Lewis wrote of him commenting on his part as the 'Unidentified Guest', and said:–

> 'He could not be more aptly named. For nearly twenty years, since he last played the part, he has remained the unidentified guest of the English stage, mysterious, tantalising and seldom present. It is said that when he worked very closely with T. S. Eliot on the first occasion he understood his beliefs in religion and was converted to Roman Catholicism.'

He has always been the symbol of deep sincerity in all he does. I remember so well going over to see him at Petersfield in the early days when he pored over the model of our theatre, and again in his dressing room before he went on stage to play the part of Lawrence of Arabia, another hero of mine, in *Ross*. *The Cocktail Party* was a joy to see despite the comment of one critic who wondered what the jolly crowd from the Goodwood races must have thought of it when they expected to see a show depicting their idea of cocktail parties as they knew them.

The Tempest: Clements took the part of Prospero and I did not think it fulfilled my idea of the part. The set and all the costumes were entirely in shades of white with very symbolic lumps of scenery which should have been right for our theatre environment. I shall not forget the splendid Ariel of Richard Kane who seemed to slither and fly through the scenes as though on air. There was certainly an ethereal atmosphere created which was difficult to define but which was very intriguing.

Olivier is once reported as saying: 'I would not like to do Prospero. I am not a verse speaker. I am more like a trumpet than a violin.'

Somehow *The Skin of our Teeth* failed to impress either the audiences, many of whom left before the finish of each performance, or the critics. Millicent Martin increased her reputation in it even though many kept referring back to Vivien Leigh's rendering in 1945.

1969: *The Caucasion Circle*, *The Magistrate*, *The Country Wife* and *Antony and Cleopatra*.

The Caucasian Circle: Topol was a welcome addition to the list of stars at Chichester and he played the part of Azdak, the judge with great force and ebullience. After the first night, when he forced the evident rawness of the peasant too much, he smoothed the performance to an impressive display of his particular qualities. There was the overhanging concern at that time as to whether Israel would erupt against Egypt and in that eventuality he would have been ordered, as a reservist, to go back to play his part as a sergeant-major. This had happened when he was in *Fiddler on the Roof* in London but we were lucky. We enjoyed his company on several occasions as he was one of the few actors who would willingly talk about other subjects rather than about himself. Peter Ustinov, Ingrid Bergman, the Thorndikes, Alistair Sim, Bill Fraser, Alec Guinness, Googie Withers, John McCallum and Aubrey Woods also stood out in this respect.

One of the visiting mayors, who had not read his programme and did not realise we could attract stars, said to me: 'If I didn't know it wasn't I would have thought that was Topol.'

The Magistrate was another spectacular triumph for Alistair Sim who squeezed every ounce out of the part of the magistrate when he found himself in embarrassing situations. Another true and typical description of his acting, besides the one I have already quoted, which brings back so vividly his performance, was written by Herbert Knetzmer in the *Daily Express*, 22 September 1969:

> 'He buckled at the knees, he shook his jowls, he giggled and guffawed and rolled his melancholy eyes and shivered and hooted like an ageing owl.'

The Country Wife made little impression on me except for the delightful acting of Maggie Smith. What a contrast between her comedy here and her dramatic acting in *Miss Julie*. The writing of the love letter was superbly detailed in every action appearing as though it was all natural and spontaneous. Ten minutes that towered above all the cavorting and silliness.

The Mitford Girls, *1981 (Lichfield)*

One of those moments in theatre which stands out brilliantly photographed in the memory as clear today as it was then.

Antony and Cleopatra was hailed as a great success for Clements and Margaret Leighton. Somehow I failed to believe in Clements' portrayal. Was I getting used to him in so many other roles? The love scene on the cushions right at the spearhead of our hexagonal stage seemed somewhat ludicrous at their age. This was one moment when I did have doubts about the nearness of our auditorium. Perhaps a sort of 'Peeping Tom' look would have been better for this scene than being in the room with the two of them.

All four plays of the season were wanted by theatres in London but it was only possible for *The Magistrate* to go to the Cambridge Theatre. Both

Maggie Smith and Topol had commitments and *Antony and Cleopatra* would eventually have been too expensive to transfer.

1970: *Peer Gynt*, *Vivat! Vivat! Regina!*, *Arms and the Man* and *The Alchemist*. A well balanced year this time with allegory, historical drama and comedy. *Peer Gynt* was very different from previous translations and renderings, therefore many deplored the changes and generally there was very divided criticism. Most people now seem to look back at it with disappointment. The opening scene with Roy Dotrice in the name part and Beatrix Lehmann as his mother was so beautifully performed that it raised great expectations for the rest of the play, but unfortunately these were not fulfilled.

Vivat! Vivat! Regina! was exactly right for our stage. Spectacular and at times very dramatic, even in scenes with a few actors, it unfolded in an absorbing way the battle between Elizabeth I and Mary even though the two never meet face to face in the play. Eileen Atkins and Sarah Miles gave superb performances and the dressing was of the highest quality. It was another world premier for us and was sold out completely within hours of being open to the public after priority booking. The queues stretched right round the building and our organisation was overstretched with the unexpected success of our publicity. Not since *Othello* did we have such a pleasant headache.

During an interview Robert Bolt said, 'I think it [the play] is relevant to our situation to-day. It is intended to explore political necessity and morality and the awful gap between the two. On a more emotional level it is about two very contrasting women in very similar situations, one who chooses the path of self-fulfilment at almost any cost and the other of self-denial and duty. Each paid a price.'

At the end of the play, when fanfares had blared, Elizabeth I has gone down one flight of stairs to posterity and glory, and Mary Queen of Scots has gone down the other flight of stairs to her execution, a lady in the audience got to her feet and was heard to say: 'My dear, exactly the same thing happened to Monica!'

This play lifted me back into the realm of all that I had hoped for with our theatre. It transferred to the Piccadilly Theatre later and to America with Eileen Atkins and Clair Bloom.

Arms and the Man particularly interested me only because I, in my small way, had directed it for the Chichester Players. I jokingly told Clements that if he wanted any advice or help I was ready to give it! Uncharacteristically he saw the joke.

The accident which befell Laurence Harvey was typical of the misadventures we had that season, and it was not the season with *Macbeth* in it. First of all, Clements had been ill at the beginning of the year and had asked me not to tell the Board or other members of the theatre before he was better, so as not to dampen the arrangements for the season. It did, however, delay the announcements of the programme a little.

Roy Hudd and Chesney Allen in Underneath the Arches, *1981*

Now Laurence Harvey, having tripped over a bed in the rehearsals of *The Alchemist*, was unable to appear in *Arms and the Man* until August, and James Warwick took over his part in the meantime. Harvey, in fact, went to the local hospital to have a piece of grit taken from his eye and when he was there suggested they might look at his injured knee. The doctor, after examining it and looking at the X-rays, said: 'Are you performing in *The Alchemist*? Harvey replied that he was. The doctor then said; 'Do you know of anyone who will buy my tickets?'

Halfway through the run of *Arms and the Man* Harvey returned to the cast using a walking stick and limping. One critic remarked how appropriate this was for the part as so many cavalry men, in those days, had their legs broken in battle when their horses collided. Of the accident Harvey said, 'There was I with a bench and an actor lying on top of me and Jonson (*The Alchemist*) and Shaw (*Arms and the Man*) squashed flat beneath me.'

I think most people found the play lightweight, and I noticed once again that as in most Shaw plays the audience felt they must display their intellect by being amused at almost every line Shaw wrote in the first half hour or so. Later they settle down and the lines get their normal appreciation.

As the play occupies less than two hours, Clements decided that the 'curtain raiser', *The Proposal* by Chekhov, should be played and this was a very amusing 'starter' for an evening of quiet enjoyment.

I found *The Alchemist* the worst of any of the Restoration plays we have ever had. As Peter Lewis said in the *Daily Mail* 23 July 1970, 'It was the biggest yawn to have lasted 370 years.' Another said, remembering the *Carry On* comedy series currently running on television, 'It was an orgy of carrying on . . . carry on ranting, carry on beard wriggling, bandy legging, fist shaking, and screaming with giggles.' The result was all too often that there was more laughter on the stage than in the audience. Owing to Harvey's absence Warwick took over the part and the director Peter Dews had to play his part.

Other mishaps that season were when Christopher Plummer, early in the year, had to withdraw from the proposed casting due to an attack of pneumonia, and during the run of *Peer Gynt* Roy Dotrice had a severe attack of laryngitis. Throughout our twenty years our local N & T specialist did very well with throat infections. Nothing, of course, to do with our pure Sussex air; just normal theatre hazards.

1971: *The Rivals*, *Dear Antoine*, *Caesar and Cleopatra* and *Reunion in Vienna*. The season was extended to nineteen weeks.

The Rivals: most of the critics praised it but obviously they did not think it was anything extra special. Margaret Leighton and Polly Adams received special mention but emphasis of praise was mainly for Carl Toms' designs and set. John Barber in the *Daily Telegraph*, 6 May 1971, wrote:–

> 'On entering the theatre and climbing the stairs one has this sudden illusion of arriving in Bath. Carl Toms has designed as a permanent set a neo-classical facade quintessential Nash in spirit which does wonders to evoke Sheridan's fashionable watering town. Through a window between giant Corinthian pillars the characters can be seen entering whilst beyond lies the graceful curves of the Royal Crescent itself.'

When Princess Margaret came for a Gala performance there was a bomb scare after just twenty minutes and the audience was turned out into the park for about forty minutes. Luckily the weather was dry but a wind played havoc with 'hair-do's' and dresses.

Anne Hillier, our publicity officer, tells a story of this bomb scare. When she was having the bar closed down, and the box office and the coffee bar, a man rushed in and demanded a gin and tonic. Anne explained that it was impossible as the sooner they got the public out the sooner the performance could start again. Pointing to the heavens he said: 'My dear young lady, if I'm to go up there I'm going to go with a gin and tonic in my hand!' He got his gin and tonic.

Dear Antoine was marked by the appearance of Edith Evans at the age of eighty-three who spoke disparagingly of the theatre to all the reporters at the press conference and seemed reluctant to accommodate herself to a medium which was strange to her. She also disliked the backstage and on one occasion said: 'I have been walking round in circles for three days and still don't know how to get on the stage.' When she was required to be revealed sitting on a sofa as the lights came up she protested to Robin Phillips, the director: 'I come on in a black costume, down a black staircase, and sit down on a black sofa in a blackout. I can't do it, Robin, I can't do it!'

In all it was a mistake to include her as her frailty meant that Clements had to keep a watchful eye on her entrances and exits and after only about three performances she gave up the part. It was taken by Peggy Marshall, her understudy, who scored a hit.

The rest of the cast as a whole was praised as one of the best we had had for a long time. It was the sort of play that I enjoyed with its twisted, almost detective, elements.

Caesar and Cleopatra brought the very distinguished actor John Gielgud. The contrast between his age and that of Anna Calder Marshall was exactly right for the purpose of the story as seen in the interplay between them, especially in the first scenes of their encounter.

The design was all white rather as if it was being played in the cold regions of Iceland; I can't think why. It was fitted out symbolically like a children's playground with rocking horses, rubber balls and slides. To see one of our greatest actors, in the part of an emperor, using the slide which did not look very stable, and declaiming his importance whilst riding a rocking horse looked ridiculous and it amazed me that he had agreed to be directed in this way. He must have seen more of the hidden meaning in it all than was apparent to the audience. Anyway the arguments were, as usual, worth listening to.

John Gielgud is well known for 'dropping bricks' which he does quite unconsciously and without the slightest malice. During one of the rehearsals when the cast was discussing how to play Shaw he looked straight at Clements, who had played Captain Shotover a couple of years before with some distinction, and said: '*Heartbreak House*, for instance. A very difficult play. Shotover's never been played properly!'

Reunion in Vienna was a sentimental Ruritanian sort of easy evening of escapism. Critics talked of it as a 'light-hearted frothy stuff' play but remarked that it was taken at a good pace and left no reason for boredom. As with all revivals many critics relied on their memories of the past in their reviews, in this case the way in which the Lunts had scored in it. The season as a whole was a tepid one for me and I found the standards of the plays, not the acting, had dropped.

1972: *The Beggars' Opera*, *The Doctor's Dilemma*, *The Taming of the Shrew* and *The Lady's not for Burning*.

The Beggars' Opera was the first musical for us and it went well, using the full area of the stage even though the scenery was somewhat too elaborate.

It was pleasant to have John Neville back, reminiscent of his appearance in the first year. Millicent Martin provided a lively reminder of her successes in television but there was criticism of the inclusion of too many exaggerated antics by the supporting cast.

The Doctor's Dilemma provided the audience with an opportunity to revenge themselves on the medical profession. Professions which deal with the more difficult aspects of living, the medical with illnesses and the law with the seedy side of human relations, are held in some awe and therefore to see them ridiculed is bound to be a source of pleasure.

Robert Selbie tells the story of how the medical profession seemed to have its revenge as well. The production was plagued with performers going ill. On one occasion there were five understudies. Clements was in great pain during an interval and at the very last minute as he was going on to perform he had, at last, to admit that it was impossible for him to act. The understudy was ready but both the other characters and the audience suddenly found they were confronted with the character Dr Blenkinsop playing the part of Bloomfield Bonington.

This play allowed Clements to play a part I am sure he would like to have played in real life, but more conscientiously of course than the character in the play. The play was quietly enjoyed, but it had no great impact on the critics.

The Taming of the Shrew gave Joan Plowright another opportunity to display her talents; both she and Anthony Hopkins received praise for their characterisations. The set was not so well liked. One reviewer spoke of it as being unhelpful to the production looking, as it did, like an uncompleted block of matt-black offices. Other phrases from the critics' articles on the play called it 'Too purposeful and not light enough', or 'An evening of little entertainment and no enlightenment'.

The Lady's Not For Burning was the best play that season as far as I was concerned. Though I am not a lover of poetry, I revel in listening to, and reading, Christopher Fry's lyrical prose. Harold Hobson correctly described it as:–

> 'Over and over again flashing phrases tumble out which send the mind racing down a hundred different exploratory ways into the unplumbed universe. Its wit glitters like a diamond; and like a diamond the play is hard and indestructible.'

Richard Chamberlain, returning to the stage for a while from television and cinema, showed his capabilities and rose above the glamour of his reputation and attracted near capacity audiences who came to satisfy their curiosity. This play rescued the season for me from being just a comfortable entertaining one to something of significance; promoting thought long after the impact of the evening.

At the beginning of the season the Board decided that it was time for a change of artistic director and told Clements that this would happen after the next two years. This meant that he would have been with us eight years in all. It was agreed not to announce this until the beginning of the 1973 season.

Because of this Clements gave way on his hitherto veto on a Christmas show and *Toad of Toad Hall* was brought in with some of the cast of the 1972 productions, such as Harold Innocent as Toad. As a trial, there being no certainty of a Chichester audience for Christmas, it was only scheduled for a run of two weeks. There was immediate heavy booking for all performances, proving what the Board and the public had been advocating for a long time that something should happen over the holiday. The pantomime at the King's Theatre, Southsea, had always run successfully for two or three months.

Clements' reluctance to extend shows at our theatre was, rightly, based on his wish to allow nothing to lower the standards of the Festival season by comparison but luckily, as will be seen in future years, we have been able to present Christmas productions of good quality.

1973: the season began with Clements announcing that he would be finishing at the end of the year. *The Director of the Opera*, *The Seagull*, *R loves J* and *Dandy Dick*.

The Director of the Opera was, I think, a mistake for Clements to start his last season with, since it belittled the Director in the play. In it he is humbled by his family, his management and by a strike of the staff. It was somewhat better nonetheless to have it at the beginning of the season as it would have been unfortunate for Clements to have left with such an impression.

Luckily he was unanimously praised for a great performance, one of the best he had done in the eight years. He was on stage nearly all the time and 'strode it magnificently'.

Felix Barker, *Evening News*, 10 May 1973, says:–

> 'It is a requiem for late middle-age. A white haircut, brilliant and (professionally) successful man . . . he is the director of a provincial Italian opera house . . . tries to escape from his (domestically) unsuccessful life. It was Anouilh's most muted and unsubtle play.'

John Tinker, *Daily Mail*, 10 May 1973, said:–

> 'Sir John conquered all early doubts about his policy for Chichester, after the loss of Olivier, and his seasons have brought joy both to the theatre's faithful audiences and to its accountants alike. Let us hope, therefore, for the gratitude we owe him, that any similarity between his present job and his current work ends with the title.'

The Seagull: Irene Worth and Robert Stephens made the play, but whilst the acting did much to carry it through the critics mainly condemned the play.

R Loves J was a musical version of Ustinov's successful play and it was generally agreed the music rather held up the action instead of helping it.

It was further hampered by the fact that the story had become outdated. At the time it was written there was a cold war with Russia at its worst and the jokes about the complications of a love match between nationalities and the antics of a spy were relevant. Now at the time of this adaptation relations between the two nations had calmed down, with the current talks between Brezhnev and Nixon introducing a spirit of conviviality and generosity. Such conditions could not have been envisaged at the time the original play was written some twenty years earlier.

Michael Billington in *The Guardian* 12 July 1973 said:–

> 'It belongs to that special graveyard reserved for those musicalisations of perfectly inoffensive plays. What strikes one is the curious needlessness of the project. Ustinov's play set in a dwarf Utopia that maintains the "balance of feebleness" was a whimsically-amiable satire on the cold war conflict between Russia and America; with the addition of music one has the feeling that a self sufficient spoof is itself being spoofed. Moreover Ustinov's joke belonged to a period in which the Great Powers were like rogue elephants indulging in an eyeball-to-eyeball confrontation in the pampas grass; at a time of détente when Nixon and Brezhnev kiss and cuddle in public the joke of intermarriage between rival offspring seems curiously pointless. An American ambassador's daughter who today weds a Russian ambassador's son would probably be greeted with a Congressional medal.'

Topol made a splendid portrayal as the General and I enjoyed a great deal of the satire in his comments to the audience. *The Stage* reviewer, R. B. Marriott, who was generally favourably indulgent in his criticisms of plays said:–

> 'It is a sluggish drawn out affair with precious little wit, unmemorable music, and with a rather dated air. It is not done well either.'

Dandy Dick was another farce with Alastair Sim and Patricia Routledge. It followed very much the pattern of *The Magistrate* but I did not think it gave Alastair Sim so much scope for his inimitable acting genius. Much publicity was given to the provision of a fresh steak and kidney pie for each performance baked by a local public house. It was said that as soon as the pie left the stage it was pounced upon by the stage crew who had won great applause after their scene shifting carried out to the tune of 'the post-horn Galop'. The play was later transferred to the Garrick theatre.

Clements' reign finished with the Christmas show *Treasure Island* with him as Long John Silver and Gordon Gostelow as Blind Pew and Benn Gunn. There was the usual publicity of the auditions for a parrot.

Clements achieved thirty-two productions, eight of which went to London. He had engaged 275 actors and actresses during that time. Unlike the *The Director of the Opera* he had shown to the world, and especially to

Chichester, his care of his wife Katie throughout. He had formed a pattern, according to his beliefs, of what was best for us and although he might have wanted to go on, it was certainly time someone else had a look at the requirements of this particular form of stage, and the future policy to keep it in the forefront of British theatres for the quality of plays as well as for the acting.

In February 1973 *The Stage* reported in a leading article:–

> 'Keith Michell, appointed as new director for the Chichester Festival Theatre, will follow the footsteps of Olivier and John Clements at least in the sense he is the successor in a very important post. The hope, and the belief, is that he will make his own footsteps, firmly and freshly, so that with his own inspiration and guidance Chichester will get another vital phase of its extraordinary life.'

So in 1974 his first programme was looked forward to with great interest and, by some, with apprehension.

It was *Tonight We Improvise*, *The Confederacy*, *Oedipus Tyrannus* and *A Month in the Country*.

Tonight We Improvise was a muted beginning to the season whereas we have always found it goes best with the first play being a resounding

Joan Plowright and Dulcie Gray in Cavell, *1982 (Reg Wilson)*

success. The rest of the programme is uplifted by it. In the same way as I felt Clements was 'put down' by the play *The Director of the Opera*, so I was certain this play was fundamentally a 'let down' for a new director already suspect because the cry had gone up, and nonsensically repeated, that he had not had experience in managing a theatre.

Here in the play the director is shouted at, derided and made to appear of no account. It began with a fifteen minute lecture by Michell on art and life and fiction, and that was a further tactical mistake. Several critics said it could easily be cut and it was certainly boring for the audience. The supporting cast was interesting with Alfred Marks, Keith Baxter, Miriam Karlin and Annie Ross. I felt it was a hotchpotch, unsatisfying evening.

The Confederacy was another of those jumbled 'mix-ups' of wives, lovers, misers and weak, suspicious husbands. It gave scope for the raucous Peggy Mount and Dora Bryan and introduced another refugee from television, Peter Gilmore.

Oedipus Tyrannus was hampered by the controversy of the director, Pilikian's insistance that it should be pronounced as Oidipus. This gave the critics a field day in discussing this change of pronunciation with headings such as 'Oi, Oi, it's Oidipus'. A case of purity versus traditional common usage.

Michell scored a personal triumph for the majority of his performances which, after the first night, increased to a complete triumph. I agreed with the verdict of *The Observer* critic who said of Diana Dors' rendering of Iocasta that he would leave it to a less charitable critic to write about.

It is interesting that the one piece of sculpture which has been presented to the theatre, and which now stands in the forecourt of the theatre, is of Oedipus. It is the work of the late Trude Bunzi and is the gift of Mr and Mrs K. Reidl, her sister and brother-in-law. The suggestion that our theatre should be the recipient of the statue came from their friends, Mr and Mrs Lustig, who are frequent visitors to the theatre, and from Mr Sam Tanner, the sculptor.

A Month in the Country made the whole season worthwhile. Beautifully played by every member of a well chosen cast it floated from beginning to end. Dorothy Tutin, whom I love to see and hear in any part, was praised by all the critics: she received the Actress of the Year Award for her performance. Derek Jacobi and Timothy West both gave their best. Several critics applauded the production and phrases such as 'the acting was magnificent' were used.

The season had been 'pulled up by its braces' and Michell was vindicated with his acting in *Oedipus* and his choice of, at least, three of the plays. We have found that no director, not even Olivier, is at his best in the first season.

Michell's great artistic sense showed itself by his inspired discovery of Jim Parker's music. Hearing a few examples of it and especially some excerpts from his new Christmas musical for young people, Michell worked with him and Wendy Toye to produce for our Christmas show *Follow The Star*. This was an instant success with the children who were able to participate in it, and the parents who enjoyed seeing the children so excited by it. It was well acted by the majority of the cast, there were tunes to remember and plenty of humour. It was repeated for Christmas in 1975 and has since been played in many cities. There were many amusing incidents during the run such as the point where the audience are scratching their heads to try and think what 'myrrh' is. On one occasion I attended when the question was asked, 'What shall we give the baby Jesus for a present?' A little voice from the back of the audience called out: 'Give him Lego'.

1975: *Cyrano de Bergerac*, *Enemy of the People*, *Made in Heaven* and *Othello*.

Cyrano de Bergerac was directed by Jose Ferrere who had in the past played the title part with great success. Herbert Kretzmar described the whole presentation as a colourful costume extravaganza. John Barber said of it:–

> 'In gallant defiance of our economic blues Chichester has flung onto the stage a romantic extravaganza of love and war with a huge cast . . . It is a gesture that this big stage can happily enlarge. Christopher Fry's translation was said to be a "powerful facet that sets the tide of eloquence flowing".'

Keith Michell came in for a great deal of praise and some criticism from those who wanted to look back at other performances. One did say, however, that 'the scene in the garden of a nunnery . . . is one of true heartbreak and Michell rises to it with a touching panache that brings the play to a sad, slow climax.'

On the other hand Irving Wardle (*The Times*), Michael Billington (*The Guardian*) and Milton Shulman (*Evening Standard*) did not like the whole production. I enjoyed it, not having seen it enacted on stage before and think of it as one of Michell's successes.

Enemy of the People I remember as one of our finest productions. Absorbingly interesting in theme and purpose throughout, it had all the elements of comedy at the beginning developing into splendid arguments and discussion which as our publicity rightly said: 'A play so ahead of its time it could have been written today.' It deals among other things in wonderfully dramatic terms with ecology and humanities in a small town.

One could easily imagine a similar affair in Chichester transposing the medicinal baths for a question of fluoride in the water supply. The personalities in this city could exactly duplicate those in the play. Given the undoubted excellence of Donald Sinden's acting (universally praised) the comedy, the drama, and the topicality, why didn't the public come to it more than they did? It was difficult to understand. I suppose because it was Ibsen. Those who did not come missed one of the best evenings in our theatre. In the theatre restaurant afterwards there were serious discussions and almost heated arguments all around us. This is what I call disturbing the public, not trying to shock them by a sniggering schoolboy style of language and sex.

Made in Heaven was, in my opinion, the very worst play we have ever produced. It seemed pointless and vapid and I was bored beyond words. People keep asking for new plays and we have done several good ones, but this was a poor example. Irving Wardle said: 'Chichester bashing is now a popular sport but this is an unspeakable piece.' Jack Tinker, *Daily Mail* 17 July 1975, said:–

> 'It is an overblown, overwritten, overspoken piece of nonsense so insubstantial one finds it hard to excuse in these times of economic austerity were it not for the occasional performance.'

It is only fair to say some critics did like it, with reservations, as a good mix of comedy with farce.

I was deeply disturbed when I heard Michell was going to include *Othello* in this season so soon after the great production by Olivier. Memories were so clear cut and vivid of his performance I thought it was risking a great deal to perform it in so short a time afterwards with Topol and himself.

Luckily the director, Peter Dews, was wise enough not to let it draw immediate comparison when he staged it in one critic's words 'colourfully set in the period of *The Merry Widow*'. So whilst the audience had to keep translating the words to the period it did avoid the pitfalls it would have otherwise encountered. Topol was, in the main, praised for his rendering of the part as a Moor which avoided the controversy Olivier ran into. Michell received almost unanimous praise as Iago, 'a subtle unobtrusive dispenser of poison'.

This season gave Michell two triumphs for his acting but not so much praise for his unbalanced programme. The year finished with a repeat of *Follow The Star* for Christmas and again it was greeted with many full houses.

1976: *Noah*, *Twelfth Night*, *The Circle* and *Monsieur Perrichon's Travels*.

At the very beginning of the year Michell took *Othello* and *Cyrano* to the Hong Kong Festival. They received a great welcome and upheld, and increased, the prestige of our theatre. The security-conscious Royal Hong Kong Police had to grant a special arms exemption permit before the Chichester Festival Theatre Company could bring the stage weaponry to the island. Immediately after the performance of *Cyrano*, eighteen imitation muskets, two sword sticks, three daggers, one knife, two dummy rifles, twenty-five rapiers and twenty-seven swords were taken to the Royal Navy's land base Tamar and locked under guard. This was the pattern of manoeuvre for each performance.

Tony Chardet, one of our directorate, was the artistic director for the

Author and wife after Freedom of City ceremony (David Evershed-Martin)

Hong Kong Festival and he arranged the visit as well as attending to his duties for Hong Kong. He was greatly missed by all when he died in 1979.

Noah with a simple set proved to be an interesting and revealing play. Gordon Jackson of television fame commanded respect and praise for his portrayal of the title part. Even though it subdued all the other biblical characters it was extremely effective. The play on the whole was enjoyable because of its obvious sincerity. Eric Thompson, the director, took all the actors to the London Zoo to study the animals they were to represent.

Monsieur Perrichon's Travels: Rex Harrison provided the great attraction in this play directed by Patrick Garland. There were many delicious ingredients in this story of gratitude and ingratitude. There was the local brass band which played before the play began, the atmosphere of the railway station and the occasion when Rex Harrison was rescued from the slopes of the Matterhorn (actually the balcony of the theatre) cleverly arranged by the Kirby Flying Ballet. A delightful evening. As B. A. Young, *Financial Times* 4 August 1976, said:–

> '*Monsieur Perrichon's Travels* is worth crossing England to collect.'

Of Rex Harrison's solemn rendering of the part, he said:–

> 'It is played with total restraint. Even when dangling over a precipice he exhibits the utmost presence of mind . . . allowing its innate comedy to reveal itself with no added decoration from him. This is comic acting at its best.'

Milton Shulman, *Evening Standard* 4 August 1976 pointed out: 'Gratitude is one of the deadliest of sins. It will sour anyone forced to experience it.'

I have certainly had occasions in my life where gratitude for help I have been able to give, ended in that person being my enemy. Sad though this is, it should not deter anyone from doing a kindness when possible, and it teaches us not to act in the same way.

Rex Harrison, writing to Selbie later, said '. . . it was all worth it. It, the season, has a very loving part in my memory which will remain with me for ever.'

The Circle: another revival but one well warranted with the important cast gathered together by the director, Peter Dews. Googie Withers, Susan Hampshire (one of my top four actresses), John McCallum and Bill Fraser were the nationally and internationally renowned players. But several others have reached heights since this production among whom were Martin Jarvis and Clive Francis. John Barber, *Daily Telegraph* 21 July 1976, said of Googie Withers and Bill Fraser, 'They are magnificent as the superannuated sweethearts.'

Jack Tinker, *Daily Mail* 15 October 1976, said when this transferred to the Haymarket:–

> 'There is a moment in this gilded production that has haunted me ever since it was unveiled at Chichester. It is that second of theatrical magic when Bill Fraser's curmudgeonly Lord Porteous moves across to Googie Wither's weeping Lady Kitty and puts his hand on her shoulder. No word is spoken to silence the silly tears she is dripping over an old photograph of her lost beauty but they dry up instantly. In that split second the audience is suddenly in possession of Maugham's real message and also in the presence of acting of the highest order.'

Like many others I have experienced such moments. Olivier as the doctor in *Uncle Vanya* with Sybil as she reprimands him for drinking too much vodka. Olivier in *Othello* as he smells a rose and Alec Guinness in a play I saw in London, *The Old Country*, when as a political exile from England he puts on a record and listens to the Eton Boating Song and shows that, despite all his pretence of not minding his exile, he is racked with home sickness.

Twelfth Night was a fairly normal presentation of the play which aroused only mild praise and criticism. Whilst some deprecated the unnecessary tricks of the supporting cast, there was praise for Jeanette Sterke, Michelle Dotrice and Gordon Jackson for playing the parts in a straightforward way.

1976 was an important year away from our theatre, and yet in many ways connected with it, such as the opening of the National Theatre in the presence of the Queen, and the deaths of Sybil Thorndike (ninety-three) and Alastair Sim (seventy-five).

Michell created during his time a very happy company and this was most apparent by his promoting and encouraging the 'New Ventures', which consisted of the younger members of the company and back stage crews who gave performances of one act plays and readings in the ballroom of the Dolphin and Anchor Hotel during the season. These were very successful and in this way they bound the company together and gave the many aspiring actors and directors a chance to show their talents. He started this trend and it has been followed ever since, now with the successful presentations in 'The Tent'.

The season finished up with another Christmas show called *Make Me A World* by the same authors of last year's success and although it did not have quite the same originality and special tunes, it enabled the children to enjoy a simple tale and to participate in the action.

1977: *Waters of the Moon*, *In Order of Appearance*, *Julius Caesar* and *The Apple Cart*.

Waters of the Moon brought Ingrid Bergman (another of my most delightful of actresses) to our theatre and she was adored by the cast and the audience on and off the stage. Despite the critics continually harping back to other renowned performances, she seemed ideal for the part and carried it through in her own particular way. Wendy Hiller gave a delightful performance in contrast of character and the whole company supported them excellently. There were protests from some about reviving such a play and Michael Billington asked:– 'What on earth is the point of reviving this kind of tepid naturalistic piece in a theatre that cries out for dash and flamboyance?' If only we could have plays of the kind he suggests all the time I would be more than delighted, but until they can be found, or written, or afforded, this play is a good 'filler'. On the other hand Herbert Kretzmer said:– 'A play of gentle melancholy, rich in humour, directed with skill by John Clements. An obvious West End candidate.'

One amusing incident during the course of the play was when Ingrid Bergman, who always had some difficulty with the English language, said, whilst watching a snowstorm, 'Oh, look, they're snowing throwballs!'

In Order of Appearance was a sort of Noel Coward's Cavalcade of *1066 and All That* affair. Eric Shorter, *Daily Telegraph*, summed it up well:–

> 'There is much good taste and good fun at Chichester. Nor is the evening in its jaunty progress from Julius Caesar to George VI without its serious moments. There is even a patch or two of emotion.'

It was a splendid light-hearted revue for the Royal Silver Jubilee celebrations and there were many thumbnail sketches of the various monarchs which are still remembered to-day, and enjoyed in retrospect. It was served up with more music by Jim Parker who had almost become the theatre's resident composer by the patronage of Michell.

Julius Caesar is remembered most for the bloodletting of the assassination. Twenty-two stab wounds and the dazzling white robes of the senators were covered in blood (needing the installation of a factory-sized washing machine) even though there are no togas as the play was set in a Jacobean period which the critics liked, but the audience, as usual, found difficult to assimilate. Peter Dews used the audience as an audience for the famous Mark Antony speech with rabble rousers around the auditorium. John Barber, *Daily Telegraph*, wrote that this scene 'so often muffed, won a great round of applause. Directing the play at Chichester, Peter Dews has taken an extremely bold line with his *Julius Caesar*. It works well so must be accounted one of the Sussex Theatre's greatest successes.'

The Apple Cart was the final success for Michell. Directed by Patrick Garland it had a strong cast including Penelope Keith, Jeanette Sterke, June Jago (another favourite of mine), Nigel Stock, Paul Hardwick and Keith Michell. It received fairly universal praise and when it went to the Phoenix Theatre later, it again received good notices.

Michell's reign was over, the Board having extended his original three year contract by an extra year. During that time he had taken plays to Hong Kong, Brussels and Luxembourg and now to Australia. He had promoted 'New Ventures' as a 'fringe company', performed brilliantly as Thomas À Becket in his production of *Murder in the Cathedral* in Chichester Cathedral (a personal triumph) and organised the Silver Jubilee Concert and several other shows at the Assembly Room in Chichester.

He had, besides a few failures, many great successes acclaimed by the critics, namely *A Month in the Country*, *Cyrano de Bergerac*, *Enemy of the People*, *Othello*, *The Circle*, *Waters of the Moon*, *Julius Caesar* and *The Apple Cart*. In the last season two plays reached an audience of 97% and the overall for the season was 88%.

Peter Dews was appointed in November 1977 to succeed Michell. Unfortunately soon afterwards Dews suffered a slight stroke which altered his forceful approach to our problems. We offered him the chance of having support by appointing Patrick Garland as an associate director for the first year. I think he was grateful to have the help. The next three years were very difficult for the Board, and Dews must have found his illness a great handicap and worry for him.

1978: *A Woman of No Importance*, *The Inconstant Couple*, *The Aspern Papers* and *Look After Lulu*.

The usual press conference held at the Martini Terrace in the New Zealand building in the Haymarket was frustrating for all concerned as two plays could not be announced. They were not yet cast and the press made much of the 'mystery' surrounding our season.

However there was a very strong cast for *A Woman of No Importance*. Jack Tinker, *Daily Mail*, 10 May 1978 said:–

> 'It has assembled on its vast octagonal arena some of the most superb women of importance the English stage can boast. Directed by Patrick Garland there is Sian Phillips, Margaretta Scott, Barbara Murray, Gayle Hunnicutt and Rosie Kerslake . . . an elegant evening swept along by Peter Farmer's settings and Mr Garland's faultless production.'

The Inconstant Couple This was another of those inconsequential plays that passed me by without any impression. The acting of Sian Phillips and Morag Hood as the couple was of a high standard but still they did not make it into a good play or production.

R. B. Marriott of *The Stage* wrote:–

> 'Perhaps if stylishly played in its native France . . . it would be meaningful and amusing . . . The couples who shift this way and that, run around the mulberry bush and in and out of temperament and emotion . . . There is not sufficient wit or element of surprise or suspense to engage one's fancy or constant attention and to disguise the thinness of the proceedings.'

The Aspern Papers: here was something to engage the attention at the time and aroused many thoughts afterwards. The truly delightful appearance of Cathleen Nesbitt, aged ninety, and a very impressive interpretation by Jill Bennett of the dreary spinster Miss Tina. Whenever either, or both, were on the stage they rivetted one's attention and the first appearance of Cathleen Nesbitt in the wheelchair was, as J. C. Trewin said in the *Birmingham Post*: 'For a moment it seemed that every light in the theatre had blazed.'

Judy Campbell, Debbie Arnold and Omar Sharif in Sleeping Prince, *1984 (Reg Wilson)*

The play, a tussle between the claims of conscience and those of gilded sensibility, was acclaimed in *The Listener* as 'the best Chichester production for the last two years'.

Sheridan Morley in *Punch*, 26 July 1978, wrote:

'We are now three-quarters of our way through the first Peter Dews season at Chichester and already it's possible to reach certain conclusions about the new regime. The main aim seems to be a series of field trials for the Haymarket. We've had a star-studded Oscar Wilde, an elegant Marivaux and now the Michael Redgrave–Henry James *Aspern Papers* (with a Coward/Feydeau farce still to come), all of which would have looked better behind a London proscenium arch.

So far, so fairly good. No theatre in recent years has been so suffocated by its audience or its geographic location as Chichester, and Dews is clearly not about to stage a theatrical revolution on those well manicured lawns. So we have a return to the John Clements era with productions designed to reassure audiences that H. M. Tennent is still alive and well and living in West Sussex and that Chichester is no more and no less than Glyndebourne for the tone-deaf.

Once though it was a great deal more than that. Built more than eighteen years ago from largely local money (much of it donated in half crowns) it was intended first to be a proud affirmation that anything Guthrie could do in Canada, by way of an open stage in a permanent tent, we could do better at home. Olivier, its first director, started to form his National Theatre Company at Chichester in the early sixties and those seasons were its finest . . . not only his *Othello* and *Vanya* but such new Ardens as *Armstrong's Last Goodnight* and *The Workhouse Donkey* suggested that here was truly a national theatre of the countryside.

With Olivier's departure for the Vic, however, came the first signs of trouble; throughout his long and very successful management John Clements did almost nothing there that had not been done better somewhere else. He turned Chichester from an exciting new theatre into a gracious revival house and that alas is what its audience has now come to expect.'

Look After Lulu: a riot of fun like *The Italian Straw Hat*, and why shouldn't we have such interludes now and again to loosen up our inhibitions with comic antics? Some of the critics took the opportunity to sneer at our audience 'doubled up' with laughter and made references to Goodwood Race week as if those who attend race meetings can only appreciate light farces.

I have always contended that the British could do with much more jollity and conviviality and that was the reason I started the Fun Day, or Gala Day, for Chichester having seen the celebrations on the lake at St Wolfgung. As has already been said by many, it is the climate we live in that refrigerates any hot blood or passion we may have had, but since we have the characteristic of being as flexible as our weather we should break out now and again and these sorts of play are as good as a tonic. What a cast it was. Geraldine McEwan (sparkling like a diamond), Clive Francis, Nigel Stock, Kenneth Haigh and, as necessary as mustard is to beef, Fenella Fielding. I loved it.

The season ended with *Sleep of Prisoners* by Christopher Fry at the cathedral which later went with *Julius Caesar* to the Hong Kong Festival. The Christmas show was *The Owl and the Pussycat Went to Sea*. Not so popular as the two previous Christmas shows.

1979: *The Devil's Disciple*, *The Eagle Has Two Heads*, *The Importance of Being Earnest* and *The Man Who Came to Dinner*.

The Devil's Disciple was a swashbuckling presentation well received by critics and public alike, especially due to the acting of Ian Ogilvy who so obviously enjoyed making the most of the part. One critic pointed out that the sub-title 'A Melodrama' was more accurate and the production made the play more of a comedy than the 'thrill-a-second' that Shaw intended. Special praise was accorded to John Clements' playing of the part of a 'weather-beaten General'.

One evening Ogilvy was standing on a barrel preparatory to having the noose placed around his head for the 'hanging scene' when he fell into the barrel as the top gave way. This 'impromptu' piece of action delighted the audience and Ogilvy, after being helped out by two of the soldiers, resumed the action of the play as though the accident had been intended. Even if the noose had been around his neck the safety catch would have acted as we had always hoped it would.

One female member of the audience asked if she could buy the gallows as she wanted them for her husband who, she said, 'suffered from a bad back!'

The Eagle Has Two Heads was another successful play for the season's opening. Directed by David William and with a 'splendiferous set and sumptuous gowns' designed by Clive Lavagna, it had the added glamour of superb acting by Jill Bennett. The very elaborate staircase, which is an essential ingredient of the final tragedy, cost us a fortune and on the first night you could feel the shudder which went through members of the Board as they contemplated it and counted the cost.

I remembered having seen the play with Eileen Herlie and I enjoyed it even more on our stage with Jill Bennett, though usually I find myself unmoved by her acting but full of admiration for her artistry.

The Importance of Being Earnest bored me in spite of the excellence of the cast which included Googie Withers (one of my favourites) Hayley Mills and Mel Martin. Luckily Dews was wise enough not to let Googie Withers compete with the ghost of Edith Evans but let her play it differently, underemphasising the famous passages. But fundamentally I was convinced it was one of those plays totally unsuited for our stage.

Keith Nurse, *Daily Telegraph* 18 July 1979, wrote:

> 'Dews' production is visually all that it should be; a world of mannered decoration. And as a reflection of a world, if not an age, of snobbish social surfaces this production . . . splendidly designed by Finlay James . . . fits the bill in more ways than one. Everyone looked the part, elegantly so, but the Wildean wit lacks bite and edge.'

Probably it was the snobbishness based on false standards which irritated me as it does in ordinary life. After one of the performances one of the audience was heard to say about Clements, who was playing the part of Canon Chasuble, 'I liked the old buffer who played the padre. Reminded me very much of John Clements'.

The Man Who Came to Dinner suffered somewhat as a play after its memorable film. The part of Sheridan Whiteside, taken by Charles Gray, is the kind of character we all love to hate and I thought his acting filled the part to its fullest extent. Again Jill Bennett had a miserable part to play but played it as if she loves that sort of part. There were some witty interludes such as Barry Justice in a speech imitating Noel Coward, which I enjoyed, and Ken Wynne's Banjo which I disliked.

Jack Tinker in the *Daily Mail* 8 August 1979, said:

'When Chichester first established its annual festival, its greatest successes were the plays that utilised the new theatre's great octagonal arena to its fullest extent. Inevitably they were diminished when they transferred to the confines of West End stages. Now sadly they seem simply designed for the fast trip to London.'

The general opinion of the season was that we were playing 'safe'.

The Christmas show was *Charley's Aunt*, a choice of Dews' which was almost unanimously opposed by the Board as being unsuitable to follow on the children's shows we had previously presented. All-in-all it did prove a failure as attendances were low and criticisms numerous. But the Board had kept to its policy of commenting on, but not controlling, the artistic director's choice. We rise and we fall by this adherence to such a principle, but at least the divisions of opinion do not become apparent to the public at the time.

1980: *The Last of Mrs Cheyney*, *Terra Nova*, *Much Ado About Nothing* and *Old Heads and Young Hearts*.

The months of January and February were ones of crisis for the Board as Peter Dews seemed reluctant to finalise his programme for the season and time was fast running out. Individual members of the Board found themselves acting as liaison agents and in the end were able to contract Joan

Cellar at author's home

Collins for the remaining play, namely *The Last of Mrs Cheyney*. Her engagement created considerable publicity because of her fame and popularity as a film actress.

Unlike the parts she had hitherto taken on the television and cinema screens, she proved to be a kindly, completely co-operative person with all the personnel of the theatre and was extremely helpful in creating a happy atmosphere. I found the play enjoyable but again thought it was not so suitable for the open stage.

Praise was particularly bestowed upon Benjamin Whitrow as the butler and others who were applauded were Elspeth March and Moyra Fraser, but all the reviews were low-toned and kept harking back to Gerald du Maurier and Gladys Cooper. I often wonder if those performances would stand up to modern standards and demands, or whether time has mellowed the memories. I remember seeing many of these artistes in the past in various roles but my playgoing was limited at the time and I did not have the advantage of being able to make comparisons. Perhaps the nostalgic references so often made about classical acting are legitimate, but it seems deadening to have them resurrected in front of every younger generation of actors and actresses.

Sheridan Morley was scathing about this play and B. A. Young said:

> 'This play moves from one melodrama to another . . . these are just for the proverbial tired businessman and then only if he is very tired and business is unusually bad.'

Terra Nova: now for a very exciting and moving new play. Only previously played in America and Alaska, it was adapted for the English audience and had its first European showing on our stage. The set was astoundingly simple and extremely effective. Pamela Howard's artistically draped off-white curtains at the back amazingly gave the impression of a wall of ice. On several occasions authentic slides were projected onto these to illustrate Scott's historic journey.

The auditorium seemed several degrees colder by the device of the set and the white stage. Hywel Bennett, who had researched everything about the expedition, fitted the part of Scott to perfection. All the rest of the cast were, without exception, almost exact impersonations of the men we knew so much about.

There were so many dramatic, and many light-hearted, moments. Especially effective was the fantasy banquet where each member ordered the finest meal that he could conjure up in his mind only to be told at the end that 'there is no food'. The only disruptive ingredient that I found in the narrative was the continual appearance of Amundsen taunting Scott.

What an experience the public missed by not coming to the play. Just because they knew the story, and its tragic end, they stayed away in large numbers, not wanting to be depressed in these days of escapism. It showed how we had, over the years, created an audience intent more on having a good evening out because of the troubled times we lived in. I can only hope there is a solid nucleus of people who will still welcome serious drama.

The story vividly recalled to me my father's enthusiasm at the time of Scott's expedition. Always vitally interested in current affairs, he had bought one of the earliest epidiascopes from Gamages, called a Mirror-scope, on which he was able to show us pictures cut out from the papers.

During a show of these pictures of Scott's adventure my music teacher called to alter a date of one of my lessons. I had constantly begged my father to let me finish with her as she always refused to let me have even the easiest 'piece' to play, but insisted on my learning only scales and endless theory of music which killed all my interest in piano playing. He called her in excitedly to see the pictures. When she asked who Scott was, that was the end of my lessons with her.

Perhaps the unfortunate title of *Terra Nova* (the name of Scott's ship) was one of the causes of its unpopularity. I heard one lady in a restaurant saying she was not going to see it because she didn't understand why it was called that. Sometimes any excuse will do.

Much Ado About Nothing: this title asked for the obvious rejoinder from one critic that he went 'expecting nothing and he got nothing'. To me it was a leaden-hearted comedy and most reviewers agreed it was tepid. Set in pretty surroundings it dragged along to the inevitable Shakespeare resolving of mixed couplings. But other people enjoyed it so perhaps it was my usual narrow prejudice against Shakespeare's comedies which dulled my appreciation though, as usual, the words were worth hearing.

Old Heads and Young Hearts, though a completely muddled and confusing story according to all the critics, had some lively comedy at times. Particularly amusing were the performances of Peter Sallis (who had adapted the play), Judy Parfitt, Lally Bowers and Frank Windsor.

The *Birmingham Post* said:–

> 'The trouble is the plot, a fairly thick mist over the evening. It could have been my fault but I was never quite sure who was who or what was happening in a 'rotten borough' election off-stage.'

The Christmas show was *Circus Oz*. It was partially successful but it increased public pressure for a pantomime or something like *Follow the Star* in which children could participate.

At the beginning of the 1980 season we announced the appointment of Patrick Garland as the next artistic director. After Patrick had known Alexandra Bastedo for eleven years they decided to marry and another link between the cathedral and the theatre was forged when they were married in the cathedral on 17 December.

1981: *The Cherry Orchard*, *Feasting With Panthers*, *The Mitford Girls* and *Underneath the Arches*.

The Cherry Orchard: the choice of this play, and its disappointing impact, was in a small way my responsibility as Garland asked my advice as to whether it should be put on since it had been produced by Lindsay Anderson in our theatre in 1966 with Celia Johnson. I had always hoped to see Claire Bloom on our stage, especially as there had been other times when her inclusion in plays had not been made possible. He may, or may not, have been influenced by my agreement to the idea but in any case Claire Bloom had always longed to do the part of Madame Ranevskaya.

John Barber, *Daily Telegraph* 16 February 1981, wrote:–

> 'if the opening play of the season *The Cherry Orchard* sounds more conventional, Mr Garland's approval is not. He believes that art comes out of personal and private obsessions and Claire Bloom has a burning obsession to play Mme. Ranevskaya, Chekhov's spoiled, feckless land owner. In her the actress sees a giddiness and irresponsibility which perhaps because of her own remarkable beauty and favoured childhood and career she feels she understands and can identify with it.'

Unfortunately the critics did not like her interpretation of the character and the praise was only mild. Phrases such as 'Not a lot of blossom in this orchard' etc headed the articles and I, for one, was disappointed that the reaction was so muted — as was the acting except for one or two cameos by Sarah Badel and Joss Ackland.

Feasting With Panthers: when I heard that Tom Baker was to take the part of Oscar Wilde in this play I could not believe the casting was right, but when I saw his performance, especially the way in which he transformed himself from the first act of defiance to the broken down remnant of Wilde in the second act, I had to agree it was an inspired piece of casting.

I enjoyed the cut and thrust of the pleading during the trial and found the text absorbing, but I was left with a nasty taste in the mouth at the end to feel I had spent an evening listening to such a sordid story. It may well be asked, after reading the chapter on 'Controversies', why I did not object to this as I did to *A Patriot For Me*. One reason is that words are different to actions and also the adults knew, without being warned, that the trial of Oscar Wilde involved the subject of homosexuality and from the beginning they were told it was not suitable for children.

The title was taken from one of his most revealing statements that 'it was like feasting with panthers, the danger was half the excitement and their poison was part of their perfection.'

The Mitford Girls: a really splendid highly-polished musical exploitation of what was a serious family history. Delightful tunes resurrected and given a new lease of life. The sisters played by a brilliant group of renowned actresses displayed the various characters, highlighting the extraordinary differences in one family, and their dedication to their chosen lifestyle.

The controversial parts of their history, connections with Hitler, the

Spanish War and Moseley, were all treated fairly and openly, even though when the members of the family who are still living came to see it they did not much like the portrayal of their particular selves. But then few people like the portraits painted of themselves. Some of them were, characteristically, very outspoken of their dislike of the revue but the public enjoyed it and it was an outstanding success. It was extended for an extra week before going to the Globe Theatre. Here it was far too cramped on the smaller stage and was not such a success as at Chichester for this reason alone.

Underneath the Arches: I could not imagine how anyone could make a revue of the *Crazy Gang*, the show which I had adored in my younger days. But Patrick Garland, who despite his more serious side loves doing musicals, revelled in the fun of it. He was probably the only one who could co-operate with Rex Harrison in *My Fair Lady* and his artistry is seen to great effect in that and *The Mitford Girls*. Whilst many criticised this as a lot of sketches strung together, it could hardly be done in any other way. The *Crazy Gang* always worked in short sketches. At least the frail story of Bud Flanagan's career strung it together. The members of our cast created the traditional *Crazy Gang* atmosphere of joyous chaos before the show, in the foyer and in the auditorium.

I was pleased to see the younger generation catch on to the spirit of it all besides the ones, like myself, who were given grand nostalgic moments. The only living member of the Gang, Chesney Allen aged eighty-seven, found himself once again, after many years in quiet retirement, appearing on the stage and on many occasions singing with Roy Hudd to the wild enthusiasm of the audience. Who talks of the stiff-necked Chichester audiences? They may not stand on the seats or run shrieking up to the stage but the applause can be deafening and uninhibited. Roy Hudd with his infectious good humour brightened everybody's lives at the theatre.

The Christmas show *Nickelby and Me*, based on the Dickens story, was not very popular and so the uneven reputation of our Christmas productions goes on until we can find the right formula.

This season was a financial disaster and we lost all our reserve funds. Luckily the future became regulated when John McKerchar, a member of the Board and a professional accountant, voluntarily took charge of the budgets and financial controls, and we again got back on the rails. With his invaluable help we have kept it so ever since.

1982: *On the Rocks*, *Cavell*, *Valmouth* and *Goodbye Mr Chips*.

The *On the Rocks* title worried me a little after the 1981 season's financial loss. I was afraid someone would report that 'Yes, indeed, Chichester is on the rocks'. However no one did, it would have been an unfair jibe as 1981 was the only time we were in difficulties.

A splendidly even gifted cast carried through an interesting and absorbing play against the odds of its topicality during the Falklands War crisis. Whilst some of the lines were too reminiscent of what was happening at that time in real life, the arguments were still relevant and the acting redeemed any faults there were in the logic of the text. Michell was praised for his part as a Prime Minister, and the rest of the Cabinet and supporting parts were played by Jean Marsh, Arthur English, Nigel Stock and Aubrey Woods.

It was one of those very few occasions when the Board granted a supplementary budget. The designer Pamela Howard asked for all the chairs of the Cabinet Room to be re-decorated the same colour as those of the No 10 Downing Street suite in the Cabinet Room; it was certainly worthwhile as they supplied the chief and most important colour in the set. Without this colouring the whole set would have been drab and dull.

Cavell was another new successful play for our theatre. A patchy play, with several inconsistencies, was rescued by a magnificent portrayal of Nurse Cavell by Joan Plowright. She dominated the action throughout, being on the stage almost all the time. One or two of the scenes seemed inexplicably out of sequence, but there were many moments of intense emotion. Again, like *Terra Nova*, the public missed a great experience because of the sombre content of the story so well known for its tragic end, an end that was still vivid in many people's minds. The truthful exposing of Nurse Cavell's character left one in some doubts as to her actions and this left some confusion in one's mind afterwards. But the memory of Joan Plowright's acting is as vivid as her portrayal of Saint Joan, and nothing can really mar the fact that Cavell was one of Britain's great heroines by her final sacrifice.

Valmouth was a most extraordinary mixture of comedy, farce and some tepid drama. I could not make any rhyme or reason of it on first seeing it. I did not know what it was all about and nor did the majority of the audience. Bertice Reading, a consummate artiste in her own style, was the essence of brashness, well supported by Doris Hare who rejoiced in her part. Fenella Fielding and Judy Campbell created outstanding characterisations.

Since listening to the record I have been made aware of some of the delightful tunes in the play but these were overlaid by the confusion of the story. Several members of the Board had the gravest doubts about it being included in the season due to its failure when it was first played at the Lyric Theatre, Hammersmith in 1958. Some of the cast now appearing were in the original production. It was then reckoned to be 'ahead of its time'. Perhaps that is still its fault. It was positively disliked by many people on this occasion as well.

Goodbye, Mr Chips brought John Mills to our stage.

I think I, and many others, would have preferred to have seen this again as a straightforward play. The music seemed to be an oft-recurring hiccup to the narrative and some of the characters were not convincing in a musical role. Well supported by a thoroughly trained and disciplined crowd of schoolboys, recruited locally, there were many moments of comedy to offset the tragedy and sentiment of the narrative. A good evening's

National Youth Orchestra 1962

entertainment and a pleasure to see the acting of John Mills.

At last we staged a pantomime. Frankie Howerd in *Jack and the Beanstalk* was a success and the children, although not able to join actively in the action, were given many opportunities to bandy words with the comedians and the wicked Aubrey Woods. Obviously after the other Christmas shows a lot of parents were tardy about booking, but as the news got round there was a better box office response. It showed that we could stage a pantomime even though the run has to be short (Chichester audiences seem to stop once the schools have gone back), and even though costs are very high to stage them in a spectacular way.

Chesney Allen died on 14 November. It was good to feel we had been the cause of renewed adulation for his talents towards the end of his life.

1983: *A Patriot For Me*, *Time and the Conways*, *As You Like It* and *The Sleeping Prince*.

I have said all I wish to say about *A Patriot For Me* in the chapter 'Controversies'.

Time and the Conways was a very pleasant play to watch and to think about afterwards. Despite its depressing conclusions that time defeats one's earlier aspirations and ambitions, there was plenty of refreshing comedy to while away the evening. Googie Withers commanded the events, but I wondered if the younger generation who watched the first act quite understood the pre-occupation house parties had with amateur dramatics in the shape of 'charades'. Nowadays parties indulge in copying television games such as *What's My Line*, *Call My Bluff*, and *Give Me A Clue*. These do not embarrass the guests with having to 'dress up', a form of exhibitionism which the British view with such reluctance.

The play made one reflect on the past and how one's life had unfolded and to what purpose. As someone once said it is a startling moment in your life when you suddenly realise you are not, after all, going to be Prime Minister or the Archbishop of Canterbury. There were some lovely performances by Julia Foster and Alexandra Bastedo.

As You Like It was best described by John Barber when he wrote in the *Daily Telegraph* on 15 July 1983:–

> 'A dappled green light plays on the permanent set, a wooden bridge garlanded with flowers and loud with the bleating of sheep and the sound of chopping wood. Patrick Garland, a director always sensitive to folk customs and pastoral conventions, gives the opening scene a look of a 'fete champetrie' by Watteau – all satins, dandified frock coats, pannier dresses and white-wigged flunkeys.'

That sums it up well except for the unusually splendid Orlando played by Jonathon Morris and delightful performances by Lucy Fleming and Patricia Hodge.

The Sleeping Prince with Omar Sharif was a completely sold out production. A dazzling permanent set in chromium and clear engraved plastic greeted the audience as it arrived and set the seal on the sparkle of the production. After the first few performances when the unfamiliarity of our stage, and his return to the stage from film appearances seemed a little unsettling, Omar Sharif took command of the play and, in very happy partnership with the fascinating Debbie Arnold, brought off a resounding success. Many critics were not so satisfied as the audiences, looking back as they usually do to the performance of Olivier and Vivien Leigh in a performance I remember seeing one evening sitting immediately behind the royal party who had come informally. Our production played for an extra week and transferred later to the Haymarket Theatre.

The season ended with *Aladdin* praised by everyone who saw it, as far as I could tell. Beautiful sets and costumes making it all as spectacular as any pantomime should be. If we could get the confidence of the public for a regular good standard pantomime, then with all our celebrity concerts, ballet, jazz sessions and plays by other companies, we shall have converted the original idea of a 'festival season' into an almost all-year-round theatre and thereby created a whole new theatre-going public in the south of England.

Summing up the influence of the various artistic directors over the twenty-two years I find myself in total agreement with the writer in the *Drama Quarterly* of August 1981 who said:–

> 'Though the annual Chichester Festival has been just about the major theatre success story of the last two decades its success can hardly be attributed to the press. There has been scarcely a year when the Chichester selection of plays has not come under fire from the drama reviewers, especially those of the trendier papers who are perpetually aggrieved over some alleged unadventureness of the choice.
>
> So far from being congratulated on establishing a thriving summer theatre where none existed before, and on the cunning arrangement of repertory that attracts 'stars' away from London for minimal salaries, successive directors have been made to feel almost guilty for putting on stuff that pleases the public . . .
>
> I cannot pretend to have liked everything that has been done over the years but the general choice of plays seems to me admirable on the face of it and to compare with any other theatre in the land. If there has been a paucity of new plays, that merely reflects the fact that good new plays are always dismayingly hard to come by and it is plainly unreasonable to deplore the preponderance of revivals when those revivals range across a spectrum that embraces not only the classics of Shakespeare and the Restoration dramatists but Shaw and Brecht, Pinero, Pirandello, Anouilh and Cocteau, Wilde and Maugham, Ibsen and Chekhov. If this were the National Theatre we would not be looking for more.'

CHAPTER 12

Behind the Scenes

One of the pleasant features of our theatre has been the loyalty and devotion of our staffs in all parts of the management. There have been a few 'comings and goings', but on the whole the staff have remained with us and especially those in charge of the offices and backstage.

Equity, of course, have pursued their negotiations throughout the years but we have been able to resolve these matters in an amicable way by them being necessarily flexible because of the unusual conditions for a Festival Theatre such as ours.

Backstage personnel were for a long time happy with their conditions but, without our being informed, a few grievances grew up and so they asked to join NATKE. I told them at the time that it should have been unnecessary if only they had let the Board know of their difficulties, which were small, as we had always been anxious to give the best working environment. This was an example of poor communications.

However, they were convinced they had to have 'their cards' in case they wished at any time to change their employment though hardly any of them have needed, or wanted, to do so. Negotiations with NATKE have also been reasonable, but I wish we could have been "obviously benevolent employers" without it.

NATKE, Equity and their members have found it difficult to realise the peculiar constitution of this theatre compared with commercial and subsidised theatres. There are no 'profits' as such as any surplus funds are immediately 'ploughed back' into the maintenance of the theatre and reserves for the next season. The Board of Directors are not paid in any way; all work voluntarily. There is therefore no need for any feeling that anyone is making money out of the theatre except those who are employed by it.

We had a very efficient and valuable costume department before it went to the National Theatre and I still believe, despite the pessimism of some of the Board, that we could have maintained such a department with new personnel to the advantage, artistically and financially, of the theatre in the succeeding years.

Typical of the unique spirit of that costume department under Mr Ivan Alderman were the following comments from him on their association with us in those early days. Writing in the Theatre Society Newsletter in 1963 he wrote:–

Management staff 1984 1. Jack Parker 2. Jan Saunders 3. Sue Perry 4. Rosemary Burt 5. Mary Bartleet 6. Doreen Eastment 7. Gypsy Madgin 8. Norman Siviter 9. Maureen Davis-Poynter 10. Jane Brace 11. Liz Winship 12. Pat Packham 13. Sue Ward 14. Ruth Wrigley 15. Alan Cramsie 16. David Bartleet 17. Adrian Whitaker 18. Bill Green 19. Karl Meier 20. Paul Rogerson 21. Andy Neal 22. Janet Edward 23. 'Dix' Dixon 24. John Gale 25. Anthony Philo 26. Patrick Garland 27. Simon Power 28. Barbara Clark 29. Jim Boutwood 30. David Grindrod 31. Nigel Hollowell Howard 32. Tim Oliver 33. Steve O'Brien 34. Colin Hedgecock 35. John Cole 36. Sharon Cosens-Shipp 37. Ann-Marie Nichols 38. Janet Burton 39. Caroline Sharman

'A short letter, what can I say? Perhaps a few words on the human qualities needed to create successful theatre workshops will convey most and explain why we might sometimes seem unruly.

The work as a whole, combining many crafts, is enormously varied, unconventional and a constant challenge and could be accurately described as 'Interpretation'. Before work on a production can commence it must be completely designed by a designer, chosen by the director, and our work is to interpret and bring into being, materially, the imaginative pictures conjured up in the designer's mind. To enter this field of work one must possess at least a few of the following qualities. Taste, ingenuity, patience, and tolerance, a strong sensitivity towards the visual arts, a knowledge of, and a feeling for, the period decoration and the antique.

Able fingers with which to paint, sculpt, model, cut and sew and generally create, and most important of all a strong sense of humour to oil the wheels and help one over the constant obstacles and difficulties, and over persons possessing these qualities, though often charming and interesting, are usually temperamentally difficult and long ago I accepted the accusation levelled at me of being 'most difficult'. A famous director once said to me, "There is far more temperament in a costume workshop than is ever to be found among the actors and I keep as far away from it as possible."

> The range of work is extremely wide, and the costumiers must be able to produce garments in any period, from elaborately complicated court regalia and ecclesiastical paraphernalia to the briefest stripper's 'G' string. Whilst the property makers conjure up anything from jewellery and personal accessories, objets d'art and furnishings, again in any given period, to vegetation, tree growth and rock formation.
>
> The pace is usually unreasonably hectic and erratic and many turn back at the first hurdle but those who stay the course will most likely become enmeshed and dedicated; and to quote again a little memory that will always stick . . . years ago whilst raving and storming after an unreasonable and exhausting effort I'd had enough! I was getting out! I'd do anything! Any old job! I'd go that day! An old wardrobe mistress helping out in the rush, put her hand on my head saying "Don't try duckie! You'll get over it! It's an octopus and you'll never get away!"'

I well remember on one occasion when the costume department suddenly decided they would like to join in the fun of my annual Chichester Gala Day procession. They got together a float, but immediately before the procession was about to start they were still dressing up with much laughter and hysterics. After a great panic they drove into the nearby market place exactly as the head of the procession was moving out causing confusion everywhere but adding much to their hilarity. Those outside the theatrical profession certainly have a lot to learn in the art of 'winding up and winding down' as a way of relieving the tensions of modern living.

As to the actors and actresses my wife and I have met them mostly at the parties given by Lord and Lady Bessborough at their home at Stansted, and at social affairs arranged by the Society. There is always a Board party for everyone in the theatre at the end of each season. Our personal parties were held, in the early days, at our home at Trefusis on the outskirts of the city or later in our 'penny plain-twopence coloured' cellar in West Street, Chichester.

Who could forget such moments as when Fenella Fielding paused dramatically halfway down the circular stairs demonstrating wide-eyed disbelief at such a 'little theatre' cellar under a house in Chichester? There have been many other cameos such as Rex Harrison, Peter Ustinov and the Mitford Girls holding court there.

On one occasion Susan Hampshire came all the way down from London especially for the party. They always started at about 11pm at night after the evening's performance at the theatre.

It was Susan's usual thoughtfulness that made her take the journey and, again as usual, she did not have any alcoholic drink. We heard from her later that she was followed by one of our police panda cars all the way to the Surrey border where they stopped her just to have a chat! We often found the police were interested when they could see we had a party, not for any excess of duty to catch anyone (everyone was very careful) but rather, I think, to spot the stars and protect them. The local police have always been very co-operative with the theatre in keeping an eye open for unwelcome visitors or, most especially, when there were royal visitors. Very friendly relationships with the crowds on such occasions and Gala Days help to make a happy city. One officious traffic warden can do a great deal of damage.

Parties never went far into the early hours of the morning as there was generally a performance next day, as well as a matinee, and rest was essential.

I have always respected the wishes of the directors in not going into rehearsals. Olivier did invite me to go in whenever I wanted to but I only did it once. I realised it is not fair to expose players to the laity when they are being directed, openly instructed and sometimes savagely criticised. It creates a false atmosphere around the auditorium.

The players I have enjoyed meeting most at the parties are those who are ready and keen to talk about worldwide subjects as opposed to talking about themselves.

I remember a friend of mine telling me how he found himself next to John Clements at a Lord Mayor's banquet at the Mansion House. He wondered what sort of conversation he could have with someone with whom he had nothing in common. So he started off by saying, 'Tell me about yourself'. Clements replied, 'You could not have chosen a better subject'.

Those personalities of the theatre who immediately come to mind who enjoyed other subjects were Peter Ustinov (whose stories of his experiences embrace everything), Rex Harrison, the Thorndikes, Ingrid Bergman, Susan Hampshire, June H Jago, Bill Fraser, Alec Guinness, Googie Withers, John McCallum, the Michells, Keith Baxter, the Garlands, and Aubrey Woods.

Of course it is perfectly understandable why the theatrical profession is self-absorbed and self-expressive. It is an extension of their art and a defence in a very competitive world. It is absolutely necessary for them to 'sell' themselves and keep themselves prominent and well appraised. A little of it is false and insincere but necessary in a career where the future is so uncertain.

I have questioned many of the supportive artistes as to what they are going to do after the season and have been appalled by the most frequent of replies that 'they did not know but would wait for the telephone to ring'. I could not contemplate such a life but I can understand their hopefulness that one day, perhaps, the telephone will ring and fame will enter their lives such as could never happen to me. An exciting prospect for them but alas, one that seldom occurs in a profession which is said to be about 60% to 70% unemployed.

I am told that there are many parents in the district who have blamed me, or blessed me, for having brought the glamour of the theatre so near to their doorsteps, enticing their offspring into such an uncertain career.

Still we can claim some great successes. Anthony Andrews, who came to great prominence in the television version of *Brideshead Revisited* once scrubbed the stage of our theatre.

Chadborn and Stoddard have come to the forefront and Adrian Noble has made a name for himself as a director with the Royal Shakespeare Company. Edward Kemp, the son of the Bishop of Chichester, has started as a playwright and I learn that the Bishop, one of our trustees, instead of blaming me is very 'chuffed' at the idea.

I have long since learnt that like the members of the services who get posted to all parts of the world, the actors also cannot lay down roots easily, so real friendships, in passing, are seldom effective. It is best not to rely on the 'dears' and 'darlings' at parties.

One of the annual debates with directors was the question of the 'billing' of stars. To get out of the awkward, and sometimes acrimonious, demands for status billing of the various stars the directors often favoured the equal listing on posters of the whole company in a pretence that they are all equal. From a publicity point of view this is illogical. All players do not get equal salaries and those with the highest box office attraction need to be prominently advertised. As one critic pointed out, 'What is the point of giving a director special prominence and not the stars? How many of the public come to the theatre because of a well known director?' Maybe they do for a certain playwright.

In one of our surveys it was significant that the name of the play was the highest incentive for people to come; next came the attraction of the theatre itself and then the star names, not the other way round as is generally believed. People like to know something about the play they are going to see and the conditions in which they are going to see it. The attraction of seeing the acting of certain stars is the next consideration. With some world renowned stars this order of preference is, of course, reversed.

Many members of the profession, especially some directors, favour a company which achieves a working relationship for a long repertoire of plays. To my mind this involves the necessity of keeping everyone happy by letting junior members have their share of leading parts and this can reduce the general standard of the productions. I believe this was tried for a while at the Royal Shakespeare and that box office takings fell as a result. It may be hard luck on the juniors and understudies but surely their talents, if exceptional, will come to the fore eventually.

The various parties given by the citizens of the city, the cathedral and by various Mayors create the atmosphere that is Chichester. Also the great care the management takes in settling the cast into bungalows, flats and houses according to their needs. These are the reasons why so many enjoy their stay with us. Mrs Geddes who has carried out the task of finding the accommodation in a voluntary capacity succeeds in satisfying all their choices of town, country or seaside.

Sometimes she does experience a sort of musical chairs turnabout when there are a few awkward customers, but on the whole the great majority are delighted with their first allotment. There is every sort of interest that can be catered for in the district.

Sailing, fishing, athletics, swimming, sun bathing or just quiet enjoyment of the country or seaside. The famous Selsey lobsters tempted many to return on day trips to the district after they have been here for a season. Plays being on alternate days give opportunities to enjoy the attractions of the locality. What a difference from playing in a crowded metropolis.

In *Sussex by the Sea* written by Ronald Hastings, *Daily Telegraph* 20 May 1967 he remarks:–

> 'Healthy houses and cottages by the sea taken by actors near the sea, swimming, tennis and sailing, a festival cricket team which everyone takes very seriously except the stage hands who are press-ganged into helping at practice and don't care much for it.
>
> "Local pride is mounting, they are falling over themselves to lend a hand," said one of the theatre staff gaily. Even the crustiest of citizens are forgetting that six years ago they were grumbling why they couldn't have a swimming pool instead. They have the pool now anyway. Last year Clements was apprehensive, and who wouldn't be with Olivier and the National Theatre departing from the town. Most people expected Chichester to go off the boil a little after these gala opening seasons. But it didn't happen and the company goes on laughing.
>
> Actors can be heard wrestling with one another to get signed on except those more than usually hard-up who have to put up with the headaches and the bad temper of summer work in London, far from the gaiety of Sussex by the Sea and the richest part of it all is that each year the Chichester Festival Theatre gets better.'

Sybil Thorndike, at the opening of the Nuffield Theatre at Southampton University, said:–

> 'Of course when we have thought of actors performing it is pure exhibitionism, but then everyone in public life is a bit of an exhibitionist. If a professor is in a class teaching, giving out something personally, then this is the same as the theatre. If he is not an exhibitionist then all the students would be snoring in their seats.
>
> The positive thing is the need to communicate something which the actor has learned through his own body, his own mould and asking the audience to partake of the same feeling.'

There have been some interesting reactions from the players themselves about working down in Chichester. They are, generally speaking, divided into those who enjoy the unusual excitement of using the techniques of the open stage, even though most are frightened of it at first, and these are mostly in the younger sections of the profession. Some of the older ones have adapted themselves to it quickly and appreciate the chance of the experience alongside their work in the proscenium theatres. Naturally there is some difficulty for them when the play is transferred to, say, the Haymarket.

James Thomas, *Daily Express* 13 July 1967 wrote:–

> 'Now that word Prestige can put a city on the map. Why do they do it for a top whack salary of £75 a week, peanuts to steadily working actors? But it is one of the oddities of this distinguished little company that in five years this Chichester Festival Theatre has acquired such world prestige that they are prepared to lead this frantic existence whilst the city dreams and ambles around them.
>
> The festival is now a 'must' for managements the world over to whom this efficient pillbox of a theatre in the round has become a magnet for talent and production techniques. And the actors actually enjoy it.
>
> They ask to come back next year to this grim slog. For where else can they exchange the remote anonymity of walking out of a drab stage door into a dark West End alley for the delight of sunbathing between calls on long lawns a few yards from the stage.
>
> Where else can actresses like Irene Worth take a five minute car ride from the theatre to a cottage with roses round the door? It is great to have parts which don't chuck one down into the vortex of so many inferior West End plays and there are not many theatres when an actor can find a challenge these days.'

Maggie Smith said in an interview in the *Daily Express* 14 September 1969 entitled 'Maggie and that dramatic lure of the great outdoors':–

> 'The unfathomable magic of Chichester that pulls her (Maggie Smith) back for the third time. You forget about the money when you walk out of a stage door and find yourself in a field instead of the Waterloo Road. We have had member of the National Theatre here who have started to ride around on bikes when they had only been used to a London bus for years. They actually realised they were healthy.
>
> But there is a lot more to it than sniffing the air and finding yourself a long way from the dreary streets which encompass an actress. This Chichester theatre, which has an apron stage with the audience on three sides, makes all our performers better artistes. They go back to London with stronger voices and they are much more capable of projecting themselves to a public which has got used to the more natural look of television.
>
> I went up to London the other day for a few hours. Suddenly I realised what noise and confusion there was. I thought about the film stars who make a fortune and have to go on doing it just to keep up with the tax man. That didn't make sense either.'

All companies, such as the Royal Shakespeare and the National have their 'occurrences' and we have had our share.

In the early days there was a time when births seemed to predominate. The Oliviers increased their family and Joan Greenwood had to depart from the second season of *Uncle Vanya* when she had a child. Joan Anderson had the same idea and I began to think we should have to abandon the idea of building a scene dock in favour of a maternity ward!

During the years there have been several romances. One of the usherettes left for Canada to marry one of the Ontario company who had come to the theatre in 1964; another much later married Christopher Timothy. I was told several marriages were rescued when the theatre opened up a new interest to one of the partners; one person suddenly found life was exciting after all and a suicide was prevented. So besides giving a lot of happiness to many thousands of people, the theatre we created has done a great deal of good. As will be seen from the list of concerts many charities have benefitted by gala concerts and performances specially arranged for them. Their funds would have been far less if the theatre had not been built to provide a place where these events could be staged.

Injuries are one of the occupational hazards which affect theatres and the people who work in it. I have recalled how Ian Ogilvy fell through a barrel and Laurence Harvey broke his leg. Dandy Nicholls in 1977 found the uneven flag stones of a newly built city precinct a danger and fell on several occasions. One actress was out of her part for some days after a piano she was moving fell on her feet and another actress fell from her horse.

In 1980 Ann Dews, wife of Peter Dews, broke her leg in a car accident. During a performance of *The Mitford Girls* a mirror ball dropped within inches of Patricia Michael when it was being flown out of position. I suppose over twenty-two years we have been lucky to have had so few incidents though all of them were minor disasters at the time.

On one occasion a Sunday concert was disrupted by the late appearance of the majority of the orchestra. Floods in the surrounding counties meant that their arrival by cars was at varying intervals, so the audience had the added interest of seeing shamefaced musicians creeping into the orchestra and joining in to supplement those who had arrived on time. It was the reverse to the fading away of an orchestra playing *Haydn's Farewell Symphony*.

As everyone realises theatres cannot exist on just what happens on the stage in view of the audience. Backstage inefficiencies could mar any performance and many are the stories of great performances let down by faulty scenery mechanism or properties forgotten to be placed by assistant stage managers. Therefore all depends on the chiefs of each department.

After eight years at the Royal Court Theatre Bill Green has occupied the position of general stage director since 1967, the second year of Clement's directorship. He is the invaluable 'king-pin' of the whole organisation and it would be difficult to find anyone to fill that role as painstakingly and with such a calm demeanour.

Bill Bray is another stalwart as chief technician. General maintenance of lighting and sound are the minor parts of his responsibility. He has had to deal with the teething troubles of three lighting consoles, each more intricate than the one it replaced. As we have been to the forefront each time we have changed the system we have always been the most up-to-date in the country, and thereby we have received the worst of the initial difficulties by having the prototypes. Proud of possessing the latest, it is disheartening to be told in a very few years that the system is out of date.

Many other theatres must find, as we do, the annoyance caused by visiting concert artistes, especially 'rock' stars who insist on using their own sound amplification. Time and again we have been criticised for faulty sound reproduction with microphones breaking down or being distorted. Our sound system is one of the finest, like the lighting, and the fault lies in the visiting groups or concert artistes.

Janet Edward and Ray Mansell, box office manager and front of house manager repectively, are excellent examples of our staff who seem to look upon the theatre as their own, caring as much for it as those who work voluntarily.

Paul Rogerson is one of the personalities of the theatre. Quiet, modest and at times retiring he seems to be the friend of everyone both in our organisation and in all the district around. Talented musically he has a great ability in finding first rate artistes for the concerts.

David Bartleet has been the accountant since 1966. Meticulous, as all financial minds must be, he is able to supply any information the Board members require and this is essential as all members keep a very detailed interest in the financial affairs of the company.

Anne Hillier was the publicity/public relations officer until 1981. She was the exciting personality who kept the life of the theatre 'peppered up' all the year round. Proof of her worth was revealed when all the critics combined to give her a farewell party and a gift. The many parties held in her honour by the Board, the local editors and television companies went on for two weeks.

Lord Cudlipp, since he joined the Board, has taken a keen interest in the publicity side of affairs for us. He devised the idea of a newspaper that appears twice a year and is distributed free in the local *Promoter* newspaper to a very wide district around Chichester. It is also supplied to all members of the Society and in all totals 130,000 copies. His expertise so freely given is extremely valuable as a result of his long and varied journalistic career.

Continuing our policy of 'going out to the public' Mrs Maureen Davis-Poynter spends all her time promoting the theatre by talks to organisations all over the south of England, interesting people in the plays and demonstrating the costumes of some of the productions. In a very friendly way she organises some of the ladies in her audiences to model the costumes and has many amusing stories when the largest will insist on trying to get into the smallest dresses.

In a theatre such as ours there can be no demarcations. Many help the members of the cast with their personal difficulties. Waiting for them at hospitals, taking them to fêtes, cricket matches and beauty contests, or playing tennis with them and standing in as dressers. Stopping nose bleeders and getting remedies for 'hang-overs'. The many behind the scenes crises that the public never see or hear about. There is never a dull moment in the theatre world.

So much for the supporting staff, and volunteers, unfortunately too many to mention individually.

I have explained in *The Impossible Theatre* how the Theatre Society was first suggested by the late Robertson-Ritchie. It has gone from strength to strength over the years and the membership now varies between 12–15,000. It started at 2,000.

The one person who has been constant throughout its history, ably backed by Mrs Ruth Wrigley, has been its secretary Mr Norman Siviter. Whilst chairmen, treasurers and members of the committee come and go he has gone on for ever. Quiet, unassuming, hating to be brought into the limelight, or to be thanked, he has maintained a loyalty to the ideals of the theatre from the time before it was built. Whatever the disagreements he must have had with the decisions of the committees, he determinedly put them aside and awaited his time to get the committees 'back on the rails'. No Society could have had a finer secretary.

Without the financial help the Society has been able to give, the theatre would have been far worse off and the struggles to keep the building and equipment up-to-date might have been impossible to overcome. Besides their many gifts of money, the priority booking of members means we have an early influx of money for the season and they are particularly helpful in booking for the slacker times such as the early parts of the week and the beginning of the season.

Many theatres have large mailing lists. How many have a theatre society of such a large membership who willingly pay £3 a year subscriptions (at the present time) to get priority booking and advance notices of all events? Once again 'going out to the public' rather than expecting them 'to come in'. Theatres must sell their goods just like any other industry and not just rely upon newspaper advertisements and posters.

CHAPTER 13
Special Occasions

The spice of life is when something special happens that breaks the routine and gives cause for pageantry and jubilation. All theatres have their openings, their anniversaries and their visits from distinguished people.

In the first two years we were lucky enough to have more than the usual share of royal visits. It was, I think, a combination of the attraction of Olivier and the new unique form of theatre (in England) which had aroused so much discussion.

Those who have experienced it know the glamour and the anxiety such visits cause and that splendid relaxed feeling of relief when it is all over and all went well. I have planned and organised all of these but, like making speeches, each situation is new and nervous-making. The initial approach was through the Lord Lieutenant and the waiting period is caused by the engagement-fixing meetings which members of the royal family are rumoured to have at certain times.

Then comes the letter saying the dates are agreed and there are the subsequent meetings with members of the royal household, generally one of the ladies-in-waiting, at Buckingham Palace or Kensington Palace. Next were the meetings with the chief executive of the County Council and combined meetings with the police and, in the case of a charity, with the organisers of the charity.

The next stages are the delicate discussions on who will be in the welcoming party, how the foyer will be cleared in time, who will present the bouquet (and what it will be), what number of attendants or representatives of the organisation will be in the reception party and who will line the foyer to the correct entrance door, who will conduct the party to their seats, hoping against hope that no member of the audience has sat in them by mistake (as happened on one occasion when the party arrived back from the interval) and the exact time of the National Anthem when the party is in position.

In the early days there was the anxiety of herding the party, in the interval, out to the marquee, later replaced by the Green Room, where once again begins the difficulty of shepherding those persons who have previously been informed they will be presented. The formal signing of the visitor's book carefully guarded by someone made responsible for its safekeeping until I could place it in the bank again, not forgetting a suitable pen (always my own fountain pen), followed by forceful persuasion of everyone to return to the auditorium whilst the visitors have a few minutes for any snatched refreshment and their other comforts.

At the end of a performance before we had the Green Room, where all the artistes and chief backstage personnel now hurriedly assemble, there was a difficulty in escorting the visitors to a dressing room to give time for the assembly of everyone on the stage. Finally came the departure and farewell handshakes to the designated people and away go the fleet of cars. With the rear lights disappearing out of sight a great sigh goes up. Do we enjoy it all? Of course we do in a super sensitive sort of way.

We did have one or two small hitches such as the late upholstering of the seats when the Queen came. Princess Margaret had a very unpleasant bumpy ride in the helicopter when she came, so much so that she had to cancel dinner at the Bessboroughs to which we had been invited.

At the second visit of the Queen the royal party arrived early due to a mistiming by one of the officials and an easy run from Arundel Castle.

There was panic among the management getting the people to move into the auditorium (so many wanting to see the arrival of the party) and getting the guard of honour lined up in the foyer. We managed it by delaying Her Majesty's entrance into the foyer. Luckily the weather was fine. The Duke of Norfolk later asked me to see that it was better organised another time. I had to inform him very tactfully that we were on time but the party arrived early. Our timing has always been meticulous but the timing in Sussex during the holiday period is very much a matter of luck as to where congestions could occur.

Princess Alexandra has, we like to think, a special relationship with our theatre ever since she laid the foundation stone in 1961. Her Royal Highness always brings with her a lively and joyful atmosphere to which everyone succumbs. Her mother, the late Princess Marina, so enjoyed her many visits and the Princess seems to have the same enjoyment of our productions.

One very special occasion was when Her Royal Highness attended our twenty-first celebrations on 2 July 1982. I organised it to be, as near as possible, like our very first opening night. First a thanksgiving service in the cathedral in the afternoon with magnificent singing by the choir under the direction of the organist and choirmaster, Alan Thurlow, before a crowded congregation. The sermon was preached by the theatre's chaplain Canon Greenacre. Unfortunately Princess Alexandra was unable to attend this because of a previous engagement but a large number of the company was present.

In the evening the Princess arrived accompanied by Lavinia, Duchess of Norfolk, our Patron and Lord Lieutenant. The usual presentation took place, the bouquet being presented by my grandson Justin, and the usherettes formed a guard of honour. A normal performance of *Valmouth* took place and I think the Princess was as bemused with the story as was everyone else, except that she had obviously read as much as was available about it before she came. I tried to answer her questions as best I could. At the end Her Royal Highness spoke to all of the cast and backstage staff making them all feel they were individually of interest to her.

Finally we escorted her to armchair seats, provided by the Royal Military Police under the supervision of their Commandant Lt Col 'Jumbo' Wood, to watch a mounted 'Skill-at-Arms' display under floodlights by the Military Police. In 1962 it was the Royal Sussex Regiment who gave a military display.

The Princess left as the firework display started and this was just about midnight. The theatre had invited all the citizens of Chichester to come and watch the display and the fireworks. Unfortunately we were about an hour later than we had expected to be and so we sat, wrapped in blankets, watching the most marvellous display Chichester has ever seen in modern times. I was horrified as the huge explosions rent the air.

As I settled down to watch the display I had to say to myself 'It has started and nothing can stop it', though I imagined the trouble we should have afterwards fom the usual people who love to snipe but I felt we should deserve the criticism as the noise was terrific. We had warned the nearby hospitals of the display and naturally thought the public at large knew of it, especially as so many of them had come to see it. And those who came did enjoy it.

There were a few letters in the press, of course, but not as many as I had expected and one or two councillors took the opportunity 'to have a go' at us by saying it must never happen again.

Christopher Fry presented us with his particular celebration of our twenty-first anniversary.

CHICHESTER '82

Twenty-one years ago the work was started
In a green place in May – the time when earth
After winter's folding grows open-hearted
And makes from inward life a summer's birth.
An amphitheatre rose, and so, each May
Since the foundation stone was laid, has come
As though in celebration of that day
The audience's anticipating hum,
The actors' exploration of a play.

The twenty-first season comes of age,
Almost a new generation's span;
Those who were infants on the world's wide stage
Have become lovers since this work began.
One era gone, another one ensues:
Olivier, Clements, then Michell and Dews
Linking the play of years with years of plays
Garlanded now to meet the approaching days.

Oedipus Rex statue (Raymond Clements)

18 July 1982 brought another great evening in the theatre. We were to have had a special star-studded Sunday night concert in aid of our building fund but this was replaced by a similar one, by request of the company, for the South Atlantic Fund to aid those engaged in the fight against the Argentinian aggression on the Falkland Islands.

This was a tremendous night when the stars named below appeared, backed by the band of HM Royal Marines C in C Naval Home Command. It was staged by Roger Redfarn with choreographers Tudor Davies and Lindsay Dolan.

Those who appeared were:– the cast of *Underneath the Arches*, Christopher Timothy; the cast of *Valmouth*, Roy Hudd, Doris Hare, Fenella Fielding, Aubrey Woods, with members of the Royal Military Police and their Commandant Lt Col W. R. Wood, Petula Clark; the cast of the *Mitford Girls*, Arthur English, Bertice Reading, Peter Glaze, Terry Scott, June Whitfield, Patrick Garland, Keith Baxter, Sir Robert Helpmann, Sir John Mills and Chief Petty Officer David Rumsey of HMS Coventry, a member of the Falklands Force.

The finale with the band and the Chichester Cathedral choir singing, with the audience, the hymn 'Eternal Father', 'Rule Britannia', 'Land of Hope and Glory', and the 'National Anthem' was a very moving and emotional drama. £15,500 was raised for the fund.

Another exciting evening was on the occasion of the Queen's Silver Jubilee. I organised this with Lavinia, Duchess of Norfolk, and after many meetings with her, Gordon Honeycombe and Martin Jenkins, a programme was devised with the following stars on Sunday 12 June 1977.

In the presence of HRH Princess Alexandra and the Duchess the London Sinfonietta accompanied the stars in cavalcade through a royal progress from 1464 to the present time.

In order of appearance John Clements, Martin Jarvis, John Moffat, Maureen O'Brien, Gary Bond, Paul Hardwick, Christine Matthews, Keith Michell, Ingrid Bergman, Charles Lloyd Peck, Nigel Stock, Jeanette Sterke, Alfred Marks, Diana Rigg, Paul Jones, Kenneth Alwyn, Caroline Van Hemert, Flora Robson, Sarah Badel, Joan Sims, Brigette Kahn, Reginald Bosanquet, Gordon Honeycombe, Penelope Keith, Hannah Gordon, Marc Urquhart, Sian Phillips, Wendy Hillier, Angela Rippon, Cicely Courtneidge, ending with a sonnet on the Coronation of Queen Elizabeth II written and read by Christopher Fry.

Lavinia, Duchess of Norfolk, was delighted to receive the £10,000 profit from the concert for her special appeal for the Silver Jubilee Fund; another example of the theatre aiding so many charities by large amounts of money through concerts, special performances and other functions.

There have been a great many gatherings of school children and parents for school prize givings, music festivals for the Chichester and district primary schools, West Sussex Youth Orchestras, fashion shows, magic circle shows, choral oratorios such as *The Messiah*, jazz festivals, circuses (without animals) recitals, one-man studies of Dickens, Beecham and Kipling all listed in the index of this book.

On 16 March Patrick Garland managed to persuade Princess Grace of Monaco to appear at the theatre in a programme of poetry and prose with John Westbrook. The programme, devised by John Carroll, was a very polished sophisticated affair. A mixture of comedy, drama and above all of beauty as befitted Princess Grace. It was her only concert in England that year and, I suppose, her very last as she was so tragically killed in a car crash in September. We were privileged to have seen and heard her on our stage.

CHAPTER 14
The Future

What of the future? My fears are that as it becomes more managed by professionals our theatre could easily lose its personality and become like many other theatres outside London. Will the voluntary spirit, the pioneering spirit we had at the beginning, be replaced by officialdom and tight-minded bureaucracy? On one occasion when I was discussing the possibility of a competition to design a fountain for the theatre, a junior member of the Arts Council staff was convulsed with laughter when I suggested it should be one which depicted a tribute to 'voluntary service'. This was a typical reaction from a civil servant. It was the belief, already implanted in him, that any voluntary effort was to be despised until such time as it was needed when all bureaucratic methods had failed.

This attitude in the Arts Council was further typified by the negligence of their officials to answer any letters from members of the Board who, like myself, worked in a voluntary way, whereas they readily answered letters from the officials.

In the future will ideals be, or have to be, forgotten for the sake of hard-headed financial considerations? I fear these things because throughout the years I have, time and time again, fought these issues on the Board sometimes single-handed and sometimes with a few supporters. Everyone has ideals but the use of 'fear' of imminent bankruptcy as a weapon is ever present and has so often proved to be false.

Prices of seats has been a constant battle. They are too often compared with the inflated prices of the London subsidised or commercial theatres. The oft-repeated warning of Dr Read, a member of the Board, that we should remember the moral of 'diminishing returns' is difficult to prove correct as the number of people booking fewer plays is constantly disguised by any additional revenue resulting from the increase of seat prices. Loss of goodwill is impossible to calculate in pounds and pence. I have been able to measure, to some extent, the feelings of our patrons by the letters I receive and the ebb and flow of donations.

It is necessary to have a well-balanced Board to include hard headed financial minds to keep the finances stabilised. There must also be a good proportion of far-sighted idealists who, nevertheless, have 'their feet on the ground'.

I have already mentioned the ever-recurring debate on artistic control, keeping the theatre unique and different from other provincial theatres.

Also the free programme, the welcoming staff, the avoidance of extravagance resulting from subsidies and sponsorships.

I am horrified, when I read the agendas of so many of the organisations I have helped, to see some of the old arguments and issues going on for ever and ever. If only some issues could be barred from discussion for a period of time, once they have been decided, a lot of time would be saved.

This theatre has been successful because it was different in stage presentation, situated in a park in a district that didn't know it needed a theatre, also because we have given, so far, considerable attention to features which the public like and want, and because, until now, it has been able to be independently self-supporting.

My hope is that the aforementioned fears will be remembered and counteracted. I hope reserves will be built up in the years to come, to take away the financial risks so that a more adventurous outlook can be under-

Five directors in the theatre with author. Peter Dews, John Gale, Keith Michell, Patrick Garland, the author (founder) and Lord Olivier (Portsmouth & Sunderland Newspapers)

taken. So many people request us to have plays by Shakespeare but the box office receipts show that people do not fully support them. New plays are few and far between because there is a paucity of new playwrights and when such plays are presented our public is wary of them.

I hope we shall get back to the standards of true drama such as we had at the beginning and that the public will find in them great enjoyment for entertainment is our aim and object.

Above all, I hope the stage will be used more and more as a three dimensional open stage. This means the selection of plays that are really suited to it. After twenty-one years it must be very obvious to everyone that too many plays best suited to the picture-frame proscenium stage, have been tried at Chichester. Too many tailor-made for future presentation on the London stages, too much scenery, too little symbolism. Whilst our sound effects have always been used with full effect the finest lighting system has not been used often as an interpretative media.

I hope, and it may be a forlorn hope, that the plays selected will not be those which are constructed as propaganda for any extremist idealogical purpose, whatever that ideology may be, or those which insidiously promote the present decadence of the country's morale. By that I mean nutrition of the canker which is eating into the British character.

By all means let the people be stimulated into thinking of some of the contemporary problems but this does not mean the theatre needs to indulge the baser feelings by raking amongst the sordid side of life which some of the playwrights, and some of the documentaries on television, have now succeeded in achieving to the lowest degree. There is so much beauty in life which need not be labelled as 'whimsy'.

As already has been said, this theatre is at its best with spectacular presentations not so easily portrayed in other theatres and I hope there will always be sufficient money to enable us to do them.

As long as the old-fashioned prejudice against open stages by some critics remains, theatres such as ours will still be held back from their rightful fulfilment. The public have proved they enjoy our theatre and are prepared to back it financially. It now only needs support from sponsors to establish it permanently and I believe this will come.

I look forward to the establishment of permanent buildings for the restaurant and Society Room but above all to the building of a studio theatre such as the ones attached to the National and Royal Shakespeare Companies and many other eminent theatres. Such small flexible theatres give the younger players, designers and producers opportunities they would not otherwise have.

If only it could be fitted up for the use of orchestras and have full facilities for plays, this would be a tremendous help to the amateurs, to small travelling companies and to solo artistes for the whole of the West Sussex area. If only there were some benefactor to make this possible sooner than later.

I hope there will be possibilities for us to commission plays and try out experimental plays, not an anti-everything beehive but one which promotes the best of playwriting for the sake of excellence alone.

I also trust we shall be able to up-grade the surrounds of the theatre with examples of sculpture and a fountain to give the atmosphere a living quality.

The area must never become a museum, a slumbering monument to the 1962 ideals and endeavours, but it must always have the fresh air of the park blowing through it bringing not the dying autumn but the hopeful spring around and into the theatre itself. To live out the rest of the ninety-nine year lease it needs to have frequent injections of new ideas and inventions. No dust and no cobwebs.

APPENDIX I

Plays and Players 1971–1984

For productions 1962/1970 see *The Impossible Theatre*

Play	*Author*	*Director*	*Designer*	*Percentage*	*Leading Players*
1971					
The Rivals	Sheridan	John Clements	Carl Toms	84	Margaret Leighton, John Clements, Angela Scoular, Joanna David, Polly Adams, Peter Egan, Edward Fox, Hubert Gregg, Clive Swift, John Tordoff, Keith McClellan, Brian Hughes
Dear Antoine	Jean Anouilh	Robin Phillips	Ann Tagg	92	Edith Evans, Joyce Redman, Renee Ascherson, Jane Baxter, Polly Adams, Joanna David, Peggy Marshall, John Clements, Michael Aldridge, Hubert Gregg, Clive Swift, Peter Egan, Harold Innocent, Paul Hastings, James Faulkner
Caesar and Cleopatra	Bernard Shaw	Robin Phillips	Carl Toms	95	John Guilgud, Anna Calder-Marshall, Pat Nye, Elroy Josephs, Charles Pinner, Brian Hayes, John Garretty, Harold Innocent, Michael Aldridge, Hubert Gregg, Peter Harlow, James Faulkner, David Sinclair, Peter Egan
Reunion in Vienna	Sherwood	Frith Banbury	Carl Toms	96	Peggy Marshall, Keith McClellan, Margaret Leighton, Michael Aldridge, Charles Lloyd Peck, Janet Lees Price, Paul Hastings, Beatrice Lehmann, John Regan, Pat Nye, Brian Hayes, John Tordoff, Nigel Patrick, Jane Hillary, Harold Innocent, Mary Hignett, Louis Hesler, Dennis Barry
1972					
The Beggar's Opera	John Gay	Robin Phillips	Daphne Dare	91	Harold Innocent, Maggir Fitzgibbon, Millicent Martin, John Neville, June Jago, Michael Aldridge, Angel Richards
The Doctor's Dilemma	Bernard Shaw	John Clements	Michael Warre	92	John Neville, Michael Aldridge, John Clements, Joan Plowright, Robin Phillips, Angela Richards, William Mervyn
The Taming of the Shrew	William Shakespeare	Jonathan Miller	Patrick Robertson and Rosemary Vercoe	94	Joan Plowright, Anthony Hopkins, William Mervyn, Brian Hayes, Harold Innocent
The Lady's not for Burning	Christopher Fry	Robin Phillips	Daphne Dare	97	Richard Chamberlain, Kim Braden, Richard Cornish, June Jago, Michael Aldridge, Harold Innocent, Anna Calder-Marshall, Brian Hayes, Leslie French

1973					
The Director of the Opera	Jean Anouilh	Peter Dews	Alan Tagg	75	John Clements, Richard Pearson, Penelope Wilton, Alan Brown, Anthony Corlan, June Jago, Maureen O'Brien, Ciarian Madden
The Seagull	Anton Chekhov	Jonathan Miller	Patrick Robertson	72	Irene Worth, Robert Stephens, Richard Pearson, Ralph Michael, Maureen O'Brien, Peter Eyre
***R Loves J**	Peter Ustinov	Wendy Toye	Tim Goodchild	96	Topol, Dudley Stevens, Richard Owens, Robert Coleman, Pip Hinton, David Watson, Rosemary Williams
Dandy Dick	Arthur Pinero	John Clements	Alan Tagg	97	Gemma Craven, Charles Lloyd Peck, Peter Eyre, Alastair Sim, Patricia Routledge, Lucinda Gane, Barry McGinn
1974					
Tonight We Improvise	Luigi Pirandello	Peter Coe	Anthony Powell	70	Keith Michell, Keith Baxter, Alfred Marks, Miriam Karlin, June Ritchie, Annie Ross
The Confederacy	John Vanbrugh	Wendy Toye	Anthony Powell	90	Peggy Mount, Peter Gilmore, Patsy Byrne, Dora Bryan, Jeanette Sterke, Gemma Craven, Richard Wattis, Nicholas Clay
Oidipus Tyrannus	Sophocles	Houkinness Pilikian	Ralph Koltai	65	David King, Keith Michell, Alfred Marks, Diana Dors, Willoughby Goddard, Richard Greene
A Month in the Country	Ivan Turgenev	Toby Robertson	Robin Archer	85	Patience Collier, Dorothy Tutin, Dereck Jacobi, Timothy West, Gemma Craven, Kay Barlow, John Turner
1975					
Cyrano de Bergerac	Edmund Rostand	Jose Ferrer	John Bloomfield	77	Christopher Cazenov, Bill Fraser, Trevor Martin, Barbara Jefford, Peggy Marshall, Keith Michell, David Willis
An Enemy of the People	Ibsen	Patrick Garland	Stephano Lazaridis	70	Donald Sinden, Barbara Jefford, Donald Houston, Bill Fraser, Peggy Marshall, Tony Robinson, Sue Jones-Davis
Made in Heaven	Andrew Sachs	Wendy Toye	John Gunter	78	Patricia Routledge, Michael Bates, Patrick McNee, June Jago, Tony Robinson, Peter Bland
Othello	William Shakespeare	Peter Dews	Finlay James	89	Topol, Hannah Gordon, Christopher Cazenov, Keith Michell, Patricia Routledge, Sue Jones-Davis, David Williams, Rex Robinson, Trevor Martin

1976					
Noah	Andrey Obey	Eric Thompson	Paul Staples	62	Gordon Jackson, Patsy Byrne, Charles Keating, David Yip, Martin Chamberlain, Deborah Grant, Cryl Branker, Jane Morant
Twelfth Night	William Shakespeare	Keith Michell	Paul Staples and Keith Michell	90	Charles Keating, Christopher Selbie, Michele Dotrice, Bill Fraser, Barbara Windsor, Andrew Sachs, Jeanette Sterke, Gordon Fraser, David Henry
The Circle	Somerset Maugham	Peter Dews	Finlay James	97	Martin Jarvis, Lee Hudson, Susan Hampshire, Clive Francis, John McCullum, Googie Withers, Bill Fraser
Monsieur Perrichon's Travels	Labiche and Martin	Patrick Garland	Eileen Diss	96	Rex Harrison, June Jago, Deborah Grant, Clive Francis, Andrew Sachs, Keith Michell, Christopher Selbie, Michael Cotterill, Bill Fraser, Tony Robinson
1977					
Waters of the Moon	N. C. Winter	John Clements	Alan Tagg	97	Adam Bareham, Maureen O'Brien, Wendy Hillier, Dandy Nicholls, Charles Lloyd Peck, Ingrid Bergman, Brigette Kahn, Paul Hardwick
In Order of Appearance	Wally Dale and Keith Michell	Keith Michell	Paul Stephens	84	Paul Jones, Elizabeth Seal, Joan Sims, Norman Vaughan, John Moffat, Tony Robinson
Julius Caesar	William Shakespeare	Peter Dews	Finlay James	75	Nigel Stock, Gary Bond, Charles Kay, Paul Hardwick, Charles Keating, Vernon Doubtcheff
The Apple Cart	Bernard Shaw	Patrick Garland	Eileen Diss	98	Penelope Keith, Keith Michell, Nigel Stock, Dandy Nichols, Adam Bareham, Paul Hardwick, Brigette Kahn, June Jago, Jeanette Sterke, Vernon Doubtcheff
1978					
A Woman of No Importance	Oscar Wilde	Patrick Garland	Peter Farmer	96	Gayle Hunnicut, Margaretta Scott, Keith Baxter, Tim Woodward, Ambosine Philpotts, Barbara Murray, Rosie Kerslake
The Aspern Papers	Henry James	David Williams		89	Jill Bennett, Cathleen Nesbit, Kenneth Haigh, Keith Drinkel
Look After Lulu	Noel Coward and Georges Feydeau	Patrick Garland	Carl Toms	96	Geraldine McEwan, Clive Francis, Nigel Stock, Kenneth Haigh, Fenella Fielding, George Howe
The Inconstant Couple	Pierre de Marivaux	Noel Williams	Bob Ringwood	76	Keith Baxter, Sian Phillips, Morag Hood, Tim Woodward, John Warner

1979					
The Devil's Disciple	Bernard Shaw	Peter Dews	Sally Gardner	86	Ian Ogilvy, John Clements, Mel Martin, David Glover, Vanessa Kempster, John Gill
The Eagle Has Two Heads	Jean Couteau	David William	Clive Savangna	70	Jill Bennett, Thomas Baptiste, Brian Blessed, Heather Chasen, Michael Malnick
The Importance of Being Earnest	Oscar Wilde	Peter Dews	Finlay James	99	Ian Ogilvy, Michael Cochrane, Hayley Mills, Mel Martin, Googie Withers, John Clements
The Man Who Came to Dinner	George Kaufman and Moss Hart	Patrick Lau	Anthony Holland	99	Jill Bennett, Charles Gray, Patsy Byrne, Thomas Baptiste, Vanessa Kempster, Barry Justice, Barbara Murray
1980					
The Last of Mrs Cheyney	Frederick Lonsdale	Patrick Lau	Susie Calcutt	96	Joan Collins, Simon Williams, Moyra Fraser, Elspeth March, Benjamin Whitrow, Charles Rogers
***Terra Nova**	Ted Tally	Peter Dews	Pamela Howard	61	Hywel Bennett, Martin Sadler, Peter Birch, David Wood, Benjamin Whitrow, Helen Ryan
Much Ado About Nothing	William Shakespeare	Peter Dews	Finlay James	70	Gerald Harper, Donald Eccles, Peter Birch, Gemma Jones, Martin Sadler, Peter Sallis
Old Heads and Young Hearts	Dion Bouccault and Peter Sallis	Michelle Simpson	Eileen Diss	88	Donald Eccles, Sally Bowers, Christopher Strauli, Lewis Fiander, Judy Parfitt, Paul Ridley, Frank Windsor
1981					
The Cherry Orchard	Anton Chekhov	Patrick Garland	Maria Bjomson	67	Claire Bloom, Joss Ackland, Sarah Badel, Emryn James, Angela Pleasance, Christopher Timothy, Lockwood West
Feasting with Panthers	Oscar Wilde	Peter Coe	Peter Coe	68	Tom Baker, Donald Houston, Lockwood West, Aubrey Woods, Frank Shelley
The Mitford Girls	Caryl Brahms, Ned Sherrin, Peter Greenwell	Patrick Garland	Stefanos Lazaridis	94	Patricia Hodge, Gay Soper, Liz Robertson, Julia Sutton, Patricia Michael, Oz Clarke, Colette Gleeson
***Underneath the Arches**	Brian Glenville and Patrick Garland	Roger Redfarn	Terry Parsons	88	Chesney Allen, Christopher Timothy, Roy Hudd, Joe Black, Peter Glaze, Tommy Godfrey, Billy Gray, Don Smoothey, Julia Sutton

1982					
On the Rocks	Bernard Shaw	Jack Emery and Patrick Garland	Pamela Howard	75	Keith Michell, Glynis Johns, Arthur English, Nigel Stock, Sue Withers, Aubrey Woods, Jeanette Sterke, Cheryl Kennedy, Jean Marsh, Lockwood West
Valmouth	Sandy Wilson	John Dexter	Andrew and Margaret Brownfoot	67	Bertice Reading, Fenella Fielding, Doris Hare
***Cavell**	Keith Baxter	Patrick Garland	Peter Rice	67	Joan Plowright, Dulcie Gray, Nigel Stock, Frank Shelley, Aubrey Woods, Alexandra Bastedo, Philip Madoc
Goodbye Mr Chipps	Roland Starke	Patrick Garland and Christopher Selbie	Peter Rice	92	John Mills, Cheryl Kennedy, Paul Hardwick, Nigel Stock, Colette Gleeson, Maria Ashton
1983					
A Patriot For Me	John Osborne	Ronald Eyre	Carl Toms	69	Alan Bates, George Muriell, Nigel Stock, Jo Webster, Sheila Gish, Nicholas Gecks, Gregory Floy
Time and the Conways	J. B. Priestley	Peter Dews	Finlay James	87	Googie Withers, Julia Foster, Eunice Roberts, Andrew Hawkins, Alexandra Bastedo, Simon Williams
As You Like It	William Shakespeare	Patrick Garland	Robin Fraser Paye	63	Patricia Hodge, Lucy Fleming, Jonathan Morris, John Geste, Aubrey Woods, Frank Shelley
The Sleeping Prince	Terence Rattigan	Peter Coe	Peter Rice	96	Omar Sharif, Judy Campbell, Nancy Nevinson, Frank Shelley, John Moffatt, Debbie Arnold
1984					
Forty Years On	Alan Bennett	Patrick Garland	Peter Rice	86	Paul Eddington, Doris Hare, John Fortune, Stephen Fry, Annette Crosbie
Oh, Kay	Guy Bolton, P. G. Wodehouse, Ned Sherrin, Tony Geiss, George Gershwin	Ian Judge	Peter Rice, Peter Farmer	84	Jane Carr, Edward Hibbert, Michael Sherry, Geoffrey Hutchings, Josephine Blake, Myra Sands
The Merchant of Venice	William Shakespeare	Patrick Garland	Pamela Howard	93	Alec Guinness, Frank Shelley, Jeremy Hawk, Burt Caesar, Martin Chamberlain, Richard Warwick, David Yelland, Joanna McCallum, Jane Carr, Leslee Udwin
The Way of the World	William Congreve	William Gaskill	Hayden Griffin, Deirdre Clancy	86	Joan Plowright, Maggie Smith, John Moffat, Hugh Fraser, Ian Hogg, Geoffrey Hutchings

*World Premieres

APPENDIX II
Royal Visits

1962–1968 HRH Princess Marina visited nearly all the productions
1961 HRH Princess Alexandra laid Foundation Stone
1962 HM The Queen and HRH Prince Philip – *Uncle Vanya* (12 May)
1963 HRH Princess Margaret and Lord Snowdon – *St. Joan* (25 June)
1964 HRH Queen Elizabeth The Queen Mother – *Love's Labour's Lost* (1 April)
HM The Queen and HRH Prince Philip – *Othello* (29 July)
1968 HRH Princess Alexandra – *Skin of our Teeth* (20 July)
1971 HRH Princess Margaret – *The Rivals* (13 May)
1977 HRH Princess Alexandra at Queens Silver Jubilee concert (12 June)
1981 HRH Prince and Princess Michael of Kent – *The Mitford Girls* (17 July)
1982 HRH Queen Elizabeth The Queen Mother – *Underneath the Arches* London (9 March)
HRH Princess Alexandra – Theatre's 21st celebration (2 July)
1984 HRH Princess Margaret – *Merchant of Venice* (10 July)

APPENDIX III

List of some of the artistes who have appeared in the Concerts and Recitals 1962–1984 Arranged by Paul Rogerson

Max Adrian; Apollo Society; Vladimir Ashkenazy; David Attenborough; Danny Abse; Amadeus String Quartet; Victoria de los Angeles; Academy of St Martin in the Field; The Aeolian Consort; Augstin Anievas; Claudio Arrau; Alexeyev Balalaika Ensemble; Kenneth Alwyn; Australian Youth Ballet; Rowan Atkinson; Allegri String Quartet; Sheila Armstrong; Antonia de Almeida.

John Barton; Sir John Barbirolli; Brighton Youth Orchestra; Sir Adrian Boult; Bath Festival Orchestra; John Birch; Janet Baker; Stephen Bishop; Harry Blech; Julian Bream; Neil Black; Bournemouth Symphony Orchestra; Alejardo Barletto; Willie Boskovsky; Daniel Barenboim; Acker Bilk; Charlie Byrd; James Bowman; Alfred Brendel; Beaux Arts Trio; Black Theatre of Prague; Kenny Ball Jazzmen; Ballet Rambert; Band of H.M. Royal Marines; Martin Best Consort; Band of the Irish Guards; Phil Bates; Chris Barber; Gary Bertini.

Chichester and District Schools Music Festivals; Lewis Casson; Fay Compton; John Case; Chichester Cathedral Choir; Shura Cherkassky; Christie Minstrels; Cremona Quartet; John Clements; City of London Ensemble; Kyung Wha Chung; Ilean Contrubas; Alan Clare Trio; Clifford Curzon; Chichester Singers; Joseph Cooper; Close Harmony; John Chilton's Footwarmers; Petula Clark; Chinese Magic Acrobats; Robert Cohen; Concert of the Royal Artillery; Cascading Strings; Court Dance Theatre of Okinawa; The Chieftans; Chamber Orchestra of Europe; Bernard Cribbens; Ricardo Chailly.

Johnny Dankworth; Dutch Swing College Band; Matt; Mattiwilda Dobbs; Andrew Davis; Meridith Davies; Antal Dorati; Lorna Dallas; Paul Daniels; Sacha Distel; Susan Drake; Donovan.

Edith Evans; Robert Eddison; English Chamber Orchestra; Early Music Consort; Dick Emery; John Etheridge; David Essex; The Enid; Mark Elder; Herb Ellis.

Christopher Fry; Pierre Fournier; Jean Fonda; Fenella Fielding; Julie Felix; Fairport Convention; Dietrich Fischer-Dieskau; Festival of Mime; Clive Francis; Lawrence Foster; Ivan Fischer; Fiddlers Dream; Anna Ford; Ella Fitzgerald; Georgie Fame; Festival do Brasil.

Joyce Grenfell; Marius Goring; Michael Garrick Quintet; Leon Goossens; Erich Gruenburg; Charles Groves; Gay Tyrolese; Juliette Greco; Stephane Grappelli; Jose-Luis Garcia; John Gielgud; Hannah Gordon; John Georgiadis; Maina Gielgud; Band of the Grenadier Guards; Gristdale Choir; Jane Glover; John Glickman; Princess Grace of Monaco; James Galway; Gabrieli String Quartet.

Christopher Hassal; Halle Orchestra; Tubby Hayes; Joan Hammond; Antony Holt; Handel Opera Society; Heinz Holliger; Barclay James Harvest; Joseph Horowitz; Hong Kong Youth Dance Group; Hinge and Bracket; Woody Herman; Owain Arwel Hughes; Hot Gossip; Philharmonia Hungerica; Yuzako Horigome; Anita Harris; Michael Habin.

Israel Chamber Orchestra; Incredible String Band; Ipi Tombi; Micha Inoue; I Musici.

Philip Jones Brass Ensemble; Terence Judd; Brian Johnston.

Miriam Karlin; Thea King; Peter Katin; Rudolph Kempe; King's Singers; Eartha Kitt; Kathakali Dance Theatre of India; Nigel Kennedy; Kneller Hall Band; Penelope Keith; Louis Kentner; Barney Kessel.

London Philharmonic Orchestra; Moura Lympany; Cleo Laine; Laurie Lee; London Mozart Players; Jacques Loussier Trio; London Symphony Orchestra; London Brass Soloists; Henry Lewis; Johnny Lambe Orchestra; Radu Lupu; Ivo Lola Ribar State Dancers; Syd Lawrence Orchestra; Little Angels of Korea; Humphrey Lyttelton; Raymond Leppard; John Lubbock; London City Ballet; Lindisfarne; Nicholas Logie; Jim Laker.

Nina Milkina; Herbert Menges; Yehudi Menuhin; Neville Marriner; Thomas Matthews; Nana Mouskouri; Harold MacNair; Menuhuin Festival Orchestra; Witold Malcuzynski; Stoika Milanova; George Malcolm; Keith Michell; Morecambe and Wise; George Melly; Geraldine McEwan; Spike Milligan; Peter Morrison; Moscow Balalaika Ensemble; Brian Matthews; Johnny More; George Melly; Mischa Maisky; Alec McCowan.

National Youth Orchestra of Great Britain; National Youth Theatre; Northern Sinfonia; New Philharmonia Orchestra; Netherlands Wind Ensemble; Nottingham Barbers; Jessye Norman; New London Ballet; Northern Ballet; National Youth Jazz Orchestra.

John Ogdon; David Oistrakh; Christina Ortiz; Oboade; Mary O'Hara; Orquestra Sinfonica Brasileri; Igor Oistrakh.

Pro Arte Society; Philharmonica of London; Polesden Lacey Players; Geoffrey Pratley; Gervase de Peyer; Victoria Postnikova; Jacqueline du Pre; Phoenix Opera; The Pentangle; John Pritchard; The Peddlars Pendulum; Norrie Paramor; Manitas de Plata; Oscar Peterson; Murray Perahia; Pasadina Roof Orchestra; Phil Zulu Troupe; Marita Philips; Carl Pini; Paco Pena; Les Paraguayos; Philippine Dancers; Ottilie Patterson; Maria de la Jau.

Royal Ballet Soloists; Arthur Rubinstein; Margaret Rutherford; Annie Ross; Jeremy Robson; Hugo Rignold; Mstislav Rostropovich; Sviatoslav Richter; Red Army Ensemble; Cliff Richard; Ruggiero Ricci; Ralph Reader; Los Romeros; Michael Roll; Buddy Rich; Bertice Reading.

Robert Spencer; Margaretta Scott; Bill le Sage; Segovia; John Smith; Elizabeth Schwarzkopf; Rita Streich; Rudolf Schwarz; Elaine Skorodin; El Sali Flamenco Company; Elisabeth Soderstrom; Swingle Singers; New Seekers; Christopher Seamin; Senegal African Ballet; Labi Siffre; State Choir of the U.S.S.R.; Steeleye Span; Harry Secombe; St John's Smith Square Orchestra; Marc Soustrot; Richard Stilgoe; Nigel Stock; Yitkin Seow; Semprini; George Shearing; Wayne Sleep; Showaddywaddy; Uri Segal; Henry Szeryng; The Spinners; Peter Skellern; Memphis Slim.

Dorothy Tutin; Sybil Thorndike; Paul Tortelier; Fou Ts'ong; Barry Tuckwell; Danny Thompson; Joan Turner; Tangerine Dream; Ling Tung; Jake Thackray; Fred Truman; Yuri Temirkanov.

Galina Vishnevskaya; Virtuosi di Roma; Vienna Boys Choir; Vivaldi Chamber Orchestra; Tamas Vasary; Sarah Vaughan.

Emlyn Williams; John Williams; Eric Winstone; West Sussex Youth Orchestra; Timothy West; John Westbrook; Iris Williams; Wall Street Crash; Westminster Cathedral Choir.

Yale String Quartet; The Yetties; Francisco Yglesia.

Pinchas Zukerman.

Forty-nine artistes and bands in seven Chichester International Jazz Concerts.

APPENDIX IV

Concerts in Aid of Charities

9 May 1964 Magic Show Theological College 1,000 00
30 April 1965 Magic Show Theological College 800 00
1965 Trelawney of the Wells R.N.L.I. 200 00
31 May 1966 The Clandestine Marriage National Society Cancer Relief 1,500 00
30 July 1968 Skin of our Teeth Sx Assoc of Youth Clubs
21 May 1968 The Unknown Soldier and His Wife Royal College of Nursing
8 November 1969 Aker Bilk Jazz Band Police Dependents Trust
28 October 1970 Ivo John Roberts State Dancers Sue Ryder Foundation 1,000 00
5 February 1971 G and S for All Police Dependents Fund 700 00
12 May 1971 The Rivals Sx and Hants Assoc Youth Clubs
18 September 1971 Concert for British Legion Covered costs
18 February 1972 Chichester Combined Charities Covered costs
26 October 1972 Marks and Spencers Fashion West Sx Girl Guides
25 March 1972 Wibold Makewzynaker recital British Heart Foundation
24 October 1973 Marks & Spencer Fashion Show British Heart Foundation
8 November 1973 Little Angels of Korea Action Research for Crippled Children 1,200 00
22 February 1974 Norrie Passmore Orchestra Fire Services Benevolent Fund
5 April 1975 Acker Bilk Jazz Band Chichester Combined Charities
14 September 1975 Keith Michell Concert C.A.R.E.
12 June 1977 Concert Queen's Silver Jubilee Lavinia Duchess of Norfolk Appeal 10,000 00
25 February 1977 Band of Irish Guards Chichester Cathedral Restoration
28 February 1977 Marks & Spencer Fashion Show British Heart Foundation
9 February 1979 Harry Secombe Concert Round Table for Hospital Radio
15 July 1979 L E–M Golden Wedding Petula Concert Red Cross and St John
27 July 1980 Marks & Spencer Fashion Show for King Edward Hospital
8 March 1981 Paul Daniel's Magic Show for Police Dependents Trust
9 July 1981 Performance of 'Mitford Girls' Out of Town Country Pursuits
14 & 15 March 1981 Chichester Singers 'Messiah' Anne Lawrence Fund
3 October 1981 Sotheby Auction for Theatre Development Fund 20,000
24 November 1981 Grenadier Guards Band West Sussex Association for the disabled
18 July 1982 Falklands Fund concert 15,500

APPENDIX V

Building Improvements and Maintenance

1966 Improvement of acoustics, ventilation and toilets 12,000
Alterations to lighting 2,000
1966 Box office, bar, scene dock, dressing rooms 56,754
1967 Air conditioning 46,754
1968 Cleaning of exterior of theatre 1,500
1969 Minerva studios repainted 596
Improvements to toilets 419
Improvements to backstage, actors' car park (£410)
1970 Thorn Q File computerised lighting console
1972 Green Room 60,000
Installation of lighting for car park 300
1973 Repairs to roof
1977 New Thorn lighting console 24,985
1978 Reconstruction of lighting and sound housing 9,000
Cladding of one side of theatre building 5,000
New doors of foyer
1979 Rewiring of electrical system 9,000
1981 Ladies' toilets' new extension 1,747
Carpeting 400
Administration building
Usherettes changing room 1,250
Sound system 12,000
1982 Alterations to administration buildings 2,000
Air conditioning of box office 1,000
Renewal of theatre roof 7,846
Renewal of theatre seats 8,335
Renewal of theatre carpeting 237
Security grills 600
New uniforms for usherettes 1,500
Extra speakers for sound 2,000
1983 Cleaning of exterior of theatre building 6,000
Double glazing 5,000
Repairs to box office roof 1,148
Computer part cost 9,000
Curtains for auditorium doors 600

APPENDIX VI
Chichester Festival Theatre

Arts Council Capital and Revenue Grants

	Production Company *Revenue* £	Production Company *Capital* £	Trust Ltd *Capital* £
To:			
31 October 1962	4,000	6,000	
31 October 1963	2,000	3,000	
31 October 1964	3,000		
31 October 1965	Nil		
31 October 1966	5,833		3,950
31 October 1967	11,458		31,050
31 October 1968	9,583		4,550
31 October 1969	6,606		7,950
31 October 1970	5,000		
31 October 1971	Nil	5,000	
31 October 1972	Nil	5,000	
31 October 1973	10,000		
31 October 1974	20,000		
31 October 1975	24,500		
31 October 1976	Nil		
31 October 1977 (includes £2,000 New Ventures)	20,000		
31 October 1978 (New Ventures only)	3,000		
	£124,980	£19,000	£47,500

No grants for theatre building since 1969
No grants for theatre productions since 1977

APPENDIX VII

Result of Survey carried out August and September 1978 over two separate weeks

A total of 19,525 paying patrons, over 15 theatre performances were asked to complete a prepared written questionnaire, of which 7,153 (36.6%) replied

TOTAL NUMBER OF REPLIES	7,153	
Place or Country of Origin		Percentage
Chichester	443	6
Sussex	2,002	28
Surrey, Hants, Dorset, Kent	3,062	43
Overseas	350	5
Other countries	1,296	18
Mode of Transport		
Train	445	6
Coach	1,062	15
Car	5,403	76
Walk	119	1½
Unanswered	124	1½
Age Groups		
Under 20	461	6
20–40	1,520	21
40–50	2,609	37
Over 60	2,546	36
Unanswered	27	—
Average number of visits to the theatre	17	
Was reason for travelling to Chichester to visit theatre only?		
YES	6,272	88
NO	881	12